Sports Sponsorship and Marketing Communications

Visit the *Sports Sponsorship and Marketing Communications*
Companion Website at **www.pearsoned.co.uk/lagae** to find
valuable **student** learning material including:

• Annotated links to relevant sites on the web

PEARSON
Education

We work with leading authors to develop the
strongest educational materials in marketing,
bringing cutting-edge thinking and best
learning practice to a global market.

Under a range of well-known imprints, including
Financial Times Prentice Hall, we craft high-quality
print and electronic publications which help readers
to understand and apply their content, whether
studying or at work.

To find out more about the complete range of our
publishing, please visit us on the World Wide Web at:
www.pearsoned.co.uk

Supporting resources

Visit **www.pearsoned.co.uk/lagae** to find valuable online resources

Companion Website for students
• Annotated links to relevant sites on the web

For instructors
• Complete, downloadable Instructor's Manual
• PowerPoint slides that can be downloaded and used as OHTs
• Additional cases

For more information please contact your local Pearson Education sales representative
or visit **www.pearsoned.co.uk/lagae**

SPORTS SPONSORSHIP AND MARKETING COMMUNICATIONS
A European Perspective

Wim Lagae

Prentice Hall
FINANCIAL TIMES

An imprint of **Pearson Education**
Harlow, England • London • New York • Boston • San Francisco • Toronto • Sydney • Singapore • Hong Kong
Tokyo • Seoul • Taipei • New Delhi • Cape Town • Madrid • Mexico City • Amsterdam • Munich • Paris • Milan

Pearson Education Limited
Edinburgh Gate
Harlow
Essex CM20 2JE
England

and Associated Companies throughout the world

Visit us on the World Wide Web at:
www.pearsoned.co.uk

First published by Pearson Education Benelux BV 2003
English language edition first published by Pearson Education Limited

ISBN 0273 687069

British Library Cataloguing-in-Publication Data
A catalogue record for this book is available from the British Library.

Library of Congress Cataloguing-in-Publication Data

Lagae, Wim.
   [Marketingcommunicatie in de sport. English]
   Sports sponsorship and marketing communications / Win Lagae.
     p. cm.
   Includes bibliographical references and index.
   ISBN 0-273-68706-9
   1. Sports--Marketing. 2. Sports sponsorship. 3. Communication in marketing. 4.
Sports--Economic aspects. I. Title.

   GV716.L34 2005
   796'.0698--dc22

                  2004056435

10 9 8 7 6 5 4 3 2 1
08 07 06 05

Typeset in 9/12pt Stone Serif by 30.
Printed and bound in Great Britain by Henry Ling Ltd at the Dorchester Press, Dorset.

The publisher's policy is to use paper manufactured from sustainable forests.

CONTENTS

FOREWORD

During the last part of the 20th century, sports have played an increasing role in the global economy. Some have resisted this development; others have followed it blindly.

The International Olympic Committee was one of the first sports organizations to understand that the world of business could be viewed as a partner in the promotion of sports, not as an enemy. We have an excellent track record and long-lasting relationships with our commercial partners.

Our sports marketing communication – because of its sheer size – may not be immediately usable for everybody, but what is characteristic of the IOC is characteristic of any sports organization. From the tiniest regional club to the large, well-known teams, all players must understand and realize that they have to take an interest in sports marketing communication. Only then can we speak of a symbiosis between sports and economics.

In order for a sports organization to succeed, it is necessary for those leaders to have an appropriate insight and necessary skills to promote and encourage sports sponsorship within the context of marketing communications. A well-trained leader should be able to speak the language of the game and also be able to communicate effectively with the corporate world. Sports sponsorship and marketing communication is playing an increasingly important role as individuals embark on this career. Wim Lagae's book should be a first step in this direction.

Dr Jacques Rogge
President of the International Olympic Committee

PREFACE

The integration of sports sponsorship in marketing communication was something that barely existed in Europe at the end of the 1980s. Sports marketing communication was at that time reduced to sports sponsorship in its strictest sense: the placing – in return for money – of logos in those media that traditionally were tied strongly to sports. Companies and organizations bought logo visibility on shirts or billboards. The prime, and very often the only, purpose of sports sponsorship was to 'be seen' and to gain brand-name recognition. However, over the past 20 years, some remarkable changes have taken place in the field of sports sponsorship. Under the pressure of ever stronger competition, business people have developed new marketing communication tools. In both the consumer and the corporate markets, we see that it is increasingly important for businesses to come up with meaningful and clearly defined forms of brand communication.

Consequently, sports sponsorship has increased in popularity and sophistication. For instance, according to Kolah (2003), global sponsorship amounted to $26.2 billion in 2003, an all-time high until then. Europe represented around one-third of this worldwide sponsorship market, with 81% of that market involving sports sponsorship. Twenty years on and sports sponsorship has thus moved into a sophisticated brand-building marketing platform. Therefore, through sports, sports and other brands have become a part of people's daily lives. In a complex promotional landscape, brands try to reach the sports consumer emotionally because the sports experience gives the brand an emotional charge.

The world of sports has gone through some important changes. Once a leisurely weekend activity, recently it has turned into an economic activity. Sports have become firmly rooted in society, and how people respond has considerably changed the face of sport. Consequently, marketing communication has reacted enthusiastically to the growth in scale and professionalism in the sports sector. The business world (as the supplier of resources) and the sports world (in need of financial support) have found some common ground in sports sponsorship. Indeed, sports sponsorship has boomed in recent years. Can you recall a significant sporting event that was not sponsored? Sports sponsorship has soared and, concurrently, its complexity has increased. More and more, brands see sports sponsorship as the logical first step towards marketing communication in sports. The next step for businesses and organizations is then to surround sports sponsorship with other marketing communication tools in order to reach their targets.

Purpose of this book

In Europe, the leverage of sports sponsorship into sports marketing communication is still a very new area of research. This book aims to shed light on this emerging field. The practice and study of sports sponsorship in marketing communication are further developed in North America than in Europe. It is expected that in Europe, this field of study will likewise become more widespread and more intensified. Various developments, which this book explores, will illustrate this point.

Sports sponsorship involves a reciprocal relationship between the sponsoring organization and the sporting organization. A win–win situation can be created if each organization is able to provide the benefits needed by the other. For instance, some benefits needed by sponsors to reach their goals are media exposure and communicative and commercial benefits, while examples of sponsor benefits are financial resources, goods and services. This exchange means that many of the cases and concepts can be seen from two perspectives. On the one hand, we see various sporting organizations asking for funds, goods or services. Sporting organizations consist of, among other things, sports events, leagues, competitions, teams, federations and individual athletes. On the other hand, we find sponsoring organizations that try to differentiate their communications through these various sports sponsorship projects.

In this book, we shall concentrate primarily on the objectives of marketing communication of brands that invest in sports sponsorship. How can sponsors utilize sports sponsorship to achieve brand- and sales-related objectives? However, the confrontation of two different worlds that very often complement one another in many sports sponsorship communication projects is very interesting and enriching from various points of view. Often, the two sides are presented in this book because it is clear that the sponsors and the recipients of the sponsorship can learn from the approaches, problems and challenges that their counterparts experience.

Target audience

This book fills a gap in the market of European books on sports and marketing. With the continuing growth of BA, MA and MSc programmes in sports marketing, sports management, sports science and other related fields, sports marketing (communication) increasingly is finding its own niche in university curricula. This book is geared towards students whose aims are to be promoted to sports-management functions, people employed in sports and sports-management jobs, and anybody who wishes to keep up with the latest developments in the fields of branding and sports.

This book will also be of interest to sports-management and marketing professionals. Every day, brand managers, advertising agencies, sponsorship consultants, sports managers, sports journalists and others who are interested in sports are confronted with problems that this book addresses. The book's methodological insights, concepts, summarized research findings and various applications can provide professionals with inspiration for their work.

Finally, this book is also easily accessible to a larger public interested in the latest developments in the fields of brands and sports. After having read this book, readers will see brands and the sports they watch in a new light.

Book structure

This book is organized as follows. Chapter 1 explores the fields of sports, marketing and communication. Sports have unique properties and basic features that correspond with services. Sports marketing communication is a dominant component of sports marketing. Marketing communication in sports entails both brand communication *of* sports and brand communication *through* sports. The success of sports sponsorship depends largely on the extent to which it has been integrated in marketing communications. The combination of factors influencing sports and those influencing marketing activities makes an integrated approach a challenge. Yet, integrated sports sponsorship communication is the key focus of this work. Case 1 reveals how (non)-sports brands activate their sponsorship investment rights in the world and European football championships.

Chapter 2 analyses sports sponsorship, the most important field of practice for sponsorship activities from the point of view of the sponsor. A sports sponsorship package would contain media carriers and affiliation rights to show brand names and logos in a sports environment. After a concise explanation of the increased importance of sports sponsorship, we analyse the objectives and target groups of marketing communications in the case of sports sponsorship. Case 2 works out the story of an imaginary tennis club that formulates sponsorship approaches by means of a well-thought-through step-by-step scenario. The strategy of how to approach sponsors applies the basic insights concerning selling sports sponsorship and allows an extensive review of the sponsored perspective.

Chapter 3 shows the interaction between sports sponsorship and public relations (PR). These thematic communication tools share some common ground in certain aspects. The unique features of sports provide a creative launching pad for relations marketing. Sports sponsorship is not only useful for marketing communications; it is also a tool used within the framework of corporate communication. In order to optimize the PR impact of sports sponsorship, event managers will use a variety of tools: after all, they are trying to maximize editorial attention for the brand name in question. Naturally, this demands a professional approach to press relationships. However, sports sponsors are not always in the spotlight because of magnificent triumphs and fantastic performances: unpredictable sporting events, such as drugs problems and serious accidents, could lead to crisis communication. Case 3 analyses the interrelation between event and corporate hospitality of the following elite sports events: the squash Open World Championships 2002 in Antwerp, the Road Racing World Championships 2002 in Belgium, and the WTA Tournament of Antwerp in 2004.

The interplay between sports sponsorship and advertising is the central focus in Chapter 4. Advertising is also an important tool for providing powerful and creative links with sports sponsorship projects, since sports advertising focuses around unique sports experiences. Sports-advertising strategy is the central topic in this chapter. Case 4 relates the story of virtual advertising in sports. On the basis of European examples, this case reveals the power of some new media in sports advertising.

Chapter 5 details all of the activities of direct marketing in the leverage of sports sponsoring. Typical for this form of exploitation is the one-on-one approach to the customer. Customer relationship management is established through classical direct media as well as through the new media (i.e. Internet communication and e-commerce, which are steadily gaining importance). Case 5 analyses official websites of European football clubs from a marketing perspective.

Chapter 6 investigates how sales promotion tools tie into sports sponsorship. It shows the need to take into account the complex character of sports sponsorship for sales promotion activities and in personal selling. Merchandising and sampling are special cases of sales promotion in the follow-up of sports sponsoring. In Case 6, we explain the sampling strategy used by Aquarius. When launching new varieties of this sports drink on the Belgian market, recreational sports which fulfil clear criteria are sponsored systematically. In the Aquarius sponsorship exploitation strategy, sampling activities are the cornerstone.

Finally, in Chapter 7, we consider the effectiveness of sports sponsoring (communication). First we look at the special case of ambush marketing. This is strategic sports communication by non-sponsored brands in a setting with many sponsors, which frustrates the effectiveness of official sponsor strategies. Measuring the exposure of sponsors is the initial focus of effectiveness measurement. Then we run systematically through the other methods of measuring the effectiveness of sports sponsorship exploitation: communication and commercial results. Case 7 illustrates how the sponsorship of professional cycling teams has evolved from a regional economic activity to an all-European activity. The strong increase in budgets for professional cycling sponsorship is explained and illustrated extensively. Effectiveness measurement is illustrated by the case of cycling team sponsor Cofidis, le crédit par téléphone.

Pedagogical features

With a theory- and practice-based approach, this book offers some general theoretical concepts about marketing communications – those that concern integrated marketing communications and those concerning the workings of sponsorship and advertising. Comprehensive cases, mini-cases, real-life examples and illustrations bring these concepts to life. The book also discusses recent developments in the sports sector. Pedagogical features include:

- **Chapter overview** sets up the chapter structure.
- **Teaching objectives** clearly outline material to follow.
- **Sections and subheadings** in the main text aid in digesting the important facts.
- **Tables and diagrams** help conceptualize concepts.
- **Mini-cases and worked-out examples** illustrate the core theme.
- **End-of-chapter key terms, review questions, discussion questions and a summary** provide reinforcement of key concepts.
- **Comprehensive follow-up cases** at the end of each chapter demonstrate real-world situations.
- **Endnotes** offer access to relevant literature to enable further study and research.

Unique features

- This book sketches the new conceptual framework of marketing communications in sports. From this perspective, sports sponsorship is not the final objective but (only) a starting point towards integrated sports marketing communication.
- The book offers a hands-on approach and transfer of North American and Australian concepts to the European context.
- The book presents many interesting European cases concerning sports sponsorship. These refer to a variety of sports and to many different forms of sports sponsorship. This work aims to highlight the theoretical background of some interesting cases of sponsorship activities within the domain of marketing communication.
- The comprehensive follow-up cases provide an overview of relevant and recent topics in Europe. Discussion questions at the end of each case provide the reader with an opportunity to test his or her working knowledge of the subject on the basis of revealing worked-out examples that show the underlying mechanisms and further activate the key terms from the chapters.

Additional material

Additional material for further study, including relevant annotated weblinks, is available at www.pearsoned.co.uk/lagae. Lecturers can also visit this site to download PowerPoint slides.

Acknowledgements

I would like to thank Pearson Education for supporting and publishing this book. In particular, I would like to thank the following: Thomas Sigel, Senior Acquisitions Editor; Natasha Dupont, Senior Editor; Colette Holden, copy editor; Annette Abel, proofreader; Peter Hooper, Editorial Assistant; Vanessa van Kempen, Pearson Education Benelux; and translator Alison Fisher.

I am grateful for the support and excellent suggestions I have received in the course of writing this book. I'd like to thank my super-reviewer and coach, Paul Emery of Northumbria University, who commented on previous drafts.

I also thank the following reviewers for their detailed written reviews and/or comments on this book: Simon Chadwick, Leeds University Business School, UK; Ruth M. Crabtree, Division of Sports Sciences, Northumbria University, UK; Ian Kenvyn, Trinity and All Saints College, Leeds, UK; Lindsay King, Division of Sports Sciences, Northumbria University, UK; Robert Lentell, University of North London, UK; Marijke Taks, University of Windsor, Canada; and Kari Puranoha, University of Jyvaskylla, Finland.

Parts of the book could not have been written without the help and support of numerous people. I would particularly like to thank the following people and hope not to have forgotten anyone: Frank Dernout; Thomas Ameye, KU Leuven; Jan Baccarne, Avans Hogeschool Breda, Tim Benijts, Lessius Hogeschool Antwerp; Philip Cornelissen, Reebok Europe; Wim Dewit, Johan Cruyff University Amsterdam; Marko Heijl, and Werner Sprangers, Punta Linea; Thijs Kemmeren, Fontys Hogeschool Tilburg; Patrick Lefevere, Quick.Step-Davitamon; Dees Naessens; Kim Pinxteren; Roland Renson, KU Leuven; Freddy Vandernjinsbrugge, Stickting Marketing; Hans Vandeweghe, De Morgen, Sport International; Bart Vanreusel, KU Leuven; Jan van Wijk, Avans Hogeschool, Breda; Jan Piet Verckens, Lessius Hogeschool; Jos Verschueren, VLEKHO Business School Brussels and Hans Westerbect, La Trobe Universtiy.

Reference

Kolah, A. (2003), *Maximising the Value of Sponsorship*. London: SportBusiness Group, pp. 17–30.

1

SPORT, MARKETING AND COMMUNICATION

Hot and overcast. I take my gear out of the car and put my bike together. Tourists and locals are watching from sidewalk cafés. Non-racers. The emptiness of those lives shocks me.' (*Tim Krabbé*)

Overview

Properties of sport

Sport as a unique service

Sport as an industry

Sports marketing within sports management

Marketing communication in sport

Of sport   Through sport

Towards integrated sports marketing communication

Aims

After studying this chapter, you will be able to:

- gain insight into the different dimensions of sport;

- explain why sport has the features of a unique service;

- distinguish the different segments of the sports industry;

- define the different instruments of sports marketing;

- distinguish clearly marketing communication of sport and marketing communication through sport;

- describe the elements of the sports promotion mix.

1.0 Introduction

During the past few decades, sport has developed from a relaxing weekend activity into a complex industry. This is evident from various phenomena. On the one hand, sport is magnified daily in the media. An illustration of this is all the news concerning David Beckham. On the other hand, the sports sector tries to take advantage dynamically of the various socioeconomic developments. For instance, the explosive growth of the fitness sector results from diverse economic, demographic and marketing evolutions. The speed with which all this happens demands creative and determined sports management. In an age in which consumers are deluged with information, it is essential for a brand to communicate distinctively. With an appealing sports project, brands can break through the immunity that consumers have developed to the innumerable advertising stimuli. Through a sports sponsorship project, a brand communicates information and avoids confusion with other competitors.

This chapter presents six elements that form the core of sport, marketing and communication. Because of its unique properties, sport occupies a special position in people's lives (Section 1.1). Therefore, owing to its basic features, sport is a unique service product (Section 1.2). Next, sport as an economic industry will be examined (Section 1.3). In this fast-growing industry, the professionalization of sports management, including the production and marketing of sport, has increased significantly (Section 1.4). Furthermore, we introduce sports marketing communications or the promotional mix as the dominant element in sports marketing. The focus hereby lies on both marketing communications *of* sport and brand communication *through* sport (Section 1.5). An important new tendency is the integrated deployment of all instruments of the promotion mix in order to take maximal advantage of the different facets of sports sponsorship projects. However, both sport and marketing factors make an integrated approach more difficult (Section 1.6).

This chapter explores the terrain of sport, marketing and communication. The general outline of marketing communications in sport is drawn, and a brief overview is given of a number of important developments, including the link between sport experience and brand value. Namely, brand communication in sport works around unique sport experiences. Through a sponsored sporting project, the consumer comes into contact with a brand in a personal and memorable manner. In other words, organizations that utilize sports sponsorship as a marketing medium are reacting to the need of the sports consumer for powerful emotions. A detailed examination of the leverage techniques of sports sponsorship will be given later in the book.

1.1 Properties of sport

We can distinguish different characteristics of participation in sport and the experience of it. The meeting of well-described needs is the first property linked to sport (see Outline 1.1).[1] Sport fulfils a number of basic needs for both the active and the passive sports person. A core need for the active sports person might be striving for health and fitness. Healthy exercise or the kick of competition can be very relaxing. Sports people want to excel in their sports. They want to perform better than a set standard: beating their competitors or bettering their personal record from last year. Improving skills and techniques might be another motive for active participation in sport. Along with motor skills, practising sports can strengthen a number of social and personal skills, such as self-confidence, self-knowledge, self-discipline and mental welfare. These motives support each other. Someone exercising to perform better than a competitor will be physically stronger, healthier and fitter under normal conditions than a person who does not exercise competitively. Someone who is successful in sport is also likely to feel more relaxed and confident.

The passive sports person, on the other hand, might be interested in sport for other motives. Like athletes, sports fans can share their experiences and emotions with each other, whether at home in front of the television or in the stadium. Primarily from this social aspect, the fan is likely to feel that spectator sport is relaxing and pleasant. In addition, the average supporter might identify very strongly with athletes who have reached a high level of excellence.

However, products and services that are not associated with sport can also satisfy these consumer needs. This is why the preference for sport is often associated with its generic components. The generic components form a second property of sport. According to the Council of Europe,[2] sport concerns: '... all forms of physical activity – informal or organised – aimed at maintaining or improving the physical condition and the mental well-being, the making of social contacts and/or the achievement of results in competitions at all levels ...'. A broader definition of sport states that any activity, experience or enterprise focused on fitness, recreation, athletics or leisure is sport.[3] Parks and Quarterman also define sport as a term that includes a variety of physical activities and associated endeavours.[4] In their approach, sport is a playful competition limited by clearly defined rules and done in sports accommodation with (usually) specialized sports equipment.

A third property consists of the very specific character of each sport. Every type of sport has special key values, each of which attracts certain groups of sport consumers. In road-cycle racing, for example, the heroic battle against the elements is important: fighting different types of weather, road surfaces and competitors. Strength, finishing, technique, respect for the rules and team spirit are key values in basketball. Depending on the country or the cultural context, consumers are attracted by the specific features of a particular sport. The interest in baseball, cricket or cycling differs greatly in social and cultural terms. Even within one region, one cultural background, or even one sports discipline, the preferences can be very heterogeneous because each specific sport symbolizes the core values of the social class that it represents.[5] For example, a sports consumer can have a passion for road cycling while showing little interest in track cycling.

The most popular TV sports programme in northern Europe in 2003 showed boxing in Hungary, women's soccer in Sweden and ice hockey in the Czech Republic, Slovakia and Finland. In Norway and Austria, biathlon and skiing, respectively, had the highest viewer ratings. This implies that although football games achieved the highest viewer ratings in a number of southern European countries, the varying popularity of sports in different countries reflects the importance of the cultural context. 2003 is an interesting reference year, because there was no distortion in the figures due to the Olympic Games or a world or European football championship.

Outline 1.1 Properties of sport

1. Meeting basic needs

- maintaining health and fitness
- relaxation/having fun
- achieving something
- acquiring motor and social skills
  - self-confidence
  - self-knowledge
  - discipline
  - mental welfare
- sharing emotions, experiences

2. Generic sport components

- component of leisure time
- competition

- form of play

- rules

- equipment

- accommodation

3. Features of specific sports

- core values

- social status

1.2 Sport as a unique service

Sport has a number of unique characteristics; the basic features are listed in Outline 1.2. Few economic activities involve the consumer as much as the sports sector. From this example it follows that sport consumers strongly identify with their sporting heroes. They also feel emotionally linked to the sport, often leading them to comment on the nature of the competition from their armchairs.

Sport consumers look for and obtain various benefits from sports competitions.[6] As mentioned previously, while recreational sports people might aim for wellbeing, a fitter lifestyle and positive social and personal skills, more competitively oriented sports people might want to defeat opponents or exceed their limitations. Fans, on the other hand, might want primarily to share experiences and emotions with other fans through their sporting experiences. The experience of sport is thus unique for each individual.

The interest in sport, as a cornerstone of leisure culture, is massive. Large sporting competitions remove demographic, sociocultural and geographic barriers. In almost every country in the world, interest is shown in the games of national teams competing in a world football championship. Young and old, rich and poor, well or poorly educated – all view the live broadcasts of football games. Just as in other economic sectors, sport companies compete. At the same time, they also rely on cooperating with each other. For example, the competing first-class football clubs assume a common stand for their sector with respect to television rights, licensing or sponsorship agreements on a league level.

The very competitive character of sport corresponds, to a certain extent, to competition in business. Doing better than the competitor, profit gain, increasing market share and turnover are primary commercial aims. To reach these goals, an organization must obtain the maximal efforts from its employees, just like a top athlete who tries to get the most from his or her career in the period that he or she is competitively active.

Company managers may want to optimize their human resource management or sales policy via sport. Hence, many unwritten sports rules are also guidelines for successful business management:

- team spirit is important;
- 'no pain, no gain';
- prepare significant confrontations in consultation;
- deal tactically;
- relax only after a successful conclusion;
- recognize the importance of situational and emotional intelligence.

Outline 1.2 Basic features of sport

- The sports consumer obtains a variety of benefits from exercising sport.
- The sports consumer is heavily involved in sport because of:
  - personal identification;
  - emotional attachment.
- The sports consumer experiences sport in a subjective manner.
- The course and outcome of sport are exciting, unpredictable and illogical.
- Sport is difficult to control.
- Sport removes geographic, demographic and sociocultural barriers.
- The sports sector is characterized by competition and cooperation.
- Sport has major business values.

The basic features of sport will be examined further from the aspect of service marketing. Based on the features of services, we will see that sport possesses the attributes of a unique service product.[7] Outline 1.3 places the basic features of sport in the conceptual framework of service marketing.[8]

Outline 1.3 Sport as a unique service

- Sport is intangible.
- The consumer does not become the owner of the sports activity.
- The consumer is involved heavily in sport.
- Sport possesses a high variability and is difficult to control.
- Sport is experienced subjectively.
- Sport production and consumption coincide (partly).
- Sport is transient.

Sport is intangible

Sport is an exertion, an 'exercise of something'. A sports game is immaterial and cannot be touched. Because of this non-tangible character, the result of practising sport cannot be judged in advance. Additionally, sport can contain a number of tangible elements, e.g. a cycling jersey or a tennis racket, which take on their full meaning only against the background of the sport, in this case cycling or tennis. Cycling and tennis games, in contrast, are essentially intangible.

The consumer does not become the owner of the sports activity

A fundamental distinction between products and services involves the fact that customers of services do not become their permanent owners. Sport forms part of the varied activities studied under service marketing. Examples of service products are wide-ranging, e.g. travelling by aeroplane, dining in a restaurant, freight transport, insurance and market research. A common feature is the intangible nature of these services. Due to this intangible nature, the sports consumer cannot become the owner of service products in the sense of active or passive sports activity.

The consumer is involved heavily in sport

Sports consumers usually feel heavily involved in sport because of their very strong identification with the standards that sporting heroes exceed and the results they achieve. Fans might quickly assume they are experts regarding the progress of a game because everyone feels like an expert in sport. This implies that, more than with other business, sports business is also approached with personal identification.

Sport possesses a high variability and is difficult to control

Meeting the needs for services involves the customer's situation, the environment, the other customers and the staff. Also, sport is exercised within a particular social framework in which emotions and experiences are shared. The pleasure of sport for a fan or spectator is determined partly by interactions with others. Sport is also unpredictable, and neither the course nor the outcome of a game can be determined in advance. Weather conditions, the condition of the day, rivalry, and chance factors ensure that no two games are identical, i.e. the final outcome of a game and its quality are heterogeneous. The less capable athlete sometimes defeats the stronger athlete of the top team.[9]

This variability of sport makes it even more difficult to control based on objective and set parameters. Because it is difficult to control, the sports marketer faces a challenge when concentrating on extending the service product that is sport. The marketer focuses on values other than winning, such as dedication, respect, team spirit and struggling against the elements.

Sport is experienced subjectively

The intangible character of sport does not allow the sports consumer to make an unambiguous evaluation. Each fan's experience is very subjective. This makes it difficult for the sports marketer to achieve consumer satisfaction. Every active participant in recreational sport and every sports fan creates a unique illusion for him- or herself. This experience is very subjective, is experienced intensely and is assumed to be real.

Sport production and consumption coincide (partly)

The production and consumption of sport usually coincide either partly or entirely. Sport is sold but cannot be produced in advance. The consumer and producer are usually both involved in the process of providing a service. Spectators of a football game and the football players all have to be in the stadium. However, the sport service could also be enjoyed afterwards; then the spectators do not have to be involved in the production of the service.

Sport is transient

Sport is a perishable service product: as soon as the sports consumer learns the outcome and the sporting event is over, the good has been consumed. If sport is not consumed immediately, then the service is lost. At best, you can remember the event or benefit from it. The service product cannot be stored to be enjoyed next month, except through videos and press reviews.

1.3   Sport as an industry

Until the 1960s, sport was geared primarily to people with (potential) sporting talent. The most important motives for competitive sport were subjective performance, the common experience of the excitement of the game, relaxation and social contact.[10] Today, however, sport means more than top sport and competitive sport. Other divergent sport modes are recreational and popular sport, fitness sport and health, adventure sport, pleasure sport and cosmetic sport (sports focusing on 'body styling').

Outline 1.4 Characteristics of the professional and voluntary sports sectors

Professional sports sector	Voluntary sports sector
Professional, paid top sport	Amateur, unpaid popular sport
Spectator sport	Participant sport
Focus on global market	Coverage of local market
Services of professionals	Devotion of volunteers
Sponsor funds	Government subsidies
Maximal profit and market potential based on economic guidelines	Maximal sport activity based on democratic rules

Traditionally, popular sport and top sport were separated (see Outline 1.4). Recreational sport, participant sport, non-profit sport, amateur sport and unpaid sport are synonyms for popular sport. Typical of popular sport is the primary focus on the athlete and working with volunteers and the coverage of the local market. The decision-making in participant sport, aimed at maximal sport activity, happens according to democratic rules, and one of the government's key tasks is to subsidize recreational sport. However, this does not exclude the possibility that popular sport can also acquire funds from sponsors.

Synonyms for top sport include professional, spectator and paid sport. Top sport involves the highest performance and the acquiring of income and status. In the management of top sport, economic guidelines are followed, for example to maximize budget, profit and market potential. For commercial reasons, top sport frequently focuses on the global market. Also, the services of professionals are required to a significant extent in top sport. It is generally assumed that top sport taps the best resources from sponsorship organizations.

Recently, top sport and popular sport have undergone a spectacular evolution. Popular sport developed from a 'young man's' activity into a valuable part of the leisure culture, applying to practically all social strata, young and old, men and women. Under the influence of developments in the social, economic and media arenas, popular sport has continued to grow and professionalize.

As a continuation of these developments, the top sport sector has also undergone further growth and professionalization. This does not exclude the fact that the organization of top sport sometimes displays amateurish tendencies. This blurs the dividing line between top sport and popular sport. The sports business sector contains diverse goods and service products, which are concentrated around three activities (see Figure 1.1). The first involves goods and service products that fit within an active sports activity. The goods developed in the framework of passive participation in sport form the second element of the sports business sector.[11] The final component contains all tangible and intangible activities in sports marketing communication. A media campaign for a sports brand and displays in stores are examples of tangible goods, while the power of the experience of sport is an intangible service product. A variation of this approach is a classification of the sports industry into core and derivative goods.[12]

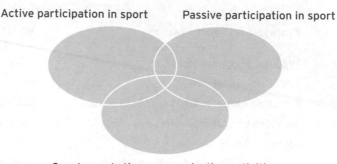

Active participation in sport   Passive participation in sport

Sports marketing communication activities

Figure 1.1 Components of the sports business sector.

The core of the sports business sector thus consists of active and passive sport participation. Derivative sports services include the construction and maintenance of sports facilities, travel in the context of sport, sports media services, sport wagers, financial services for sport, intermediaries and sports marketing agencies.

1.4 Sports marketing within sports management

Sports management

As an introduction to the term 'sports marketing communication', we will describe briefly the terms 'sports management' and 'sports marketing'. The specific dimensions and features of sport determine the outlines of sports management, which consists of both the production and the marketing of sport services. Sports management is '... a field concerned with the coordination of limited human and material resources, relevant technologies, and situational contingencies for the efficient production and exchange (marketing) of sport services ...'[13]

According to this definition, the essence of sports management consists of the coordination of four elements: deployment of personnel and material resources, technology, support services and the organizational context (Outline 1.5).

Outline 1.5 Sports management skills

- Human resources management

- Training and coaching techniques

- Sports management support services

- Coordination of the sport context

Source: Chelladurai, P. (2001) *Managing Organizations for Sport and Physical Activity: A Systems Perspective*. Scottsdale, AZ: Holcombe Hathaway.

Human resource management affects everyone in sport who is involved in the production of sport services: customers, salaried employees and volunteers. In addition, there is the management of the technology in sport. Sport technology includes training and coaching techniques. Support services of sports management include marketing communication, services concerning sports law and financial services. A final aspect of sports management is the coordination of the sporting environment. The sport context includes the environment in which a sports organization functions, such as market conditions, government regulations, cultural norms and social expectations. A manager with responsibility for a sports product or service must be proficient in the planning, organizing, directing, delegating, monitoring, budgeting and evaluation of the outlined activities.[14]

Sports marketing

Sports management implies the production and marketing of sport (Figure 1.2). A definition of sports marketing must be preceded by an examination and definition of marketing. Marketing is a management process that identifies, anticipates and implements customer needs in an efficient and customer-friendly manner. The umbrella term 'marketing' includes the process of planning and implementing the conception, pricing, promotion and distribution of ideas, goods and services. These goods and service products are exchanged and meet the needs of individuals and organizations.[15] Kotler and colleagues define marketing as a social and managerial process by which individuals, groups and organizations obtain what they need and want through creating and exchanging products and value with others.[16] At the heart of the marketing process is the mutual exchange between two parties. This is the act of obtaining a desired object from someone by offering something in return. The marketing discipline aims to optimize the

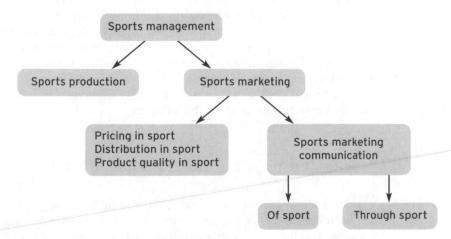

Figure 1.2 Sports marketing communication within sports management.

agreed-upon conditions, time and place of agreement of these transactions. Marketing in the non-profit, voluntary and government sectors, such as police departments, colleges, museums and charities, has become very important.

Marketing is a broad and complex term that is given a concrete expression through the elements of the marketing mix. The marketing mix traditionally contains the components price, product, place and promotion. On the one hand, sport discovered the marketing discipline; for example, successful fitness centres implement in their marketing strategies the most sophisticated techniques of geo-marketing (place), price-setting, product quality and promotion. On the other hand, the marketing world is making use of sport; for example, Guinness communicates through sports sponsorship programmes.

The marketing of sport involves the specific application of marketing principles and processes to market goods and services directly to sports participants and spectators or end users.[17] From the needs and requirements of sports organizations, the sports manager creates products which are exchanged with third parties. In this description, sports marketing refers to the marketing of sport forms and products.[18]

However, generally a broader approach is used, in which sports marketing implies not only the marketing of sport but also all marketing activities utilizing sport. Sports marketing consists of '… all activities designed to meet the needs and wants of sport consumers through exchange processes. Sport marketing has developed two major thrusts: the marketing of sports products and services directly to consumers of sport, and a marketing of other consumer and industrial products or services through the use of sport promotions …'.[19] Both in the marketing of sport and in marketing through sport, the needs of the sports consumer are considered. Gray defines sports marketing as '… the anticipation, management and satisfaction of sport consumers' wants and needs through the application of marketing principle and practice. Sport marketing begins with the customer – whether an individual or organisation – in mind …'.[20]

That sport usually possesses the features of services forms an interesting starting point for the relatively young discipline of sports marketing.[21] Sport marketers must take the properties and features of sport into consideration when elaborating their strategy. As in every marketing approach, in sports marketing the consumer is key. The group of sports consumers is not homogeneous and contains different sectors, because sport consumption occurs at different levels of involvement with sport. Along with active participation in sport, fans may watch sport or collect sport archive material.

1.5   Marketing communications in sport

Marketing communications or promotion can be described as establishing contact with consumers and organizations (trade) to influence their knowledge, attitudes and behaviours in a direction that is favourable for the marketing policy. The commercial communication of an organization contains both marketing and enterprise communication. Enterprise communication, or corporate communication, is a broader term for marketing communications.[22] The aim of corporate communication involves building up trust and goodwill among internal and external relationship groups. Public relations (PR) activities are often employed for this goal.

Not only marketing communications but also product-quality, price-setting and distribution techniques – the other instruments of the marketing mix – can improve or strengthen a brand. The success of a marketing communication strategy is, after all, linked to the manner in which the promotion mix fits with the other marketing instruments. In essence, marketing communication contains all of the instruments through which the marketer spreads information regarding the product, price and distribution. A poor-product quality cannot be compensated for by a professional deployment of the promotion mix. Also, the price and the choice of distribution channels partly determine the success of a marketing strategy.

Figure 1.3 shows the individual tools that constitute the sports marketing communications or sports promotion mix.

Figure 1.3 The sports marketing communications mix.

Sports sponsorship is any commercial agreement by which a sponsor contractually provides financing or other support in order to establish an association between the sponsor's image, brands or products and a sports sponsorship property in return for rights to promote this association and/or for granting certain agreed direct or indirect benefits.

Public relations consists of identifying, establishing and maintaining mutually beneficial relationships between the organization and the various stakeholders on which its success or failure depends. Stakeholders are organizations or groups of individuals with whom the organization wants to create goodwill through acts of hospitality and/or a press approach.

Advertising is any paid, non-personal communication through various mass media by organizations who hope to inform and/or persuade a particular target group. The content of advertising is determined and paid for by a clearly identified sender.

Direct marketing communications are a personal and direct way to communicate with customers and prospects. Possible classic ways of using direct marketing communications are personalized brochures, direct mailings and tele-marketing. New ways to communicate interactively with different stakeholders are being offered by the Internet.

Sales promotions are the set of activities conducted by marketers to stimulate sales in the short run. Sales-stimulating campaigns include price cuts, coupons and sampling. Point-of-purchase communications, personal selling, exhibitions and trade fairs could also provide extra value to the sales force, distributors or consumers, aimed at increasing sales in the short run.

In the leverage of sports sponsorship, advertising remains very important. Nevertheless, in the past few decades, new instruments in the promotion mix have been developed and added to advertising. These instruments have typical features and both strong and weak points, which will be elaborated further in the text. Sports sponsorship is usually the cornerstone of a sports marketing com-munications strategy and the logical introduction to sports marketing communication. In a sporting environment, a sponsorship organization may usually communicate only its brand name and logo. This limited message should be supported by other communications tools.[23] It is therefore important to sur-round sports sponsorship with other promotion instruments. However, in some cases, there is no direct link between, for example, sports advertising or sports hospitality and sports sponsorship. Since we do not deal with these cases in this book, our approach to sports marketing communication is restricted to the field of sports sponsorship communication.

Classic models of marketing communications operation propagate a series of effects that must be achieved with the help of promotion techniques.

It is widely accepted that consumers move through three major stages in their response to promotional instruments: cognitive, affective and behavioural stages. Outline 1.6 shows two major models of how consumers respond to pro-motions: the hierarchy-of-effects model and the 'classic' AIDA (attention, interest, desire, action) model. For instance, the hierarchy-of-effects model

Outline 1.6 Marketing communications models: the hierarchy-of-effects and the attention, interest, desire and action (AIDA) models

Stages	Hierarchy-of-effects model	AIDA model
Cognitive stage	Awareness	Attention
	Knowledge	
Affective stage	Liking	Interest
	Preference	Desire
	Conviction	
Behaviour	Purchase	Action

Source: Pope, N. and Turco, D. (2001), *Sport and Event Management*. Boston, MA: McGraw Hill; and De Pelsmacker, P., Geuens, M. and Van den Bergh, J. (2004), *Marketing communications*, 2nd edn. Harlow, UK: Pearson Education.

suggests that consumers move through a series of sequential steps, e.g. 'think', 'feel' and 'do', in their response to a marketing communication stimulus.[24] In the cognitive phase, improving brand recognition and knowledge is key, while the affective phase is oriented towards the promoting of the brand attitude and preference. Finally, the behaviour phase involves stimulating buying or the intention to buy.[25]

Communication operation differs according to the extent of the consumer's involvement with a brand. We can work with situations of both high and low involvement around sport. If the consumer's involvement is low (in the case of an unimportant decision or a product with a low social or financial risk), cues are used in the marketing communication. These are traditional endorsers with a certain meaning that draws attention. Famous athletes and experts are common examples.[26] For products and services with a high consumer involvement, the functional distinguishing characteristics first and foremost make the difference. Because of its unique features, sport permits an interesting image transfer. This is why sports sponsorship has grown into a creative and powerful medium for brand communication.

Marketing communication of sport

Just like sports marketing in the broad sense, marketing communication in sport contains marketing communication of sport and marketing communication through sport (see Outline 1.4). In the case of marketing communication of sport, the different forms of sport position and sell themselves through various marketing communication media. These brands (sporting events, federations, clubs, teams and individual athletes) utilize instruments of the promotion mix to sell themselves professionally and to position their products and services on the brand map. An illustration is enhanced market value for sponsors of the Belgian tennis players Kim Clijsters and Justine Henin (see Mini-case).

Mini-case study – Henin and Clijsters: sportive top, commercial subtop

Sports marketing sometimes resembles the stock market, gambling on the right athlete, who hopefully fulfils all sporting and commercial expectations. That good timing can be worth its weight in gold can be illustrated by the main sponsors of the Belgian tennis players Henin and Clijsters. For example, Siemens Belgium-Luxemburg concluded a contract several months before the start of Roland Garros 2001, just before the breakthrough of Clijsters and Henin at the Grand Slam level. The total sponsor sum was estimated then at €500,000 over two years. In exchange, both tennis stars wear the company logo on their sleeves and are available four days a year for publicity activities. The contract has since been extended to 2004, but it remains a fixed sum regardless of their performance or ranking, which is not usual in sports marketing.

Belgacom was also an early investor (January 2002) in Clijsters and Henin. The contractual sum is secret, but it is considered peanuts compared with the international status that Henin and Clijsters have achieved and what they represent in television scope. In the meantime, Clijsters and Henin have enhanced their market value. In May 2002, Clijsters signed a contract with Fila International, which immediately set her as a figurehead on the same pedestal as Capriati, although not in equivalent financial terms. However, Henin concluded a good deal when she moved from Le Coq Sportif to Adidas in mid-April 2003, when she signed a five-year contract. Adidas does not publish concrete figures, but insiders in the tennis world estimate that Henin receives €1 million per year from Adidas. In this way, Adidas is covering its bets: Kournikova is their glamour babe, Henin the serious one.

Because of its massive television attention, tennis is a very marketable women's sport. However, although the Belgians score very highly on the tennis court, their aura off the court still leaves something to be desired. To achieve true hero status, Clijsters and Henin have to conquer the sports press, doing, for example, what the Williams sisters have done. Thus, Clijsters and Henin still seem to be lacking the necessary international allure for worldwide brands. However, the relationship between Clijsters and Lleyton Hewitt has helped, creating interest for media other than the sports press.

Table 1.1 Top five Women's Tennis Association (WTA) players (ranking and prize money)

Rank	Tennis player	Points, end season 2003	Rank	Tennis player	Prize money in 2003 (€)
1	Justine Henin-Dardenne (Belgian)	6.553	1	Kim Clijsters	3 248 071
2	Kim Clijsters (Belgian)	6.628	2	Justine Henin-Dardenne	2 800 369
3	Serena Williams (US)	3.916	3	Serena Williams	1 785 376
4	Amélie Mauresmo (French)	3.194	4	Amélie Mauresmo	1 103 044
5	Lindsay Davenport (US)	2.990	5	Lindsay Davenport	1 027 024

Note: dollars converted to euros at the exchange rate at the end of the year.

Source: Federal Reserve Bank of America.

Marketing communication through sport

In the case of marketing communication through sport, non-sports brands use sport forms to increase their brand value. Although their core business clearly is not sport-related, non-sports brands quality for the sports industry because of their sponsorship role. In this approach, sports sponsorship grows into a platform for the business and marketing communication of an organization. Marketing communication through sport has become very attractive. In periods with (too) many media and advertisement stimuli, sports sponsorship communication acts as a distinctive signboard. The Formula 1 team BMW Williams sponsored by the anti-nicotine patch NiQuitin CQ is one such example of marketing communication through sport.

Marketing communication through sport is a form of affiliation marketing. A brand is associated with a sport object to produce an image transfer.[27] Marketing a brand uses sport to enter the consumer's social environment in a friendly manner. Non-sports brands recognize a number of features in the service product sport that suit their business strategies. Sport experience is associated with emotions[28] that simplify associations with brand names and give the brand a unique meaning.[29] Not only one's own brand experiences, but also those of reference groups, have a great effect on the brand image created. Reference groups include family, acquaintances and well-known television celebrities, such as top athletes. Sport arouses feelings that even the wildest marketer cannot stimulate with an advertisement. Intense feelings such as euphoria, heroism and drama arise spontaneously during sport, and because of these powerful emotions, advertisers want to associate brands with sport.[31]

Mini-case study – Formula 1 team sticks on nicotine patch: NiQuitin, a range of stop-smoking products, sub-sponsor of the BMW Williams team

The car-racing team BMW Williams has scored a first in the Formula 1 world. The Williams' cars on the circuit have been decorated since April 2003 with commercial signage for NiQuitin, a range of stop-smoking products from the pharmaceutical giant GlaxoSmithKline. Williams dropped sponsorship by tobacco companies three years ago, but it is the first team to be sponsored by nicotine patches and nicotine gum. The 'stop-smoking cars' were first seen at the San Marino Grand Prix. This stunt is exceptional for racing, which traditionally has been very dependent on tobacco sponsorship for its income. Five of the ten teams competing in Formula 1 in 2003 were sponsored by large tobacco groups such as Philip Morris. British American Racing is owned entirely by British American Tobacco (BAT), which markets brands such as Lucky Strike.

But bad news has been threatening Formula 1 for some time. In just a few years, tobacco advertising will no longer be allowed on the circuit. According to a European Union guideline, every form of tobacco advertising will be forbidden from 2005 or 2006. Since the European guideline was approved by the European Council of Ministers, the Formula 1 circuit has been trying to attract other sponsors. The Frank Williams team took the initiative to ask GlaxoSmithKline to be a sponsor after another sponsor had pulled out. The NiQuitin logo will be affixed to the sides and bonnet of the car. GlaxoSmithKline does not intend to become the main sponsor of Williams (BMW will retain this title) but the value of the sponsorship deal with Williams has not been announced.

Williams obtains other benefits from the deal with GlaxoSmithKline along with the sponsorship money. Many international figures in the anti-tobacco lobby have welcomed the initiative. 'Finally, car racing will be associated with health instead of death and disease,' said Gro Harlem Brundtlandt, the director-general of the World Health Organization in a statement. This provided Williams with quite a lot of free positive PR.

Source: Based on Smeets, F. (2003), 'Formule 1-team kleeft nicotinepleister op', *De Morgen*, 17 April 2003.

1.6 Towards integrated sports marketing communication

Supplementing sports sponsorship with other thematic instruments is therefore necessary to achieve cognitive and affective goals. PR and advertising work more in the long term than the short and are especially suited to support sports sponsorship. Sports sponsorship leverage is a complex process, because of the different time-effectiveness of the promotion mix instruments, e.g. instruments of action communication aim at immediate changes in behaviour and must be effective in the short term. The remaining structure of this book, reproduced in Outline 1.7, reflects the elements of the sports marketing communications mix (or the sports promotional mix).

Outline 1.7 Instruments of sports sponsorship leverage

Sports sponsorship and thematic communication

Sports sponsorship and action communication

The integrated deployment of all instruments of the promotion mix is an important new tendency in marketing communication. An important development is that due to the advertising clutter, the power of impersonal advertisement via the mass media is lessened. Other significant challenges are the appearance of new, interactive media, such as websites and email, the increased importance of relationship marketing and the need for distinctive communication. So, in different market situations, companies have evolved a completely integrated system of marketing communication that links up with sports sponsorship.[30] These various promotion components can be used to take advantage of the different facets of the sports sponsorship project.

Possibilities for integrated sports marketing communications

A creative implementation of the promotion mix is likely to result in consistent expressions in terms of content and design and in maximum communications impact. Mutual strengthening of the instruments employed could lead to a synergistic effect, which means that the total effect on the knowledge, attitude and behaviour of the target group is much stronger than the sum of the effect of the individual elements.[31]

Each promotion instrument may affect the other parts of the marketing communication. Integral marketing communication in sport means that sports sponsorship is a lever for the other instruments of marketing communication. In other words, sports sponsorship is an investment that demands investment. The size of the sponsorship leverage package depends on, among other things, the content of the sports sponsorship, the marketing aims, the brand awareness and the brand image. This sponsorship development budget is in addition to the cost of the sports sponsorship, which usually just covers the investment in rights. The extent of integration of sports sponsorship in marketing communication is an initial measure with which to evaluate the effectiveness of sports sponsorship (see Chapter 7).

Outline 1.8 Time-effectiveness of sports sponsorship and other marketing communications instruments

Aim	Long term	Short term
'Think'/'feel'	Sports sponsorship	Fairs, exhibitions
	Advertising	
	Public relations	
'Do'	Personal selling	Sales promotion
		Direct-marketing communication
		Point-of-sales communication
		Internet communication

Leverage of sports sponsorship with other instruments is also essential due to the different time-effectiveness of these instruments (see Outline 1.8). Sports sponsorship is more likely to be effective in the long term because of its implicit and indirect message. With sponsorship, a brand sends an indirect message to the customer after the customer has come into direct contact with a sports sponsorship project.

Barriers to integrated sports sponsorship communication

Specific environmental factors in sport and in its marketing make an integral marketing communication in sport difficult (Outline 1.9).

Outline 1.9 Barriers to an integrated sports sponsorship communication

- Persistent sport hobbyism

- Reticence by advertising agencies with regard to sports projects

- Fear of uncontrollable factors in sport

- Inertia due to triumphs or logo visibility in media

- Deficiencies in communication and coordination

Persistent sport hobbyism is the primary explanation for the failure of integrated marketing communication in sport. This means that managers could act in an economically irrational manner due to being dazzled by the sports event.[32] Since, at the top of a company, there is some room to manoeuvre,[33] allowing personal objectives to be fostered alongside company goals, decision-makers could adopt an amateur approach to the selection and development of sports sponsorship offerings. This amateurism or hobbyism was typical of 'old sponsor cultures', when the sports manager's job was finished after the purchase of the promotional sport rights.[34] Because of hobbyism, sports sponsorship projects could be an end in themselves instead of a means of promotion. Indeed, the success or failure of integrated communication depends on the managers' ability (or lack of it) to maintain a rational distance from the sports sponsorship events. The many emotions that sport arouses could also explain why companies sometimes remain too long in sports sponsorship. Despite the fact that every extra euro to acquire sponsorship rights results in a reduced return (and could have been invested in other means of promotion, e.g. leaflets, advertising or personal selling), the company continues to support the sports project. Cycling sponsorship provides illustrations of investments with a poor yield. The Italian cycling world was in uproar at the end of 1995 after the director of the textile company MG, main sponsor of the top cycling team MG-Boys, died. His death resulted in a swift suspension of the sponsorship.

A second barrier to an integral policy might be that the advertising agency advises the client, out of self-interest, not to use sport as a signboard. Advertising agencies are often not enthusiastic about committing part of the communication budget to sports sponsorship, because they do not receive a commission for investing in the promotional sport rights. From this, traditional media campaigns may be a more lucrative alternative for advertising agencies.[35] Many marketing communication agencies do not yet have the experience to surround sports sponsorship powerfully and creatively and therefore advise their clients not to choose sport.

A third reason why implementing sports sponsorship is not easy might be the dependence of the sponsor on the sport. The behaviour of the sponsored team on and off the field might affect the sponsor's image, and, for example, doping or bribery scandals could tarnish the brand image; for example, hooliganism could put the sports club, and the sponsor, in a bad light.

The fact that the companies often expect just logo visibility and do not sufficiently utilize the properties and characteristics of sport might be another drawback for an integral policy. For too long, the sports sponsorship project was an island within the organization. There seem to be multiple causes for this non-professional attitude, e.g. lack of knowledge about the means and the working and effectiveness of the instrument of sport, combined with a limited amount of practical experience and a lack of sponsorship-evaluation methods. Also, the fear that yields would be disappointing is likely to be a stumbling block to elaborating a professional sponsorship policy.

Finally, the coordination and planning of sports marketing communication are perceived to be very complex and labour-intensive, both inside and outside the company. On the other hand, buying media space as part of an advertising campaign seems less complex than investing in the right sports project. It is evident that sports sponsorship might uncover any internal tensions within an

organization. For example, the union representative who has just been refused his or her request to increase the number of company parking spaces will not be happy when the athlete to whom the company is paying high sponsorship fees is constantly in the news in a negative light. In addition, sports communication sometimes demands specialized outsourcing, which could make coordination and planning more difficult. Strong egos and territorial problems between, for instance, press, PR and marketing communication managers could also make integrated communication difficult.

1.7 Summary

Sport satisfies a number of fundamental needs for consumers, including health and fitness, relaxation and pleasure, achievement, acquiring skills, and sharing experiences and emotions. At the same time, a series of characteristics of sport can be identified that affect the marketing process. Some of these characteristics reflect attributes associated with unique marketing services: sport is intangible, unpredictable and difficult to control, while the consumer is heavily involved and sport production and consumption coincide. The fact that sport is a unique service product has significant consequences for the sports marketer, who cannot control the core product and should place marketing emphasis on product extensions. Marketing communication is a dominant element of the job description of the sports marketer. It consists of marketing communication of sport on the one hand (sports brands) and marketing communication through sport (non-sports brands) on the other. Usually, sports sponsorship is the pivotal element in the sports promotion portfolio. Sports sponsorship, supported by PR and advertising, aims primarily to achieve cognitive and affective effects. The idea is to influence the target group's brand knowledge and attitude.

Through action-oriented communication, which also combines with sponsored sports projects, an organization tries ultimately to stimulate increased sales. Thematic sponsorship communication instruments typically are employed for a longer period, while instruments of action communication, in contrast, are implemented only for short periods. A creative use of the instruments of marketing communication as an extension of sports sponsorship might result in a synergistic effect. In this case, the total knowledge, attitude and change in behaviour of the target group might be greater than the sum total of the effect of the individual instruments. However, specific sport factors, such as being dazzled by the glamour, glitter or logo visibility of the sports sponsorship project, could be barriers to an integrated promotional approach to sports sponsorship projects. Also, factors inherent in the organization of marketing communication, such as the coordination costs and the self-interest of advertising agencies, might inhibit an integral policy.

Key terms

Core values
Emotional attachment
Generic sport components
Integrated marketing communication
Interaction
Marketing communication of sport
Marketing communication through sport
Participant sport
Personal identification
Promotion mix
Service marketing
Social status
Spectator sport
Sports advertising
Sports consumer
Sports direct marketing
Sports industry
Sports management
Sports marketing
Sports marketing communication mix
Sports marketing leverage
Sports public relations
Sports sales promotion
Sports service
Sports sponsorship communication
Subjective experience

Questions

Synergy
1. On the basis of Outline 1.1, discuss how two basketball players might perceive the properties of sport differently, in terms of meeting basic needs and generic and specific sport components.

2. Discuss the elements of sport that you believe contribute most to the uniqueness of sports marketing.

3. Find the names of some sports organizations to illustrate the different sport modes in the sports industry.

4. Explain and illustrate the difference between sports marketing and sports promotion.

5. How does the sports marketing communication mix differ from the traditional marketing communication mix?

Endnotes

1 Mullin, B.J., Hardy, S. and Sutton, W.A. (2000), *Sport Marketing*. Champaign, IL: Human Kinetics.
2 Council of Europe (1993), *Comité pour le développement du sport*. Strasbourg: Council of Europe.
3 Meek, A. An estimate of the size and supported economic activity of the sports industry in the United States, *Sport Marketing Quarterley*, 6(4), 15–21.
4 Parks, J. and Quarterman, J. (2003), *Contemporary Sport Management*. Champaign, IL: Human Kinetics.
5 Renson, R. (1976), Social status symbolism of sport stratification, *Hermes*, 10, 433–43.
6 Scheerder, J., Taks, M., Vanreusel, B. and Renson, R. (2001), Is de actieve sportbeoefening in Vlaanderen gedemocratiseerd? Over de sociale gelaagdheid van de sportdeelname gedurende de periode 1969–1999, *Tijdschrift voor Sociologie*, 22(4), 383–20.
7 Dejonghe, T. (2001), *De noodzaak aan exogeen opgelegde economisch-geografische principes bij het professionaliseren van het door endogene factoren ontstane wereldsportstelsel. Gevalstudie: het lokalisatievraagstuk van het topvoetbal in België*, doctoral thesis. Ghent: University of Ghent.
   Dejonghe (p. 289) classifies (top) sport as person-related, immaterial, non-sustainable consumer–oriented services with an economic function.
8 Lovelock, C., Vandermerwe, S. and Lewis, B. (1996), *Services Marketing. A European Perspective*. Harlow: Pearson Education.
9 Shilbury, D., Quick, S. and Westerbeek, H. (1998), *Strategic Sport Marketing*. St Leonards: Allen & Unwin.
10 De Knop, P., Van Meerbeek, R., Vanreusel, B., *et al.* (1992), Marketingtendensen in de sport, *Praktijkgids Sportmanagement*, 1, 4.
11 Shilbury *et al.* (1998), op cit.
12 Chelladurai, P. (2001), *Managing Organizations for Sport and Physical Activity. A Systems Perspective*. Scottsdale, AZ: Holcomb Hathaway.
13 Ibid.
14 Parks and Quarterman (2003), op cit.
15 Brassington, F. and Pettit, S. (2000), *Principles of Marketing*. Harlow: Pearson Education.
16 Kotler, P., Armstrong, G., Saunders, J. and Wong, V. (1999), *Principles of Marketing*. Upper Saddle River, NJ: Prentice Hall.
17 Gray, D. (2001), Sport marketing: strategics and tacties. In: Parkhouse, D. (ed.), *The Management of Sport: Its Foundation and Application*. Boston, MA: McGraw-Hill, pp. 300–336.
18 Shilbury *et al.* (1998), op cit.
19 Shilbury *et al.* (1998), op cit.
20 Shilbury *et al.* (1998), op cit.

21 Burnett, J. and Menon, A. (1993), Sports marketing: a new ball game with new rules, *Journal of Advertising Research*, 33, 21–36.
The term 'sport marketing' was first used in the American specialist journal *Advertising Age* in 1978 and described the activities of consumer and industrial product marketers who were using sport as a promotional vehicle or sponsorship platform (commonly referred to as marketing through sport). The term originated in marketing practice and was first elaborated in the 1980s and 1990s in the American academic literature, as in the *Journal of Sport Management* (first published in 1987) and the specialist journal *Sports Marketing Quarterly* (first published in 1992) and in standard textbooks. In the European academic world, attention is regularly paid to aspects of sports marketing (primarily sports sponsorship), as in the *International Journal of Sports Marketing and Sport Sponsorship* (first published in 1997) and the *European Sport Management Quarterly* (formerly the *European Journal of Sport Management*, first published in 1994).

22 Argenti, P.A. (1996), Corporate communication as a discipline: toward a definition, *Management Communication Quarterly*, 10(1), 73–97.

23 Floor, J.M. and van Raaij, W.F. (1998), *Marketing-communicatiestrategie*. Groningen: Stenfert Kroese.

24 Pope, N. and Turco, D. (2001), *Sport and Event Marketing*. Roseville, NSW: McGraw-Hill.

25 Logman, M., Matthijssens, P. and van Raaij, F. (1999), *Marketingcommunicatie in zakelijke markten*. Alphen aan den Rijn: Samsom.

26 Derksen, G. (1992), Reclame, reclame-communicatie en onderzoek. In: Roomer, J. and Van Tilborgh, C. (eds), *Intern/Extern: Het integreren van communicatie in bedrijven, organisaties en instellingen*. Deventer: Kluwer Bedrijfswetenschappen, p. 8.

27 Roe, C. (2001), *Trends in Sponsorship: the Emergence of the Experience*. Brussels: Congress Institute for International Research.

28 Smith, A. and Westerbeek, H. (2002), *Sport Business in the Global Marketplace*. London: Macmillan.

29 Pine, B.J. and Gilmore, J.H. (2001), *De beleveniseconomie*. Schoonhoven: Academic Service; Schmitt, B. (1999), *Experiential Marketing*. New York: Free Press; Roe (2001), op cit.

30 De Pelsmacker, P., Geuens, M. and Van den Bergh, J. (2004), *Marketing Communications,* 2nd edn. Harlow: Pearson Education.

31 Poiesz, T. and van Raaij, W.F. (2002), *Synergetische marketing: Een visie op oorzaken en gevolgen van veranderend consumentengedrag*. Amsterdam: Pearson Education.

32 Segers, K. (1998), *De macht om zich met het nutteloze in te laten: Bedrijfssponsorship als particulier kunstinitiatief aan het einde van de twintigste eeuw. Een onderzoek naar haar betekenis en efficiëntie in België,* doctoral thesis, Brussels: VUB.

33 Lagae, W. (1997), Het pokerspel van de professionele wielersponsorship. In: Van Tilborgh, C. and Duyck, R. (eds), *Marketingjaarboek 1997*. Zellik: Roularta Books, pp. 86–94.

34 Crimmins, J. and Horn, M. (1996), Sponsorship: from management ego trip to marketing success, *Journal of Advertising Research*, 36(4), 11–20.

35 Van Spauwen, B. (2001), *Waarom reclame niet werkt*. Tielt: Lannoo.

Case 1 Sponsoring the football World Cup and European Championship

Key learning points

After studying this case, you will be able to:

- understand the hierarchical relationships between official sponsors and suppliers of top sports events;

- illustrate the central ideas behind sports sponsorship communications

- distinguish between business-to-consumer and business-to-business brands.

Recently the European and world football championships have grown by leaps and bounds into a marketing communication feast. Various categories of sponsors have invested in and communicated through these international football championships. The world and European football championships were, or are, being organized in the following countries between 1996 and 2010.

World football championships:
  1998 France

  2002 Japan and South Korea

  2006 Germany

  2010 South Africa

European football championships:
  1996 UK

  2000 Belgium and the Netherlands

  2004 Portugal

  2008 Austria and Switzerland

In the study described by Easton and Mackie (1998), the attitude of consumers with regard to sponsoring and sponsors was investigated (Figure 1.4). The public had a realistic attitude towards the sponsors: 83% of respondents were aware that sponsoring has commercial aims and 77% regarded sponsoring as a means to create a better image. Nevertheless, 77% and 70% of the respondents realized that sponsoring is essential for, respectively, the tournament in particular and the sport in general. Finally, the public also distinguished between sponsoring and advertising. Approximately three-quarters of the interviewees felt that sponsoring was a more distinctive manner of promoting than advertising. In contrast, 58% of the respondents did not distinguish between sponsoring and advertising.

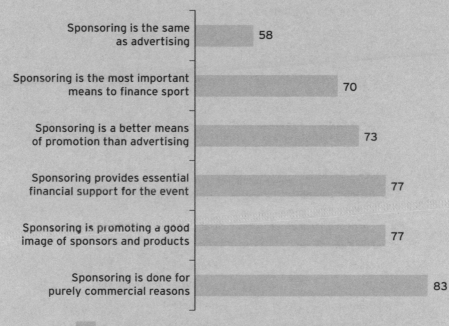

Sponsoring is the same as advertising — 58

Sponsoring is the most important means to finance sport — 70

Sponsoring is a better means of promotion than advertising — 73

Sponsoring provides essential financial support for the event — 77

Sponsoring is promoting a good image of sponsors and products — 77

Sponsoring is done for purely commercial reasons — 83

Percentage mostly or entirely agreeing with comment

Figure 1.4 General perception of the sponsoring of Euro '96.
Source: Easton, S. and Mackie, P. (1998), When football came home: a case history of the sponsorship activity at Euro '96, *International Journal of Advertising*, 17(1), 99-114.

Easton and Mackie (1998) surveyed the perception of the brands sponsoring Euro '96: Carlsberg, Canon, Coca-Cola, Fujifilm, General Motors, JVC, McDonald's, MasterCard, Philips, Snickers and Umbro. Brands that sponsored the European football championship had the image of a strong brand (Figure 1.5). Four-fifths of the respondents felt that these products could be bought anywhere in the world. They considered the sponsoring brands to be market leaders (64%) and producers of high-quality products (40%). There was also a certain amount of identification with the sponsoring brands by about half of the interviewees.

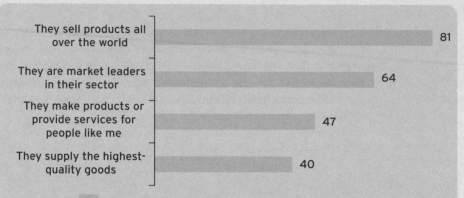

Figure 1.5 Perception of the products and services of the Euro '96 sponsors, *Source*: Easton, S. and Mackie, P. (1998), When football came home: a case history of the sponsorship activity at Euro '96, *International Journal of Advertising*, 17(1), 99–114.

Table 1.2 Official partners and suppliers for France '98

Official partners	Official suppliers
Eurocard/Mastercard	Danone
Fuji Film	EDS
Gillette	France Télécom
JVC	Hewlett–Packard France
Philips	La Poste
Opel	Manpower
McDonald's	Sybase
Adidas	
Snickers	
Coca-Cola	
Canon	
Budweiser*	

*Because of the Evin Act, which forbids advertising of alcoholic products, Casio replaced Budweiser as boarding sponsor in the stadium.

Tables 1.2 and 1.3 show the composition of the official partners and suppliers for France '98. It is interesting to see how a number of these official partners took up the key values of the event. For Coca-Cola, for example, the football World Cup formed a significant communication stepping stone. Coca-Cola's most important goal for communication was to address its target group and maintain the high brand preference. Not being present at an event of such size, and thus giving a competitor a chance, would be a disaster for the marketing giant. Coca-Cola also wanted to show that it understands and shares its clients' passion for football. 'Refreshment' was the key word. On the one hand, Coca-Cola's message was an attempt to guarantee emotional refreshment by making a link to the consumers' passion. On the other hand, Coca-Cola means physical refreshment as the football player or leisure sports person turns to the soft drink to cool down after exertion. The communication involving the World Cup focused primarily on the main target group of 12- to 19-year-olds.

Table 1.3 Official partners and suppliers for Euro 2000

Official partners	Official suppliers
Carlsberg	Adecco
Coca-Cola	Adidas
Fujifilm	Cisco
Hyundai	Connexxion
JVC	KLM
Eurocard/MasterCard	Lever Fabergé
McDonald's	Nashuatec
Philips	Nestlé
PlayStation	Total Fina
Pringles	Telfort
PSINet	
SPORTAL.com	

France '98 formed a cornerstone of Coca-Cola's worldwide marketing activity. Through promotion activities and local marketing activities, fans from over 60 countries were brought together to share their passion for the world's largest and most exciting football event. To stress its universal character, Coca-Cola sponsored a tour of the World Cup through three continents. This provided an excellent opportunity for fans in Nigeria, Saudi Arabia, South Korea, the UK, the Netherlands and France to share in the aura of the World Cup. To express the physical and emotional refreshment, a number of country-specific actions were undertaken. The Cup was first kissed by the star Ronald Koeman on Dutch soil. Then the Cup toured the Netherlands, where fans could share their passion by holding the Cup for a moment. In the football-mad Netherlands, a day for fans was held on 7 June 1998 in the Amsterdam Arena. Special activities were arranged for children. In a competition, children could qualify to play a preliminary match or to be a ball boy or girl or a flag bearer in a game at France '98. A striking action by Coca-Cola Belgium involved the first prize in its promotion. The main question consisted of calculating how long it would take the Belgian goalkeeper Filip De Wilde to run a lap around a football field. The winner was allowed, together with a partner, to attend a match in the first round of every World Cup final for life, with flights, tickets and accommodation paid for entirely by Coca-Cola.

By becoming involved as the official World Cup '98 sponsor, Adidas wanted to communicate that it produces more than just football products. Adidas is the undisputed market leader in the football market. Nike was on the lookout to grab a larger share of the market, which until recently was not so aggressively manipulated. Adidas was the sponsor, supplier (balls, ball boys and girls, and 12 000 volunteers) and licence holder (Adidas was the only brand allowed to sell official World Cup clothing) at the World Cup. By clothing the contemporary stars Kluivert, Zidane and Van der Sar, Adidas wanted to communicate that international top football players are very selective in the materials they use. Direct communication was done with the primary target group (boys between 12 and 19 years old) through a music channel. Youth tournaments were held at a test centre for Adidas products in Belgium and the Netherlands, and a football village was constructed in the shadow of the Eiffel Tower to organize a youth tournament during the World Cup.

France '98 was a platform for McDonald's to express its association with the top athletes from around the world and with a unique sports event. Via restaurant decoration and special World Cup packaging, it wanted to convey pleasure and suspense to the customers in 75 McDonald's countries. Also, it stimulated the effect across the breadth of football, with social programmes and sport-oriented community work in cities in France. Promotion actions consisted of offering a Mc WC Special (special hamburger, served with salsa; this mildly spicy sauce was supposed to suggest an association with Brazilian football) and a WC Meal. Restaurants were also decorated using a World Cup theme. The McDonald's Young Photojournalist Contest (sponsor pooling with Fuji) involved a competition for children aged between eight and 14 from the Netherlands, the UK, Italy and Argentina. Children sent in photographs whose subject was football. The Mc Goal! Goal! Goal! initiative rewarded attractive football through gifts to the SOS Children's Village, the official charity programmme of the Fédération Internationale de Football Association (FIFA).

The joining of forces between official sponsors and a government partner was a new trend that was becoming apparent. The Cities Foot Youth Tournament, for example, was organized after pooling the sponsorship of Adidas, McDonald's, Danone and the Ministry of Youth and Sport. The sponsors organized a football tournament for French youths born after 1984 in 128 French cities, in which the winning team would be combined with youth teams from Brazil, Mexico and South Africa. The initiative attempted to promote integration and solidarity, community work, festivities in cities and sporting encounters. *T'es Jeune, t'es Foot* was another pooling initiative sponsored by Coca-Cola and Crédit Agricole. This tried to realize the dreams of thousands of young football players: participating in World Cup '98, for example as a ball boy or girl. Via a quartet of actions, the two sponsors wanted to give young football players a unique football experience.

Finally, a few remarks about the sponsoring motives of the official suppliers Nashuatec and Adecco. Nashuatec wanted to communicate through sponsoring Euro 2000 that it not only produces photocopying, printer and fax apparatus but also produces hardware and software and consulting services. Nashuatec Benelux supplied the tournament with 450 remanufactured fax and photocopying machines and printers and 70 technicians to manage the flow of documents. By providing second-hand machines, Nashuatec wanted to demonstrate that these devices had been restored perfectly. Euro 2000 was a stepping stone for the company to invite 2500 business contacts and to conduct targeted image campaigns.

As the official supplier of Euro 2000, it was Adecco's task to recruit 330 volunteers per stadium. In and around the eight stadiums, there was a recurring need for chauffeurs, hosts, ticket collectors, warehouse workers, etc. The volunteers were rewarded for their work with an Adidas outfit, food and drink, and reimbursement of expenses. Recruitment was conducted through advertisements in local newspapers, with application options including forms in the Adecco offices and on the Internet. Adecco received in exchange the right to use the logo and the mascot. As exclusive supplier, it also obtained logo visibility via boarding.

Questions for discussion

1. Visit http://fifaworldcup.yahoo.com. Make a sectoral analysis of the official sponsors and suppliers of Germany 2006.

2. Visit www.hyundai.com. What are the key benefits for the South Korean car brand Hyundai of being the official sponsor of country football tournaments? Identify how Hyundai surrounds this sponsorship investment.

3. Which key football values were taken up by Coca-Cola during France '98? Visit www.coca-cola.com and give the essence of the sponsor's communication of Coca-Cola.

4. Compare the image transfer that a business-to-business brand and a business-to-consumer brand want to achieve through sponsoring an international football championship.

References and further reading

Business Week (1998), The real match, *Business Week*, 8 June 1998.

Easton, S. and Mackie, P. (1998), When football came home: a case history of the sponsorship activity at Euro '96, *International Journal of Advertising*, 17(1), 99–114.

Interesting websites

www.euro2004.com
http://fifaworldcup.yahoo.com

2

SPORTS SPONSORSHIP

Monday 19 July 1982, 15th stage of Manosque-Orcières Merlette

From the frying pan into the fire. The director of the soft drinks brand Capri-Sonne (our sponsor) has arrived. At his side the company's publicity manager. Two short speeches are made. The verbal talent of those two surprises me. Not one improper word. Their faces radiate kindness. Nevertheless, their message was clear and business-like. It can be summarized as follows: We have not yet won – that was true. It is about time that we win – we think so too. Investing in a team that doesn't win is a bad investment – we agree completely. A dissatisfied sponsor manager is unpredictable – goes without saying. At the end of this year the contracts expire – fact. The management will remain here on the Tour for three days to follow the team's performance closely – squirm, squirm, squirm. We wish everyone success in the near future.

(Peter Winnen, cyclist)

Overview

Sports sponsorship: an exploration

The growth of sports sponsorship

Goals and target groups of marketing communication in sports sponsorship

Buying sports sponsorship

Selling sports sponsorship

Aims

After studying this chapter, you will be able to:

- explain why sports sponsorship is a rapidly growing instrument of marketing communication;

- identify the goals and target groups of marketing communication reached by sports sponsorship;

- evaluate different forms of sports sponsorship based on criteria;

- understand the corporate management of sports sponsorship;

- be able to approach, as a person in charge of a sporting organization, potential sport sponsors in a structured manner.

2.0   Introduction

Sports sponsorship currently has a special place in marketing communication. For too long, sports sponsorship has been driven by the passions of top managers, who have also enjoyed the glamour and glitter of sporting projects. The preference for sport was, perhaps, historically associated with their passion. Within this hobbyistic approach, the sponsored activity was one alongside the other elements of marketing communication. Since then, the integration of sports sponsorship in the promotional mix has increased greatly. Working around sport forms has grown into a creative and powerful instrument of marketing communication.

Depending on the context, the term '(sports) sponsorship' has different meanings (Section 2.1). Sports sponsorship has experienced a spectacular rise (Section 2.2), and it is an ideal instrument to achieve various goals and reach target groups of marketing communication (Section 2.3). We shall focus in this chapter on tactical and strategic aspects of sports sponsorship. Under what conditions is sports sponsorship a well-considered platform for the marketing communication of an organization (Section 2.4)? The management of sports sponsorship demands considerable discussion, since for both the sport sponsor and the sponsored sport, a sponsor contribution has significant juridical and fiscal consequences.[1] However, these aspects fall outside the scope of this book.[2] When a sporting organization approaches potential sponsors, this should also be carried out only after considerable discussion (Section 2.5).

Key ideas and terms of selling sponsorship are illustrated in Case 2, which tells a story from the world of recreational sport. Contrary to the main focus of the text, we analyse this case from a recipient's viewpoint. Indeed, to open up new sources of income, local tennis club Baseline decided to recruit sponsors, which demands good ideas and much discipline.

2.1 Sports sponsorship: an exploration

Sponsorship

Sponsorship is normally considered to be a business agreement between two parties. The sponsor provides money, goods, services or know-how. In exchange, the sponsored party (individual, event or organization) offers rights and associations that the sponsor utilizes commercially. The idea of reciprocation echoes Sleight (p. 4),[3] who defines sponsoring as '... a business relationship between a provider of funds, resources or services and an individual, event or organization which offers in return some rights and association that may be used for commercial advantage ...'.

A sponsor therefore expects communicative elements in exchange from the sponsored party. In this case, there is mutual benefit for the sponsor and the recipient. Sponsoring is described by Otker (p. 77) as '... buying and exploiting an association with an event, a team, a group, etc. for specific marketing (communications) purposes ...'. Bradley and colleagues (p. 123) describe sponsoring as '... the financing of an event, personality, activity or product to improve customers' awareness and attain media coverage, most commonly in the arts and sports ...'.[5] In this definition, improving brand awareness via sponsoring and the visibility of the culture or sport-sponsoring project is key.

Any definition should distinguish commercial sponsoring from corporate philanthropy. Patronage implies that an individual or organization donates funds for altruistic benefit.[6] Patronage is associated with a magnanimous intention. The patron makes funds or equipment available for an organization or an individual and expects for this a minimal contribution in return, such as good standing in the community or an artwork. Until the start of the 1970s, sponsorship was considered a special category of donation. Patronage is more typically associated with cultural activities and usually takes place more discreetly than sponsoring. However, even with a donation, the recipient should benefit.[7] Charity, where an individual or corporation makes a donation and publicizes the fact, is – just like patronage – different from sponsoring, according to the previous descriptions, because a commercial orientation is absent.[8] There is also an important difference between subsidizing and sponsoring. By subsidizing sport, the government supports the sports sector to achieve sport policy aims. Subsidizing in the sense of a 'sport-for-everyone' philosophy is an example of this.

Despite the fact that the meaning of the term 'sponsorship' can be traced back to Roman private law (the 'sponsor' supplies security if the debtor cannot meet his or her debt obligations),[9] it is still a relatively new concept in marketing literature and the sports industry. In the international specialist literature of the past few years, interest in sponsoring as a theme for research has grown greatly.[10] Sponsoring is the most recent instrument in the promotion mix. Irwin and colleagues (p. 15) state that '... sponsorship may be considered as the newest entry in the contemporary sport promotion mix ...'.[11] Meanwhile, sponsoring has grown into a mature instrument of the communication mix. This implies that sponsors are no longer satisfied with a standard package as reciprocation, but impose increasingly higher demands on the sponsored projects.

Global sponsorship market

Despite the difficulties of quantitative analysis of the sponsorship market, information on the evolution of sponsoring expenses around the world has been provided by three independent reliable sources, namely the International Events Group (IEG), Sports Marketing Surveys (SMS) and the SportBusiness Group. These organizations have been collecting data on the amounts invested in sponsoring. The sport-sponsoring amounts reported are a 'cost of entry'. To utilize the sponsoring opportunity fully, the costs for the sponsoring rights have to be supplemented with other instruments of marketing communication.

That sponsoring is a relatively rapidly growing communication instrument can be seen from the data from IEG. In 1984, the market for sponsoring worldwide was estimated at €3 billion.[12] Total sponsor amounts for 2002 were estimated at €20 billion (see Figure 2.1).

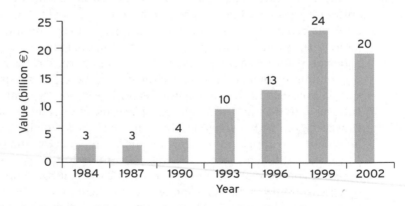

Figure 2.1 Evolution of the world sponsorship market 1984–2002.
Note: dollars converted to euros at the exchange rate at the end of the year.
Source: Sponsorship Research International (2001), *2000 Worldwide Sponsorship Market Values Report*. London: SRi/SportBusiness Group; and Kolah, A. (2003), *Maximising the Value of Sponsorship*. London: SportBusiness Group.

Table 2.1 Value of sponsorship rights throughout the world

	2000 (in € billions)	%	2003 (in € billions)	%
Europe	8.3	31.5	5.9	28.2
North America	9.3	35.1	8.3	40.1
Central and South America	1.9	7.2	1.7	8.4
Asia–Pacific	6.4	24.2	3.7	17.9
Other	0.5	2	1.1	5.4
Total	26.4	100	20.8	100

Note: dollars converted to euros at the exchange rate at the end of the year.
Source: Sponsorship Reasearch International (2001), *2000 Worldwide Sponsorship Market Values Report*. London: SRi/Sport Business Group; and Kolah, A. (2003), *Maximising the Value of Sponsorship*. London: SportBusiness Group.

From a continental perspective, investments in sponsoring both in 2000 and in 2003 were highest in the USA, with a share of 35 and 40%, respectively, of the world total (see Table 2.1). According to sector, in 2002, worldwide soft drinks were the most important sports sponsors, followed by cars, telecommunications, personal care, banks, beer, other financial services, sports clothing, finance companies and insurance agencies.

Sponsorship investments in Europe were estimated at €8.2 billion for 2000 (see Table 2.2). Sponsorship expenses were highest in Germany, the UK and France in 2000. Sponsorship investments in the Netherlands, Spain and Italy were at a similar level.

Table 2.2 Value of sponsorship rights in Europe in 2000

	Sponsorship (€ m)	% of Europe
Europe	8245	100.00
Germany	2513	29.79
UK	1337	16.21
France	1105	13.40
Other European countries	926	11.24
The Netherlands	601	7.29
Spain	547	6.63
Italy	541	6.56
Switzerland	269	3.27
Sweden	209	2.53

Table 2.2 continued

	Sponsorship (€ m)	% of Europe
Denmark	122	1.48
Finland	76	0.93
Ireland	56	0.68

Note: dollars converted to euros at the exchange rate at the end of the year.
Source: Sponsorship Research International (2001), *2000 Worldwide Sponsorship Market Values Report*. London: SRi/SportBusiness Group; and Kolah, A. (2003), *Maximising the value of Sponsorship*. London. SportBusiness Group.

In the UK, expenditure on sponsoring increased greatly during the 1980s and 1990s. In 1980, the UK sponsorship market was estimated by Mintel at €80 million;[13] in 1999, it amounted to €521 million (see Figure 2.2).

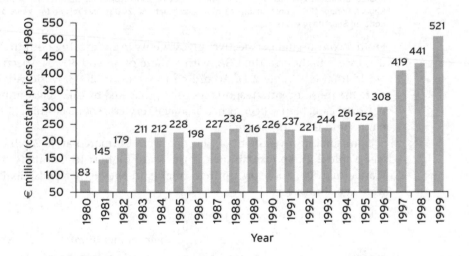

Figure 2.2 UK sponsoring market for 1980–99.
Note: pound sterling converted to euros at the average exchange rate in December of the year. Calculation of the constant prices of 1980 on the basis of the GDP-Deflator of the Ministry of Finance based on the national accounts.
Source: Mintel (2000), *Sponsorship 2000 UK*. London: Mintel International Group.

Worldwide, the annual growth of sponsoring between 1990 and 1999 was estimated by Irwin and colleagues (2002) at 10–15%. In the 1990s, the annual growth in advertising and sales promotion was only 6%. Sponsorship rights form only a small part of the marketing communication portfolio. In Europe in 2000, the share of sponsoring in advertising budgets was 8%.

① 2.2 Growth of sports sponsorship

Sport is the area in which sponsorship has developed furthest. Depending on the year being studied, the country and the definitions, the share of sports sponsorship within sponsorship as a whole lies approximately between 50 and 70% of the total. In 2000, for example, the share of sport in sponsorship in both Germany and the Netherlands was 59%. Along with sport sponsoring, cultural sponsoring is an important field of application. Public and social sponsoring (cause-related marketing) and sponsoring of education are other fields of application. The sponsoring of television programmes, in contrast, is often classified under sponsoring but is actually associated more closely with advertising.

The term 'sports sponsorship' is linked seamlessly to the concept of sponsorship. Sports sponsorship can have different meanings depending on its context. It is ' … any commercial agreement by which a sponsor, for the mutual benefit of the sponsor and sponsored party, contractually provides financing or other support in order to establish an association between the sponsor's image, brands or products and a sponsorship property in return for rights to promote this association and/or for the granting of certain agreed direct or indirect benefits …,'[14] directly or indirectly arising from the playing of sport. Sports sponsorship includes the right to display a brand name and/or company logo on media carriers in a sporting environment. In this case, 'sports sponsorship' means the same as 'promotional sport rights'. Promotional sport rights also include the right to mention the logo or the brand name of a sports project, for example, in advertisement campaigns, at points of sale or as part of PR activities. The duration of the sponsorship rights and the extent of sectorial and regional exclusivity are other key elements in a sponsorship agreement. Sports sponsorship is the logical entry into sports marketing communication. Some sports-sponsoring packages contain the most important elements of the sports promotion mix.

Promotional sports rights or sports sponsoring are distinguished from licences (promotional licensing). A sports licence is the purchase by an organization of the name or logo of a sports club or event. Companies or organizations wanting to display these symbols on their products pay for this privilege and obtain a licence. Through such official images, the company expects to stimulate sales. The European football championship Euro 2000, for example, had three categories of commercial partners.[15] The 12 official partners and 10 official suppliers were the official sport sponsors. There were also licence holders, who bought the right to sell official Euro 2000 products. The licence holders also bought the right to communicate using the official logo, the mascot and the trophy of Euro 2000.

The term 'endorsement' is also associated directly with the term 'sport sponsoring'. Translated literally, endorsement means ambassadorship. Celebrity endorsement means that a brand is associated, via sponsoring, with a famous athlete. A brand aims to capitalize on the emotional dependence of sport consumers and the inspirational nature of top athletes. For example, along with his

Real Madrid salary of €15m in 2003, David Beckham received additional income from sponsorship contracts with individual companies wanting to exploit his fame and image. Important private sponsors of Beckham were Vodafone (€1.4m), Pepsi (€2.8m), Marks & Spencer (€4.2m), Adidas (€4.2m), Brylcreem (€1.4m) and Gilette (€3m) (www.sport.be/business).

Sports sponsorship has deep historical roots. In ancient Greece, the elite supported athletic events, while in the Roman period, the elite sponsored, or even owned, the gladiators. The first modern commercial use of sports sponsoring has been traced to the placement of advertisements in the official programme of the 1896 Olympic Games in Athens.[16] The first recorded use of sports sponsoring in the UK occurred in 1898, when the year's Football League Champions Nottingham Forest endorsed the beverage company Bovril. Sport sponsoring began to break through around 1950.[17] In the UK, the first major sports sponsoring involved the 1956 Whitbread Gold Cup in horse racing.[18] Initially, the sports brands, newspapers and car makers were the first to approach sport. A major boost to sport sponsoring arose actively out of the prohibition of television advertising of alcohol and tobacco products. Consequently, tobacco companies turned to sponsoring. Sports sponsoring took off in the 1970s, when non-sports brands discovered sport as a means of communication. In Case 3, these developments are illustrated for teams in professional cycling.

The quantitative importance of measuring sport sponsoring is not a simple thing to understand. For the following reasons, sponsoring data must be handled carefully:

- Sponsors do not always state (correctly) how much they have invested in a sport object.

- Sponsored sport organizations do not always state correctly how much sponsors are actually contributing.

- Budgets for sports sponsorship can include leverage activities.

- Budgets for sports sponsorship at the regional and local levels are not systematically recorded in a sport-sponsoring centre.

- The sponsoring industry is surrounded by non-disclosure and confidentiality agreements.

- In contrast to advertising costs in mass media, sponsoring expenses are more difficult to verify.

If information about the amount spent on sports sponsoring could cause trouble, then companies often prefer to underestimate or not disclose these budgets. Also, for the recipient, disclosing the funds obtained can involve a delicate balancing exercise. The sponsor's contribution can also change, depending on the individual case. In a number of cases, sponsoring can be deceptive. One Belgian study revealed that marketing managers have also included under the heading 'sponsoring budgets' the costs for PR (in 66% of cases), reimbursement of consultants (46% of those interviewed) and press relations (44% of the sample).[19]

Applications of sports sponsorship

Taking into account the sometimes limited reliability of sports sponsorship data, it is still possible to elaborate upon a few applications. Comparison over time allows us to follow the sums invested in sports sponsorship, which illustrate a steep rise in investment budgets. Olympic Games sponsorship is the first interesting application. All Olympic Games sponsorship is included in The Olympic Program (TOP). Primarily large companies retain the right to communicate their partnership with the Olympic Games during the Olympiad. An Olympiad is a period of four years in which the Summer Games, the Winter Games and the Paralympics are the most important events. Table 2.3 shows that the budget of TOP V is six times the budget of TOP I.

Table 2.3 Evolution of sponsoring sums of Olympic programs

TOP	Location	Period	Sum ($ million)	Partners
TOP I	Calgary, Seoul	1985-88	95	9
TOP II	Barcelona, Albertville	1989-92	175	12
TOP III	Lillehammer, Atlanta	1993-96	350	11
TOP IV	Nagano, Sydney	1997-2000	500	10
TOP V	Salt Lake City, Athens	2001-04	600	11

TOP, The Olympic Program.
Source: www.olympic.org/uk.news/index_uk.asp

A second application involves the UK sports sponsorship market, which has risen from €71 million in 1980 to €686 million in 2002, implying an average annual growth rate of 10.9 % (see Table 2.4). Key Note predicted that the annual growth rate of sports sponsorship would continue to increase by 5–6% until 2006, which would bring the total UK market for sports sponsorship in 2006 up to £550 million.[20] When classified into sectors, the financial institutions are the most important sport sponsors, followed by sporting goods manufacturers, alcoholic drinks, electronics/IT, car manufacturers and catering/leisure.

Table 2.4 UK sports sponsorship market for 1980-2002 (in € million at constant prices of 1980, year-on-year % change (prices in euro)) (original value in pound sterling in brackets)

Year	Value	Year-on-year change (%)	Year	Value	Year-on-year change (%)
1980	71 (30)	–	1992	300 (239)	-14
1981	132 (60)	86	1993	326 (250)	9
1982	170 (85)	29	1994	332 (265)	2
1983	202 (100)	18	1995	323 (285)	-3
1984	207 (110)	3	1996	399 (302)	23
1985	232 (125)	12	1997	486 (322)	22
1986	212 (145)	-9	1998	503 (353)	4
1987	244 (160)	15	1999	601 (377)	20
1988	295 (180)	21	2000	652 (400)	8
1989	298 (210)	1	2001	680 (421)	4
1990	328 (223)	10	2002	686 (442)	1
1991	347 (238)	6	1980-2002		10.9*

* Average growth rate 1980-2002.

Note: pound sterling converted to euros at the average exchange rate in December of the year. Calculation of the constant prices of 1980 on the basis of the GDP-Deflator of the Ministry of Finance based on the national accounts.

Source: Dunn, M. (2002), Sports Sponsorship: Market Report 2003, 3rd edn. Key Note.

The explosion in sports sponsorship budgets for top sports events is also seen in football. One main sponsor for the World Cup 2002 in Japan and South Korea had to pay approximately nine times as much as for the World Cup 1994 in the USA. The total of investments from all official sponsors grew from 146 million euros in 1994 to 275 million euros in 1998 and 488 million euros in 2002.[21] This trend of steeply rising budgets is also confirmed for European football championships. The sponsorship rights for Euro 2000, organized in the Netherlands and Belgium, amounted to double that for Euro 1996, organized in the UK. Considerable sponsor sums are also being pumped into the top football teams. Table 2.5 shows the annual investment (season 2002–03) of the main sponsors of important football clubs in Europe.

Table 2.5 Sponsorship of some European football clubs, 2002–03

Club	Sponsor (sector)	Sum (million euros)
Bayern München	T-Mobile (telecommunications)	15.8
Juventus	Fastweb (telecommunications)	12.9
Real Madrid	Siemens Mobile (telecommunications)	11.5
Manchester United	Vodafone (telecommunications)	10.8

Source: www.sport.be/business

These applications confirm the image of a gradual to explosive increase in budgets for sports sponsorship. A number of factors might explain this increased interest (Outline 2.1). Both brands and sport have become globalized. Because international events transcend national and cultural boundaries, brands communicate via sport. Brands also have discovered that sports sponsorship is a powerful medium to augment the brand experience and to stand out positively as a brand. Because sport is both a key activity and a catalyst for other activities, television channels transmit more hours of sports programming compared with some decades ago. With the liberalization of the economy, the commercialization of sport generally has been accepted by the public. The prohibition of advertising alcohol and tobacco products also produced a reorientation of promotion budgets towards sports sponsorship.

Outline 2.1 Explanations for the increased interest in sports sponsorship

- Globalization and professionalisation of brands
- Decreasing effectiveness of traditional advertising via mass media
- Globalization of sport
- Professionalization of sport
- Increased acceptance of commercialization of sport
- Increased television coverage of sporting competitions
- Changes in the media landscape
- Breakthrough of distinctive communication through sport
- Breakthrough of experiential communication through sport
- Ban on tobacco advertisements

Europe has been ascribed a more significant role as a magnet for sports sponsorship budgets in the period 2004–07. Catalysts include the 2004 Olympic Summer Games in Athens, the Euro 2004 football championship in Portugal, the 2006 Olympic Winter Games in Turkey and the football World Cup 2006 in Germany. It is also expected that interest in top European sports events, such as Wimbledon and Roland Garros in tennis, the Champions League in football and

the Tour de France and the World Cup races in cycling, will continue to grow. Europe also accommodates top sporting events in golf, rugby, athletics and skiing, which will become more important.

2.3 Goals and target groups of marketing communication in sports sponsorship

The motives for sports sponsorship vary widely.[22] Within a professional approach to sports sponsorship, the selection of the sport form depends on the marketing communication goals and the intended target group. Whether it makes sense to turn to sports sponsorship depends on the goals of marketing communication and of corporate communication (we shall return to this in Chapter 3). We shall not consider hobbyistic or personal motives, which still occur in the 'old sport' sponsoring culture. An important restriction in sports sponsorship is that a brand communicates a limited message, usually nothing more than the brand name and the logo. Therefore, sports sponsorship acts first and foremost on cognitive goals (see Outline 2.2). Because sponsoring acts indirectly and implicitly, a brand also strives for effective goals. Behavioural goals of sports sponsorship are explained in detail in Chapters 5 and 6. The marketing communication aims of sports sponsorship are listed in Outline 2.2.

Outline 2.2 Marketing communication goals in sports sponsorship for brands and products

- Cognitive goals

  Increasing brand awareness, e.g. Daewoo and football sponsorship

  Clarifying brand interpretation, e.g. Cofidis, le credit par téléphone and cycling sponsorship (see Case 7)

- Affective goals

  Support and change brand image, e.g. ING running tour (endurance and effort)

  Accentuate brand experience, e.g. The North Face and Conrad Anker – 'Never stop exploring'

- Behavioural aims

  Increasing brand loyalty, e.g. Coca-Cola and country football championship (see Case 1)

  Support and stimulate sales, e.g. Aquarius (see Case 6)

  Create distribution space, e.g. Quick.Step and cycling sponsorship

Brand value is created first through passive and later through active brand awareness. A business-to-consumer product will sell well only when the brand is sufficiently well known to the general public. Familiarity among specific target groups is important for business-to-business products. Every brand strives for as great a brand awareness as possible. In many sporting environments, the repetition of a brand name is the factor that increases brand awareness.

The sporting world presents a powerful forum to clearly bolster the brand name. For example, in the mid-1990s, an unknown South Korean car manufacturer, Daewoo, entered the saturated car market in Western Europe. Sponsoring of Roda JC in the Netherlands and of FC Lierse in Belgium was a cornerstone of Daewoo's marketing communication strategy. To make it clear that Daewoo is a car brand, the name Daewoo was placed on a car image on the football players' jerseys.[23]

Sport offers the possibility to associate a dynamic, young or friendly image of a sport with a brand. Each branch of sport embodies a number of values, which can have a positive effect on the sponsoring brand. Mountain climbing might be associated with effort and perseverance. For example, The North Face (slogan: 'Never stop exploring') has been sponsoring ice-wall climber Conrad Anker for years.[24] Gymnastics, on the other hand, has an image of purity, and sailing an image of relaxation and freedom, while brands that want to project masculinity might concentrate on motorized sports. Another example concerns international banker ING, sponsoring the most popular city marathons via an ING Running Tour. Through this project, values such as endurance, discipline and effort are transferred from the world of the participant to the brand.

However, sports sponsorship ensures added brand value not only in consumer markets but also in commercial markets. Air-conditioning manufacturer Daikin, co-sponsor of the Lampre cycling team between 1999 and 2002, offered a communication stepping stone to the distributors of its products in the key European countries. Values such as flexibility, effort, character and endurance were transferred from the sport of cycling to the brand.

Behavioural aims are achieved by utilizing sports sponsorship in combination with other instruments of marketing communication. The possible advantages that a brand gains from sponsoring will usually have an effect, after a while, on turnover and profit. Depending on the particular phase of life of a brand, the sport sponsor aims for an increase in top-of-mind (the first brand that an interviewee recalls spontaneously), spontaneous or assisted familiarity. By binding itself with a unique sports project, a brand attempts to distinguish itself from the competition in its communication strategy. This gives it a competitive advantage over rival brands. The classic example is Coca-Cola, which sponsors top sports events to stay ahead of its competitor Pepsi-Cola. Sales support via sports sponsorship can take various forms.

The motives for sports sponsorship listed in Outline 2.2 are not exhaustive. A brand that utilizes sports sponsorship creatively achieves a wide range of aims. Cycling team sponsor and laminate manufacturer Quick.Step wanted to achieve more and better distribution space in do-it-yourself businesses in key European countries, along with improved brand awareness.

Becoming familiar with and studying target groups forms an essential part of a marketing communication strategy. Every sports sponsorship strategy stands or falls according to a clear description of the goals as well as the target groups. Outline 2.3 reveals the connection between different groups of sports consumers on the one hand and the consumer and the commercial market on the other. Prospects, customers, sales people and suppliers are the traditional target groups of marketing communication. The trade press is an example of a group falling under the category 'other'.

Sports consumers can be classified according to interest in the sports event.[25] Someone who plays basketball will notice the brand names on the equipment of basketball players more quickly. A spectator in the sports stadium or along the track comes directly into contact with expressions of sports sponsorship. Passive sports players come into contact with sponsor expressions via the media. A passionate football fan will not want to miss a live transmission of the Champions League. Other sports fans limit themselves to the summary or only watch the highlights. The viewing figures for a live broadcast of a cycle race, for example, are above average during the last hour of the race. Finally, there are the passive sports players who are primarily interested in stories that 'go beyond sport'. This target group comes into contact with sponsor expressions via family magazines or lifestyle programmes featuring sponsored athletes.

Outline 2.3 Target groups of sports marketing communication

Segmentation of sports consumers	Target group and marketing communication				
	Prospect	Customer	Sales person	Supplier	Other
Active sports player					
Spectator					
Interest via media					
Live broadcasts					
Summary, highlights					
Incidental sport					

2.4 Buying corporate sports sponsorship

The management of sports sponsorship at the corporate level should be undertaken only after detailed consultation. Figure 2.3 shows the different stages to be followed in a systematic sports sponsorship plan in marketing communication.

Figure 2.3 Sports sponsorship plan in marketing communications.

Once a sponsor has decided to sponsor a particular sport, the sponsor must go about it quite strategically. The tactical tips have been summarized in the ten sponsor commandments (see Outline 2.4).[26]

Outline 2.4 The ten commandments for the sports sponsor

1. Above all, communicate thy sponsoring.

2. Follow thy personal preference in a sponsor decision only as a last resort. If thy personal preference succeeds, let thyself be surrounded by critical colleagues.

3. Holy be the link between brand and sports sponsorship.

4. Dear sponsor, be honoured.

5. Be interfering and demanding.

6. Never promise the recipient eternal loyalty.

7. Watch out for and be inspired by free-riders.

8. Be especially wary of fellow sponsors.

9. Invest primarily in sponsoring rights 'that live'.

10. Manage thy sports sponsoring dynamically and flexibly.

Selection of a form of sport

The sponsoring project that best reaches the desired target groups must be selected. Here we can distinguish between consumer and commercial markets. In the business-to-consumer environment, an organization tries to reach both its existing customers and potential customers. The existing customer database can then be arranged further by function of the turnover realized or of the purchasing frequency per customer. The commercial market involves significant actors such as sales people and suppliers.

Sports sponsorship can be subdivided into a number of basic forms: the sponsoring of individual athletes, sports clubs or teams, the sponsorship of sports events and sports organizations (leagues, unions, federations, competitions, prizes, etc.) and the sponsorship of sports facilities. Classified according to value, the sponsoring of sports organizations (federations, leagues, competitions) was the most important sports sponsorship category in 2002, with a share of 44%. Team (25%) and event sponsoring (22%) were other important categories, followed at a distance by official partners (4%), sponsorship of individual top athletes (3%) and sponsorship of official suppliers (2%).[27]

Gradually, sports facilities are also being sponsored, including football stadiums, foyers, sports auditoriums and sports halls. Venue branding is a normal affair in Canada, the USA and Australia. The Colonial Stadium, for example, named after an Australian insurance company, is a multisport stadium in Melbourne where primarily Australian-rules football and cricket are played. In Germany, strong German brands have invested in football stadiums since 2000. Examples include the AOL-Hamburg Arena, the Volkswagen Arena and the Allianz Arena. For five million euros, the naming rights for the new stadium for Bayern Munich in Fröttmaning were granted to the insurance group Allianz in Munich. Volkswagen Arena is the name of the new home base of the footballers from Vfl Wolfsburg. In Hamburg, the naming rights for the new stadium were granted to AOL for approximately three million euros annually. The top sports centre Stad Rotterdam and the Philipsstadion in Eindhoven are Dutch examples of venue sponsoring. Nevertheless, venue sponsoring in continental Europe is still in its infancy. With the increase in public–private partnership (PPP) in the construction and maintenance of the sporting infrastructure, a breakthrough is expected here in the near future.[28]

The sponsor's contribution takes the form of monetary funds or products or services. The sponsor's contribution can be fixed or can depend partly on the success of the team or event. For example, the official partners of Euro 2000 made significant financial contributions, while the official suppliers provided goods and services amounting to an agreed commercial value. Depending on the case, the financial contribution usually can either be spent without restrictions or should be devoted to a specific goal (financing transfer or expanding the sports programme). Examples of a material contribution with a clearly agreed commercial worth are products that the particular form of sport can use, e.g. tennis equipment or canteen infrastructure. Services, e.g. an exchange agreement with the media, or know-how, e.g. a secretariat to run the salary administration, can also be provided.

For a potential sponsor, there are five criteria that might be used to evaluate a sports sponsorship form (see Outline 2.5): the fit between the sport and the brand, the essential features of the sport, the possibilities for integration in the marketing communication, the duration of the impact period, and the estimate of the costs. Depending on the type of brand (business-to-consumer or business-to-business) or of the sponsoring aims, other selection criteria could additionally be given priority.

An interested sponsor might first investigate the essential features of a particular sport. What is the socioeconomic profile of the target group of the sport? Which key values and social statuses are associated with the sport? Do the sport values correspond with the central brand values (brand fit)?[29] Is there a match between the geographic reach of the brand and of the sport? The existence of synergistic values between sponsor and sponsored also seems to be very important. If both sponsor and sponsored are able to deliver the benefits needed by the other entity, then they can become engaged in an exchange of benefits and can create a win–win situation.

Outline 2.5 Evaluation criteria for forms of sports sponsorship

I. Correspondence between the brand and the form of sport

   1. Target group

   2. Key values and social status

   3. Aims and target group of sponsoring brand

   4. Geographical reach

   5. Synergistic values

II. Essential features of sport

   1. Multisponsor environment

   2. Media attention

   3. Experience power

III. Possibilities of sports sponsorship leverage

   1. Theme communication

   • PR

   • Advertising

   2. Action communication

   • Direct marketing communication

   • Sales promotions (merchandising, sampling, etc.)

IV. Duration of impact period

V. Estimation of (opportunity) costs

1. Costs of sport sponsoring

2. Costs of integration into marketing communication

- New channels

- Existing channels

Then there are the essential features of the particular sport. What position does the recipient occupy in the multisponsor environment (categories of sponsors, number of sponsors per category, sector exclusivity)? How strongly are the media interested in the sport? Even the experience power of the particular sport deserves attention. Inherent to a sporting experience are the powerful emotions aroused in the sports consumer. Organizations apply experience marketing to take advantage of the consumer's need for memorable experiences. The sports consumer also strives to spend his or her time on quality pursuits. The selection of a particular sport with distinctive experience features is the key to success. The experience power of this sport is linked to the interests of the target group, the brand characteristics and the commercial activity.[30]

The promotional spin-off of the type of sports sponsorship or sports sponsorship leverage is a third point of attention. To what extent can theme and action communication link up with sports sponsorship? A consumer market, for example, will be more interested in a sports project with a broad public because certain sales-promotion actions link up perfectly with it. For instance, when entering new markets, sports drink Aquarius utilized sampling as a technique of sponsorship-driven sales promotions (see Case 6).

A fourth selection criterion is the duration of the impact period. An event sponsor must communicate its sponsoring credibly some time before, during and after the sporting event. The sponsor of a national football competition, for example, is not in the limelight for several weeks in the summer. A sponsor of a football event enjoys a shorter communication period than a sponsor of a football team. It is essential to establish first the periods of prominent sponsor notification. At the same time, the sponsor must conceive a strategy, e.g. to bridge the quiet periods communicatively and keep the sport in the public eye.

Finally, there is the cost associated with a particular sport. This consists not only of the investment in promotional sports rights but also of the support budget. The support budget includes all costs associated with integration in the marketing communication. This concerns not only the costs for the existing channels, e.g. the efforts of the promotion department, collaboration by the office managers, or modification of existing advertisement campaigns, but also the costs of the new channels, e.g. recruiting a person to be responsible for sponsoring, outsourcing or additional action communication.

From this, each sponsor should compare the opportunity costs of a sponsorship programme. Opportunity costs refer to all alternative applications of the resources invested in sponsoring. For instance, the marketing manager should check whether the resources devoted to sport might not be employed more efficiently in an advertising campaign or point-of-sales communication. More specifically, each sponsorship manager should analyse the sports sponsorship portfolio under consideration. For example, the sponsorship manager should weigh the high risks of individual sponsorship (e.g. a cyclist) against the risks of team sponsorship (e.g. a football team versus a cycling team) and the low risks of event sponsorship (e.g. official partner of a European championship). High-risk sponsorship properties could receive negative press, which may damage part of the brand image, such as a doping scandal or a bribery affair. Such incidents can cause a sponsor to terminate the agreement prematurely. For example, the doping scandals exposed during the Tour of Italy in 2002 were the direct stimulus for the multinational construction company Mapei to terminate its cycling sponsorship early at the end of 2002. Before the scandals were exposed, Mapei had intended to continue as a sponsor until the end of 2004.

Mini-case study – The strategies of sponsoring winter sports: the cases of Viessmann, Ruhrgas, Buderus and Luk

The races take place 'smoothly'. Otto starts 'like greased lightning' and shoots through the ice channel 'as if machine-driven'. 'One link fits into another.' That is how one TV reporter commented on the driving style of Sylke Otto, 'luge driver', when referring to the company Luk. These clichés apply to the suppliers of the car sector that have supported the luge sport and the German Olympic champion for 20 years. Luk installs couplings for components for business systems and for vehicle hydraulics. Thus, it is appropriate that viewers experience Otto's rides as a dynamically occurring technical process.

For other winter sports sponsors, linguistic links to highlight the affinity (synergy) between company and the sponsored object are superfluous. Energy supplier Ruhrgas, for example, utilizes the force of the association of its product with snow and cold. Ruhrgas is the title sponsor of the world championships in ski-jumping and biathlon. In addition, it is one of the six main sponsors of the ski-jumping tournament and one of the top partners of the biathlon team of the German ski league, DSV.

Manufacturers of heating appliances Viessmann and Buderus – direct competitors for market leadership – are also strong winter sports sponsors. Buderus has supported the DSV teams in ski-jumping and cross-country skiing and had a presenting sponsorship for the world cup in ski-jumping. Viessmann wants to upgrade its extensive winter sports package as presenting partner of the world cup in ski-jumping. For years, Viessmann has been the main sponsor of the world cups in cross-country skiing and the

German national luge team, among other achievements. Viessman is also the presenter of the world cup for biathlon and sponsors individual athletes.

The sponsoring of sports in snow and ice seems to be worthwhile. Viessmann, Ruhrgas, Luk and Buderus emphasize the relatively favourable cost-benefit ratio. This concerns primarily the extensive media coverage of the various winter sports. When the football and Formula 1 seasons are over, there is a profusion of live transmissions of bobsledding and luge by the various television stations. The sponsors of biathlon and ski-jumping illustrate such media coverage. IFM Media analysis found during the season 2001-02 that 260 hours of broadcasting time, primarily on the commercial station RTL, were devoted to biathlon, with a maximum of four million viewers. Similarly, ski-jumping enjoyed more than 400 hours of television transmission and drew approximately 9.5 million viewers for the final jumps of the tournament.

Finally, the highlights of ski-jumping include the advertising messages reserved for the few main sponsors. 'We are not one of many' is Viessmann's explanation for its engagement with luge.

Another argument in favour of winter sports is that scandals are rare – with the exception of doping in cross-country skiing. Also, the German biathletes, bobsledders and luge drivers are as successful as the ski-jumpers Hannawald and Schmitt, which gives them a dynamic image.

Ruhrgas has been engaged in ski-jumping since 1992 and in biathlon since 1994. Continuity is a key component of the sponsoring strategy of Viessmann, Buderus and Luk. For example, Luk has been supporting winter sports for two decades. Its presence at ski-jumps, shooting stands, ski runs and ice rinks has improved brand awareness and, above all, created a positive dynamic image for the end user. The exploitation of winter sports sponsoring is another important consideration. Technical companies want to address professional sectors and offer an identity platform for employees. This is why Buderus selects sponsor platforms that offer the possibility to bind national and international business and project partners directly to themselves.

Attention is paid to the integration of sponsoring in communication. Viessmann employs biathletes Frank Luck and Georg Hackl for testimonials during the summer. Furthermore, its red and white logo has begun to adorn the cap of Niki Lauda, although he is rarely seen in the summer season. Sports sponsorship is exploited by Buderus at fairs and events and via giveaways, while Ruhrgas communicates its support for sport on the Internet and on printed announcements.

> Along with winter sports sponsorship, sponsoring managers often also select summer sports to sponsor. Ruhrgas is the strategic partner of FC Schalke 04. Buderus has a strategy for sport communication involving the national football team. Luk is also present as a sponsor in motor sports and cycling. The main emphases of the relationship sponsor Viessman, in contrast, are exclusively luge, biathlon and ski-jumping.
>
> *Source*: Based on Nic Richter (2002), Sport business, *Horizont*, September 30-32

Budgeting for sports sponsorship

Concerning the budgeting of a sponsorship investment, there are a number of guidelines. The most logical is that a sponsor invests as much as is necessary to achieve the goals, given its budget restrictions.[31] Sponsoring practice teaches that the allocation of a budget occurs primarily in relation to the sport that an organization wants to sponsor. The sponsor contribution depends on the position in the sponsor hierarchy (main, co- or subsidiary sponsor), the title rights of the sponsor (the name of the sponsor incorporated in the title of the event, the sponsor presents the prizes), the media, the aura of the sport, the nature and features of the sport, and the duration of the agreement. Other criteria for the budgeting of sponsoring expenses:[32]

- depend on the events that a company wants to sponsor;
- include a percentage of the advertising and marketing communication budget (32% of those interviewed);
- depend on the sponsoring efforts of competitors (16% of those interviewed);
- include a percentage of the turnover (11% of those interviewed);
- include a percentage of the company's profit (6% of those interviewed).

The relevance of these five selection criteria varies from company to company. Some criteria are more important for brands that are active in consumer markets, while others are very sensitive for brands in commercial markets. The business context and the phase of the brand's product lifecycle are other specific elements. This does not detract from the fact that the criteria in Outline 2.5 provide a handy reference framework. An arrangement of these criteria based on their significance is the next step in the decision-making process.[33] Decision-makers ascribe a score to each selection criterion and can then add up the scores of each sport alternative. In this way, they create a more objective ranking, which, ultimately, leads to the selection of a sponsoring form.

The setting or adjustment of the limit of duration of sports sponsorship is another strategic worry for a sponsor. In this context, the question also arises of when is the best time for the sponsor to start and end the sponsorship agreement. In 2001, the average duration of the 50 most significant sports sponsorship agreements lasted for 4.2 years. In 2002, the average duration had risen to 6.7 years.[34] On the one hand, new agreements for sponsoring sports facilities were concluded, in a number of instances for a period of 20 years or longer. On the other hand, this indicates that sponsors are investing more time and money in the development of a partnership with the recipients. Termination of a sponsorship agreement is recommended when:[35]

- the marketing communication aims have been achieved;
- the marketing communication aims cannot be achieved with sports sponsorship;
- the general brand strategy has changed (change of brand name, new positioning, etc.);
- the sponsored sport object is no longer trustworthy;
- collaboration with the sponsored sport object becomes difficult;
- the original commercial collaboration has degraded into hobbyism;
- a better alternative presents itself.

2.5 Selling sports sponsorship

Those in charge of sporting organizations usually want to stimulate their organizational funds to achieve the following goals:[36]

- to receive financial support;
- to receive goods;
- to receive services;
- to achieve exposure;
- to create an association with the sponsoring brand.

Plan for sponsor recruitment

The demand for sponsorship is usually greater than the supply. Therefore, it is very important for recruiters of sponsors to approach potential sponsors systematically, starting from the mission of their organization. In order to put together a motivated sponsorship procurement committee, the management and the members of the sponsor recruitment organization should be informed. This committee should first present the unique selling features of their organization before identifying potential sponsorship opportunities. For instance, before approaching prospective sponsors, a sports organization could go to the media to offer exclusive rights, or 'contra-deals' might be worked out at the local level, where both sponsor and sponsored may provide opportunities in kind to each other. For example, a golf-course provider may offer free membership for *x* members to a hot-air-balloon company that provides *x* free flights per annum.

In order to keep the sponsorship recruitment process efficient, recruiters should undertake their screening activities, with respect to the current sponsor group, their network of acquaintances and the competition in the local surroundings, selectively. When approaching potential sponsors, empathy and customization are very important. From the first contact with the prospect, recruiters should take a business-like approach. Finally, once the contract has been signed, recruiters should do more than they promised and nurture the new sponsors. To do this, the sponsor committee should elaborate a partnership strategy that demands a creative and time-consuming engagement. The different steps represented in Outline 2.6 are elaborated in depth in Case 2, describing the sponsorship acquisition of Tennisclub Baseline.

Outline 2.6 Step-by-step plan for sponsor recruitment

Step 1 Mission takes off.

Step 2 Informing management and members.

Step 3 Determining unique selling features.

Step 4 Identifying the number of potential sponsorship opportunities.

Step 5 Targeting specific sponsors.

Step 6 Approaching potential sponsors via a customized approach and with empathy.

Step 7 Nurturing sponsors.

Categorizing official sponsors

Official sponsors can be placed in a number of categories (see Outline 2.7). According to the benefits offered, a sponsoring brand might become title sponsor, main sponsor, co-sponsor or subsidiary sponsor. There are three different approaches to determining the price (in cash or the commercial worth of goods and services) of the sponsor contribution.[37] Case 3 provides examples of the market prices of different VIP packages. The 'cost-plus' method calculates a fee on top of the cost price of the constituent elements of a sponsor package (income from tickets, meals, parking fees, VIP packages, etc.). The 'competitive market' approach uses the prices of similar packages of competitors as the reference point. The 'relative value' method concerns the commercial worth (exposure, PR power, etc.) of the constituent elements of the sponsoring package. The type of contribution (cash versus goods or services) provides another means to categorize sponsors.

Outline 2.7 Placing of official sponsors into categories

Depending on the amount of the contribution	
Depending on the type of the contribution	Olympic sponsors:
Cash sponsor	Coca-Cola/McDonald's
Goods sponsor	Panasonic/Samsung
Services sponsor	Sports Illustrated/Swatch
Depending on the category	UK football sponsors
Title sponsor	Barclaycard Premiership
Main, co- or subsidiary sponsor	Fly Emirates (Chelsea
Supplier	shirt sponsor)
Licensing partner	Umbro (Chelsea kit sponsor)
Media partner	Fossil (Chelsea watches)
	Sky digital (Chelsea TV)

Sources: www.athens2004.com; www.arsenal.com

Towards a sports sponsorship contract

How best to approach potential sponsors demands considerable strategic discussion. Outline 2.8 lists the different steps involved in converting a contact with a prospective sponsor into a contract with a new sponsor. In Case 2, these concepts are illustrated with the example of a local tennis club, which approached and recruited sponsors.

Outline 2.8 Sponsor acquisition: from contact to contract

1. Cold call:

   ● Short introduction

   ● Is the target group of interest?

   ● May I send a proposal?

2. Letter and short proposal.

3. Second phone call: interested in personal presentation?

4. Presentation of sponsorship proposal: content and form.

5. Negotiation techniques to settle the sponsor contract.

6. Drawing up sponsor contract.

The major themes of the content and form of a basic contract for sports sponsorship are shown in Outline 2.9. This checklist contains the personal details of the contractual parties, the contributions exchanged, the extent of exclusivity, payment arrangements and the duration of the agreement.

Outline 2.9 Content and form of basic contract for sports sponsorship: checklist

- Contract parties: legal forms, Chamber of Commerce registration number, personal details of signatories to the contract.

- Mutual key offerings: society or club states sponsored activities, communication possibilities offered by the recipient, exposure versus payment conditions involving money or goods, loan or transfer of title, invoice or supply data, payment or supply deadlines. Sponsor often will want guarantees regarding number of entrants, competition class, etc. and the maximal exertion requirement by the recipient.

- Extent of exclusivity.

- Determining name registration and limiting conditions, bonus system, production costs (also other advertisement carriers).

- References: applicable regulations, league regulations, etc.

- Settlement of differences: arbitration committee for sports sponsorship according to arbitration regulations.

- Duration of the agreement: set period or unlimited, conditions for premature annulment or termination due to bankruptcy, act of God, urgent reasons, etc.

- Specific clauses: manner of communication of sponsor name and logo, ban on negative publicity, provisions for non-compliance or incorrect contractual implementation (in specific cases a termination clause), approval of general meeting of members, etc.

- Possible options for extension.

- Setting time points for evaluation.

- Personal details of contacts.

- Place of signature, date and signature of sponsor and recipient.

- Recording the number of copies.

- Appendices listing the agreed offerings, possibly illustrated with images.

Promotional signage

The age of stadium board advertising and sports shirts as the sole or most important communication carriers of sports sponsorship belongs to sport's archaeological past. Currently, there are many diverse possibilities for communication

carriers, both in recreational sport and in top sport, which are utilized for promotional aims. As part of the sports sponsorship agreement, the recipient provides communication carriers.

> Promotional signage includes printed messages or logos identifying a sponsor or event on any of the following types of materials: banners, street-poles, attachments, bill-boards (fixed or movable), scoreboards, electronic message boards, posters and dashboards or rink-boards. It also includes impressions such as on-ice or on-field message, rotational courtside messages, on-field or on-court logos, and virtual signage ... The definition of signage has also been expanded to include logo placement opportunities ... [38]

Thus, the brand names and the logos of sponsors adorn, for example, caravans, inflatables, placemats, mousepads and bus shelters. In a sporting environment, there are so many possibilities for communication carriers that they cannot all be described. We find brand names and logos from sponsors on racing cars, caps, the transport fleet of a sports team, sweatbands, wrist bands, bathing caps and tennis racquets. The increase in the number of branches of sport and the increased commercialization of sport have created many new possibilities (see Chapter 4).

2.6 Summary

Sports sponsorship involves the purchase of promotional sports rights by a sponsor. The sports sponsor expects clear communicative returns from the recipient. The use of the sponsor's logo and brand name in the media carriers of a particular sport is the core of the sponsorship package. The permitted media carriers for the logo and the brand name differ according to the sponsorship package purchased. The additional association and exploitation possibilities are also associated with the contents of the sponsoring package. Sports sponsorship is the most important area of application of sponsorship. Sports sponsorship realized faster growth in the 1990s, as a small corner of marketing communication, than advertising and sales promotion actions. The increased importance of sports sponsorship is associated with developments in the fields of marketing communication, media and sport. The professionalization and globalization of the sports sector, the breakthrough in experience communication and relationship marketing, and the more sceptical view of advertising in the mass media are just some of these developments.

The selection of a particular sport must fit into a well-conceived plan for sports sponsorship. Such a plan is based on the goals and target groups of marketing communication. Usually, sponsoring first achieves cognitive aims, then affective aims and finally behavioural aims. Sports for sponsorship are selected for their correspondence with the brand, their basic characteristics, the potential for integration in marketing communication, the duration of the impact period and the cost price. Central characteristics include the target group reached by the sport, the sport's key values and social status, its geographic range, the multisponsor environment and the media attention given to the sport. The promotional spin-off of a sponsoring form involves the possibilities for linkage to thematic and action-oriented communication instruments. The duration of the impact period and the estimate of the (opportunity) costs of sports sponsorship are other important selection criteria.

Via sports sponsorship, sports managers attempt to obtain financial support, goods or services. Sponsoring by the mass media ensures exposure. Sponsoring brands also can transfer desired associations to the recipient. How to approach potential sponsors should be discussed thoroughly in advance, starting with the mission and ending with the sponsor offer. In the negotiations from contact to contract, professional communication is essential. Once the contract is signed, the new sponsor must be nurtured.

This chapter has discussed sports sponsorship and outlined the nature of sports sponsorship communication. Hereafter, this book examines in detail the marketing communication mix variables that combine to form the nucleus of a core sponsorship leverage strategy. In Chapter 3, we will discuss the interplay between sports sponsorship and public relations.

Key terms

Accommodation sponsoring
Action communication
Affective aims
Behavioural aims
Brand fit
Brand confusion
Brand irritation
Budget evolution
Business-to-business
Business-to-consumer
Cognitive aims
Endorsement
Event sponsoring
Impact period
Licences
Management by hobby
Marketing communication goals
Marketing communication target group
Multisponsor environment

Opportunity cost
Segmentation of sports consumers
Selection criteria
Sponsoring market
Sports sponsorship
Sports sponsorship form
Synergy
Team sponsorship
Theme communication

Questions

1. Illustrate with examples the possible marketing communication goals of sports sponsorship.

2. What criteria does a potential sponsor use to select between different sport forms?

3. What is the added value of an integral approach to sports sponsorship communication?

4. Which factors make an integrated approach difficult?

5. Which steps are involved when a not-for-profit sporting organization systematically approaches potential sponsors?

Endnotes

1 For an international overview of contributions concerning juridical and ethical aspects of sponsoring, see Cornwell, T.B. and Maignan, J. (1998), An international review of sponsorship research, *Journal of Advertising,* 27(1), 1–21.
2 Fiscal and juridical aspects were analyzed thoroughly for the Netherlands in Adfo Sponsoring (1998), *Praktijkgids 1999.* Alphen aan den Rijn/Diegem: Samsom, and for Belgium in Taks, M., Hemelaer, R., Lagae, W. and Wille, L. (2000), *Jaarboek Sportsponsoring 2001.* Diegem: Kluwer.
3 Sleight, S. (1989), *Sponsorship. What It Is And How To Use It.* London: McGraw-Hill.
4 Otker, T. (1988), Exploitation: the key to sponsorship success, *European Research,* May, 77–85.
5 Bradley, J., Dibb, S. and Simkin, L. (1996), *The Marketing Planning Workbook: Effective Marketing for the Marketing Manager.* London: Routledge.

6 Arthur, D., Scott, D., Woods, T. and Brooker, R. (1998), Sport sponsorship should ... a process model for the effective implementation and management of sport sponsorship programmes, *Sport Marketing Quarterly*, 7(4), 49–60.

7 Meenaghan, T. (1998), Current developments and future directions in sponsorship, *International Journal of Advertising*, 17(1), 3–28.

8 Arthur *et al.* (1998), op cit.

9 Adfo Sponsoring (1998), *Praktijkgids* 1999. Alphen aan den Rijn/Diegem: Samsom.

10 Cornwell and Maignan (1998), op cit.

11 Irwin, R., Sutton, W.A. and McCarthy, L. (2002), *Sport Promotion and Sales Management*. Champaign, IL: Human Kinetics.

12 De Pelsmacker, P., Geuens, M. and Van den Bergh, J. (2001), *Marketing Communications*. Harlow: Pearson Education.

13 Mintel (2000), *Sponsorship-UK*. London: Mintel International Group.

14 SportBusiness Group (2003), *Maximising the Value of Sponsorship*. London: SportBusiness Group.

15 Courtois, A. (2001), Euro 2000: een economisch effect voor België, Nederland en de commerciële partners. Presented at the Institute for International Research, Brussels, 15 February 2001.

16 Sandler, D. and Shani, D. (1993), Sponsorship and the Olympic Games: the consumer perspective, *Sport Marketing Quarterly*, 2(3), 38–44; and Pope, M. (1999), Overview of current sponsorship thought, *Cyber-Journal of Sport Marketing*, 2, 7.

17 Seghers, K. (1992), *Sponsoring in België: een stand van zaken*. Brussel: VUB Press.

18 Marshall, D. and Cook, G. (1992), The corporate sports sponsor, *International Journal of Advertising*, 11, 307–24.

19 Van Haverbeke, W. (1990), *Sponsoring Sports or the Arts. A Comparative Study about Business Sponsorship of Sport and the Arts in Flanders*. KU Leuven: Centrum voor Economische Studiën, Algemene Reeks.
   Van Haverbeke elucidates the sponsoring budget of 101 sponsoring companies in Flanders and Brussels. Three-quarters of the companies interviewed had sports sponsorship projects running.

20 Dunn, M. (2003), *Sports Sponsorships: Market Report* 2003, 3rd edn. Key Note.

21 *De Standaard* (2002), Was het de moeite waard? Kosten-batenanalyse van het WK, *De Standaard*, 29 June 2002.

22 Arthur *et al.* (1998), op cit; Abratt, R., Clayton, C. and Pitt, L. (1987), Corporate objectives in sports sponsorship, *International Journal of Advertising*, 6, 299–311.

23 Adfo Sponsoring Actueel (2001), *Trends op de sponsoringmarkt*. Alphen aan den Rijn: Samsom.

24 www.thenorthface.com.

25 For more information on segmentation of sport consumers, see Hunt, K., Bristol, Y. and Bashow, E. (1999), A conceptual approach to classifying sports fame, *Journal of Services Marketing*, 13(6), 439–52; Tapp A. and Clower, J. (2002), From 'carefree casuals' to 'professional wanderers': segmentation possibilities for football supporters, *European Journal of Marketing*, 36(11/12), 1248–69; and Quick, S. (2000), Contemporary sport consumers: some implications of linking for typology with key spectator variables, *Sport Marketing Quarterly*, 9(3), 8.

26 Lagae, W. (1999), De tien sponsorgeboden. Presented at the Institute for International Research, Limette, 1 September 1999.

27 Kolah, A. (2003), Sports marketing surveys. In: SportBusiness Group, *Maximising the Value of Sponsorship*. London: SportBusiness Group, pp. 24–6.

28 Van Hulzen, M. (2002), Sportaccommodatie vernoemen naar sponsor is lucratief, *Sportaccom*, 15(3), 15–17.

29 Adfo Sponsoring Actueel (2001), op cit.

30 Pine, B.J. and Gilmore, J.H. (2001), *De beleveniseconomie*. Schoonhoven: Academic Service.

31 De Pelsmacker *et al.* (2001), op cit.

32 In this example, I refer to a study of Belgian companies conducted in 1990; see Van Haverbeke (1990), op cit.

33 De Pelsmacker *et al.* (2001), op cit.

34 Kolah, A. (2003), Sports marketing surveys word sponsorships monitor. In: SportBusiness Group, *Maximising the Value of Sponsorship*. London: SportBusiness Group, p. 38.

35 Taks, M., Hemelaer, R., Lagae, W. and Wille, L. (2000), *Jaarboek sportsponsoring 2001*. Diegem: Kluwer.

36 Shilbury, D., Quick, S. and Westerbeek, H. (1998), *Strategic Sport Marketing*. St Leonards: Allen & Unwin.

37 Stotlar, D. (2001), Sponsorship. In: Parkhouse, B. (ed.), *The Management of Sport: Its Foundation and Application*, 3rd edn. New York: McGraw-Hill, pp. 337–52.

38 Mullin, B.J., Hardy, S. and Sutton, W.A. (2000), *Sport Marketing*. Champaign, IL: Human Kinetics, p. 189.

Case 2 Tennisclub Baseline: how to serve a smashing sponsorship deal

Key learning points

After studying this case, you will be able to:

- elaborate in depth the different steps in a sponsor recruitment plan;

- distinguish between the different categories of sponsors;

- develop a partnership strategy for existing sponsors.

On Sunday mornings, there is a huge crowd at Tennisclub Baseline (TCB). Parents drive back and forth to ferry their children to mini-tennis on time. The introductory courses for kids are an enormous sporting success. But paying for the kids' trainers, frequently replacing the training equipment and renting sports facilities have put the club's budget in the red. Nevertheless, management has decided against raising the membership fees again. Soliciting sponsors is the most important item on the agenda at the crisis meeting. Ms Volley, chair of TCB, argues for finding additional sponsor income. Soliciting sponsors is a time-consuming, difficult and delicate task that could thoroughly shake up TCB's culture. Also, the demand for sponsorship money is much larger than the supply. So, TCB is acting in a very competitive environment. TCB will therefore emphasize what the club has to offer sponsors and work on distinguishing itself from competitors. The chair has complete confidence in this course of action. Over the past few years, she has expanded the management of TCB. She proudly considers the following management qualities at TCB:

- a stable managerial operation that takes member involvement seriously;

- presence of human resources;

- considerable knowledge (connections) and emotional intelligence;

- well-developed governing committees;

- a permanent secretariat with office facilities;

- easy contact with the management.

Ms Volley has advised her board that an amateurish approach to soliciting sponsors could seriously disrupt TCB. Therefore, TCB will have to estimate carefully the costs of the sponsor policy. If the known costs of soliciting sponsors outweigh the uncertain benefits, then TCB had better look for other sources of income. The organization of a sports event, setting up a stand at the annual fair, door-to-door sales and improving the functioning of the canteen are traditional alternatives. To increase the chances of success, the chairperson has created a multistep plan:

1. TCB's mission.

2. TCB informs its members

3. Unique selling features of TCB.

4. TCB identifies potential sponsorship opportunities.

5. TCB targets specific sponsors.

6. TCB approaches potential sponsors via a customized, empathic approach.

7   TCB nurtures its sponsors.

Step 1: TCB's mission

The TCB mission statement states:

> TCB wants to be a leading and innovative club for recreational and competitive tennis for players at every level. Our ultimate goal is to offer our members tennis programmes (coaching, training, relaxation) suited to their individual needs to give them a great relaxed feeling. Thus, approaching our members on an individual basis is important to us. To sum up: 'Play to your advantage at TCB'. Another aspect of TCB of which we are proud is our youth programme ('Instant fun at TCB').

In order to archieve these organizational goals, TCB will welcome financial support, goods or services via new sponsorship arrangements.

Step 2: TCB informs its members

Informing the members is important to prevent resistance to sponsoring, to stimulate the involvement of the management and the members, and to use the existing network. By organizing an information evening, expanding the sponsor committee, or putting up notice boards/suggestion boxes in the hall, changing rooms and canteen, the board can win over sceptics and put together a motivated, coordinated sponsorship procurement scheme. A broad support base for sponsoring actions promotes collaboration between the different committees in the club and avoids collaboration problems. For example, TCB's sponsor committee was invited last year to a barbecue to celebrate the champion. The committee was dismayed to discover that the meat had been purchased from the largest competitor of the main sponsor.

Step 3: Why sponsor TCB?

A first unique selling feature of TCB is the excellent management qualities in the board. The members' satisfaction is the second trump card that TCB wants to play. The following points illustrate customer satisfaction:

- over ten years' experience in certified coaching of players;
- focus on both recreational and competitive tennis;
- individual training and progress;
- individualized training programmes and technical guidelines;
- an expanding and flourishing youth programme:
    - 200 players under age 18;
    - 15 youth interclub teams (6-16 years old);
    - two provincial youth champions;
- trophy for youth-friendliest club in 2001;
- first-class training and competition courts and accommodation;
- excellent location and good car parking;
- play area for small children;
- card tables for seniors.

A third strong point of TCB is that existing sponsors are treated well. In the TCB Business Club there is a platform for networking. TCB Business Club captivates and flourishes because the board has invested in the sponsors' quality time. A representative of the current group of sponsors has offered to welcome new sponsors into the sponsor group. Their motto is: 'From new contacts to new contracts'.

Step 4: TCB identifies potential sponsorship opportunities

TCB is looking primarily for structural sponsorship of the club. Contrary to event or project sponsors who sponsor TCB only for a specific one-week event, structural sponsors support the club continuously during the agreed sponsorship period. TCB wants these structural sponsors to grow into partners of the club. TCB gives sponsors communication advantages from which the sponsoring organization will clearly benefit. However, TCB does not beg money from companies. Therefore, the TCB board will first perfect the club's communication platform, since exchange sponsoring agreements with a local media partner (radio, newspaper or magazine) always increase the club's commercial attractiveness. For a local club like TCB, it is also important to first discuss a sponsor file with local government.

For structural sponsors, TCB uses the following hierarchy:

- match
- sponsor = main sponsor
- set sponsor = co-sponsor
- game sponsor = secondary sponsor

This classification is based on the sponsor's contribution (in cash, in kind, in media access). Examples include:

- the costs of the new changing rooms and showers (supported by the local plumber) can be high, e.g. match sponsor;
- the costs of the club shirts, e.g. set sponsor;
- the costs of inserts in free local papers and spots on the local radio, e.g. game sponsor.

TCB is willing to consider different types of sponsor contribution:

- financial sponsoring: payment in cash;
- material sponsoring: equipment, such as nets, balls, gravel, and sanitary facilities;
- exchange sponsoring: media access, such as local papers and other local carriers;
- know-how: accounting and financial support and advice.

Along with structural sponsoring, TCB wants to obtain sponsoring for specific events or training sessions. The following sport projects are possibilities:

- summer and winter training ('Supported by...');
- competition and multisport training ('Offered by...');
- mini-tennis ('An initiative of...');
- tournaments (title sponsor: 'Dunlop TC Baseline Tournament').

Only in the next phase will TCB utilize communication carriers. The TCB board elaborates different packages for the main sponsor, co-sponsor(s) and material sponsors:

- advertising boards on the courts and display or sponsor boards at the entrance to the club;

- announcement posters (activities, tournaments, training);

- membership cards, stationery, compliments cards, Christmas cards;

- presenting partner of club events (name association);

- placemats on the tables in the cafeteria;

- sports bags for members;

- polo shirts and tracksuits;

- club towels, sponges and gadgets;

- advertisements in the local media;

- promotion folder and programme book for the club;

- press file containing all articles published about the club;

- website of the tennis club;

- photographic and video material of the club;

- club van;

- advertising messages during events.

Equally important is elaborating PR packages for the different categories of sponsor. The sponsorship decision-makers of TCB distinguish between the negotiated return and an unexpected (more than promised) return for the sponsors:

- negotiated return:

- advertising panel;

- logo present on tennis equipment;

- presenting partner of club events.

- unexpected (more than promised) return:
  - 'sponsor day': tennis clinic for personnel of sponsoring companies;
  - 'another view': the club as location for meetings;
  - 'going out with the club': the club as a social platform;
  - 'business club' information;
  - evenings: reception and networking.

Step 5: TCB targets specific sponsors

To keep the sponsor recruitment process efficient, TCB works selectively. After all, the club's energy is not unlimited. The reality of sponsor recruitment teaches that a small management core can deal with the most important recruitment efforts and that the number of potential sponsors is infinite. Three screening activities should be undertaken:

● Screening the current sponsor group: usually it is less difficult to keep or upgrade an existing sponsor than to find a new sponsor.

● Screening the network of acquaintances, including members, family and acquaintances of members, and suppliers.

● Screening the competition in the local surroundings, including:

  - sponsors of other local sports clubs;

  - federation sponsors;

  - sponsors of tennis clubs in other districts.

Step 6: TCB approaches potential sponsors via a customized approach and with empathy

From the first contact with the potential sponsor, TCB takes a business-like approach. A good and well-conceived sponsoring proposal is its calling card. TCB will be judged on it. Therefore, it is extremely important that the whole proposal is representative and attractive. What should such a proposal look like, and what should it contain? Before TCB contacts a potential sponsor, it must know at what level the company operates. A locally oriented company does not have the budget to sponsor a national club; likewise, a national headquarters is not interested in the small scale of a local club. Therefore, TCB first examines the company's size and range and its target groups.

TCB goes through the following procedure when preparing a sponsoring proposal:

1. Inventory of what the club wants from a company (money, products, services, know-how, network) and which members know and/or could recruit potential sponsors.

2. Collecting information about the company's communication policy (other sponsor projects, advertisements, website, annual report, employees).

3. Noting everything the club can offer the company to achieve its objectives.

4. Writing a letter with specific suggestions for a presentation.

5. Calling for a response and to make an appointment for a presentation.

6. Presenting the club and noting the company's wishes.

7. Sending a proposal with an individualized package (the offer).

Especially difficult tasks that require concentration are the drafting of the letter (point 4) and preparing an attractive sponsor proposal (point 7). Therefore, the members of the TCB sponsor committee first made a synthesis of accessible and relevant contributions in sports management magazines and participated in sponsoring and fund-raising workshops. From these courses, the TCB sponsor cell gleaned much inspiration to approach sponsors professionally with an improved likelihood of success.

The sponsorship letter: contents

Ideally, TCB would be introduced to a company by someone who is involved with the club in one way or another, e.g. another sponsor, a member of the board, a member or a parent of a member. In the letter that TCB sends to potential sponsors, TCB can refer to the common link. This should have a positive effect in most cases because TCB distinguishes itself in this way from other clubs writing to the same potential sponsor without a reference. The letter from TCB:

- is not longer than one and a half A4 pages;

- spells correctly the name of the company and contact person throughout;

- refers to a mutual acquaintance;

- is enthusiastic, with a catchy introduction and succinct language, and without jargon;

- establishes clear benefits from sponsorship;

- concludes with the remark that the TCB board would like to discuss this further face to face and that somebody from the board will call to make an appointment;

- names one contact person and is signed by the board.

The contents of the letter must make it clear that TCB has thought seriously about the opportunities that TCB can offer the company. TCB does not ask for money but shows how the company can utilize the club to achieve its goals.

Then the TCB sponsor committee considers the immediate questions that a company might pose when reading the letter and tries to answer them. As the letter cannot be too long, it may not always be possible to put all the information that the company wants into the letter. Therefore, it is advisable to enclose one or more leaflets and possibly also photographs.

Appendix 2.1 gives an example of a sponsorship letter.

The sponsorship letter pays attention to:

- the information about TCB;

- the TCB sponsor offer (structural or event sponsoring);

- why TCB or the mini-tennis tournament is interesting for the company;

- commercial and social aspects;

- target groups reached by the club (adults, juniors, men, women, families, companies, etc.), indicating for each target group what consumer products they are interested in;

- the frequency of media attention (once in a while, regularly, every week);

- the type of media attention (regional television and radio reports in local newspapers, own media), also stating the range or the circulation of the medium:

- the costs and the duration of contract that is desired;

- the global sum per sponsoring package or per project;

- the sponsoring term.

The sponsorship proposal: what should it contain?

Ms Volley, the TCB contact mentioned in the letter, then contacts the company for a response and to make an appointment for a personal presentation of the club. Two or (at most) three representatives of TCB must give the presentation. Based on the discussion, an individualized proposal can be prepared, which TCB should send out as soon as possible. If it is good, then the company will, hopefully, become enthusiastic during the discussion. TCB therefore must capitalize on this. However, it is important to give the company time to consider the proposal carefully and to decide whether it will become a new partner of the club.

What does TCB offer, and what is it going to cost the sponsor?

A sponsor file contains a brief reference letter in which the first discussion is summarized. The TCB sponsoring proposal includes the following aspects:

- Introduction: short summary of the club's history, the level, ambitions and partners/sponsors with which the club has previously collaborated (how many, from what sectors, etc.).

- Link with the company: what and whom can the company reach via the club (e.g. 25% of the members buy a new bicycle every three years; 40% of the members regularly surf the Internet, etc.)?

- Offer: with clearly described returns in exchange for sponsoring (preferably in an outline form).

- Money: financial calculation of the proposal (sponsor contribution, duration and what exactly will be done with the money).

The contract

The TCB sponsor committee sometimes has to deal with the failure to keep verbal agreements. Empty sponsor promises can be avoided only by confirming them in a contract. To prevent misunderstandings and problems with communication, it is important to prepare brief written reports of all meetings between sponsor and recipient. Both parties can set down the most important points and agreements, together with a list of actions to take.

Checklist for contents of the sponsor contract:

- Report all basic data correctly in the contract: name of sponsor and recipient, club's legal form, people authorized to represent the sponsor/club and their function.

- State clearly the scope, duration and termination options of the agreement.

- Describe clearly the key contributions and returns.

- Specific clauses: manner of communicating sponsor's name and logo, forbidding of negative publicity, provisions for not or incorrectly fulfilling the contract, (under certain conditions, an annulment clause), approval by general meeting of members, etc.

- Possible options for extension.

- Place of signing, date and signature of sponsor and recipient.

- Recording of number of copies.

- Enclosures in which the agreed actions are listed, if possible with clarifying photographic material.

Step 7: TCB nurtures its sponsors

Finally, once the contract has been signed, TCB does more than it promised. The PR manager at TCB gives the sponsors ideas and makes them aware of the many options presented by TCB. After signing the contract, at a cele-bratory meeting, perhaps with press present, TCB works on the partnership. It makes sure that the sponsor is satisfied and presents a successful exam-ple to other potential sponsors. This again demands a creative and time-consuming engagement by TCB. In other words, the current sponsors must be nurtured, and to do this the sponsor committee must elaborate a partnership strategy. To act on the sponsor efforts, not only time and energy but also some of TCB's budget must be invested. This is used to pay for extra activities for the sponsors. Involving the sponsors in the functioning of TCB can take a variety of forms and does not always have to be expensive.

Consider the following examples of an action plan:

- Send a Christmas present, birthday card or invitation to the tennis club's New Year's party.

- Classify the club sponsors into VIP categories: pay a 'golden' VIP more and different attention than a 'silver' or a 'bronze' VIP.

- Work with set club contact people for different VIP categories.

- Hold discussions with the various contacts and other members of the society.

- Send the sponsors the club magazine or prepare a VIP club magazine for sponsors.

- Send a press file and evaluation material (newspaper articles and photos of activities) to the sponsors.

- Stimulate networking between the groups of sponsors and ensure syn-ergy in the multisponsor environment.

Questions for discussion

1. Is the management of TCB right to choose sponsor recruitment, or should it explore other possibilities?
2. Which trump cards should TCB play more often, or in a different way, in the communication?
3. Which other instruments would you use to nurture the match, set and game sponsors of TCB?

Appendix 2.1 TCB sponsorship letter

[logo TCB] Tennis Club Baseline
Kjöpmannsgatan 37
N 7001 Trondheim
Telephone (03)-77. .. ..
Fax (03)-77. .. ..
info@TCB.com
www.TCB.com

Lumber Limited
attn: Mr. Henry Goodlife
Managing Director
Karl Johans gate 7
0234 Oslo

Our reference: RO/fl/SB-008

Date: Trondheim, 16-11-2003

Meeting to present Tennis Club Baseline

Dear Mr Goodlife,

Last week Lumber Limited served an ace: you promoted Victor Schotte to marketing manager. That he has been an energetic and enthusiastic member of Tennis Club Baseline will come as no surprise to you. During our last youth tournament it was, in fact, Mr Schotte who recommended that we contact you.

Tennis Club Baseline is growing. We have seen a steady growth in membership (adults and youth) since 1980 and we welcome new athletes. Our members take part in local as well as regional competitions, and some even play in international competitions. Understandably, a club like Tennis Club Baseline needs financial freedom. We would like to set up a meeting to show you the advantages that you as a sponsor can receive in return.

Three members of our sponsorship committee, Ms R. Jones, Ms L. Smith and Mr Davies, our sponsorship manager, member secretary and club treasurer, respectively, would like to visit Lumber Limited. They are available each working day, excluding Wednesdays, between 9.30 a.m. and 11.00 a.m. and after 4.00 p.m. Of course, their presentation is non-binding.

If you have any further considerations, please contact your marketing manager for 'information from the ground up'; if you prefer, you can consult our website, www.tcb.com, where you will find answers to all your questions.

Yours sincerely

Dina Volley
Chair

3

SPORTS SPONSORSHIP AND PUBLIC RELATIONS

Success is no coincidence (*Joop Alberda, chef de mission*, the Netherlands Olympic team, Athens 2004)

Overview

Corporate public relations

Types of public relations in sport

Sports sponsorship and hospitality

Sports sponsorship and publicity

A push-pull approach to press relationships

Sports sponsorship and crisis communication

Aims

After studying this chapter, you will be able to:

- understand the goals and target groups of corporate communications in sports sponsorship;

- understand the forms of public relations of and through sport;

- explain why sports sponsorship is a platform for relationship marketing;

- explain the difference between publicity and advertising in sport;

- relate the deployment of press instruments to the objectives of publicity;

- elucidate the steps to be followed in the case of crisis communication in sport.

3.0 Introduction

The exploitation of public relations (PR) by sports sponsorship was for a long time steeped in an atmosphere of hobbyism. The benefits went to friends of decision-makers, who also enjoyed the selected sports project. The first investments in football boxes, for example, were more a perk of senior management than a well-considered instrument of marketing communication. Since then, organizations have taken a more systematic and targeted approach to PR. PR in sport involves relationship marketing on the one hand and media relations on the other. Relationship marketing in sport is about enhancing relationships and transferring unique experiences to the public. A press approach in sport aims to generate publicity around a sports sponsorship project.

Through sports sponsorship, organizations achieve other goals and reach other target groups compared with those of marketing communication (Section 3.1). Generally, there are various forms of PR involved in sport (Section 3.2). However, we deal with PR (hospitality and press relations) solely from a sponsorship perspective. Indeed, sports sponsorship is also an interesting medium to reach relationship groups and is likely to work around unique sporting experiences (Section 3.3). The awareness of the image of sports and non-sports brands is determined not only through the instruments of marketing communication but also through publicity via editorial reporting of sports sponsorship projects. Yet, publicity in sport can not only amplify the effect of marketing communication campaigns but also damage it (Section 3.4). With an active press policy, a range of instruments can be implemented to generate interest and promote good relations (Section 3.5). However, sport is not always portrayed positively, and negative publicity can seriously destroy the image of sporting organizations and sponsors. Crisis communication in sport has correspondingly evolved into an important focus of concern (Section 3.6). The organization of VIP hospitality is the main focus of Case 3, analysing four elite sports events: the World

Championships Road Racing organized in Belgium in 2002, the Golden League athletic meeting in Brussels in 2003, the squash Open World Championships of 2003 in Antwerp, and the WTA Tournament of Antwerp in 2004.

3.1 Corporate public relations

PR consists of planned and sustained efforts to build up and defend an organization's reputation. The care of all groups involved on the one hand and good relations with the press on the other are key to a PR approach. PR consists of promoting the organization's interests. The 'good' side of an organization is highlighted, while the 'less good' side is not emphasized or is concealed.[1]

In a number of cases, the term PR refers only to technical or executive functions. Examples of this include receptions, company parties, events, publications and press relations. Therefore, in the specialist literature, the term PR is sometimes replaced by 'impression management'[2] or 'reputation management'.[3] Shank (p. 391)[4] defines PR of sport as '... the element of the promotional mix that identifies, establishes and maintains mutually beneficial relationships between the sports organizations and the various publics on which its success or failure depends ...' PR through sport also fits into an interactive communication strategy, making use of the various media to obtain understanding, attention and support for the values and aims of an organization among clearly specified groups.[5]

Stakeholders

Organizations operate within a complex relationship network and are far less independent nowadays than in the past because their relationship groups have become more diverse and more complex. Every organization has different relationship groups, depending on the type of products, services or ideas involved, the market and the objectives (short-, middle- and long-term).[6] Companies want to ensure that the interests of all groups are respected. Every actor that is influenced directly or indirectly by, or affects, the company's performance is a stakeholder.[7] Shareholders form only one of the many parties interested in the company's results. Other contractual relationship groups are employees, customers and suppliers. Examples of public groups include the government, conservation groups, consumers, local residents, press and media. The challenge lies in creating synergy between these differing groups of people.

A dividing line – sometimes artificial – can be drawn between the activities of internal and external PR.[8] Internal PR aims to improve collaboration between employees and their motivation, since the ongoing evolution in an organization demands considerable communication between the different departments and all employees. Internal communication also involves the ambitions, job satisfaction, career planning and problems of employees. Internal PR activities are aimed primarily at staff members and their families, management, board of directors and former employees. External PR targets all groups and people surrounding an organization who have an impact on its survival and growth. However, the dividing line between internal and external PR is very vague, because the activities of internal and external PR overlap strongly. When processing requests for sponsorship and organizing sponsored activities, for example, there is a continuous interaction between internal and external relationship groups, which makes the division between internal and external PR less relevant the longer it lasts.[9] This interaction between internal and external PR ensures synergistic effects that benefit the company identity and the company image.

Corporate public relations

Sports sponsorship is employed not only to achieve the goals of marketing communication; it is also an instrument of corporate communication. Under PR fall all activities devoted to favourably influencing relationship groups (corporate PR) or the direct support of marketing objectives (marketing PR). Corporate PR and corporate communication are synonymous.[10] Corporate PR aims to create goodwill among the diverse public groups. Outline 3.1 lists these target groups and goals of corporate communication in sports sponsorship. By involvement in a sporting project, traditional target groups (employees, the press and its opinion leaders, sports fans, sector relations, the general public and politicians) are merged with sports fans and all stakeholders associated with the sporting project. Through a sponsored sporting project, a company could come into contact with new relationship groups and may discover better links to existing target groups.

Outline 3.1 Target groups and goals of corporate communication

Target groups	Goals
Employees	Accentuate employees' involvement
	Ease staff recruitment
Press and opinion leaders	Create goodwill
	Generate positive publicity
	Defuse negative publicity
Fans	Rising up the loyalty ladder
in sports environment	Increase brand awareness
TV-viewers	Improve goodwill
Sector and business relations	Build relations with other organizations
	Improve and extend a company's goodwill within the sector

Target groups	Goals
General public	Increase company awareness among the public
	Promote or boost the company logo
	Increase involvement with the local community
Politicians	Improve goodwill
	Lobby

3.2 Types of public relations in sport

Generally, sport is a medium that can strongly support various forms of PR targeted to different audiences, as listed in Outline 3.2.

Outline 3.2 Forms of public relations (PR) in sport

Media PR	Special Olympics, Belgium, informs the press about their activities in order to generate positive publicity.
Retention communication	In the run-up advertising campaign to Euro 2000, all employees of Nationale-Nederlanden, main sponsor of the Royal Dutch football league, received an orange T-shirt on which was written 'Welcome to the lion's den'. Furthermore, competitions were created to win tickets.
Recruitment communication	Adecco, sponsor of the Turin 2006 Olympic Winter Games, will handle the recruitment, selection and training of the volunteers, and the professional development of the TOROC (Torino Olympic Committee) personnel.
Fusion communication	Vodafone Group Plc, one of the world's leading mobile telecommunications companies, communicates through sports when taking over local brands.
Public affairs	Cigarette brand Marlboro invites politicians to its skyboxes at the Silverstone Circuit during the British F1 Grandprix.

Financial PR	Analyses in the financial press of the T-mobile share are illustrated with a picture of the T-mobile-sponsored cyclist Erik Zabel.
Marketing PR	To introduce the official Euro 2004 match ball Roteiro, Adidas organized a well-targeted press campaign.

Sport and media public relations

Media PR is the oldest form of PR and remains extremely important. Developing and maintaining good contacts with the audiovisual media, the written press and the specialist press is the immediate goal of media PR, since organizations aim to generate favourable publicity for the brands and all of an organization's projects and events that benefit the company's image.[11] Journalists and the media form a significant intermediary public group.

Sport and retention communication

Retention communication forms the core of internal PR. As part of a sustainable enterprise, organizations consider their employees as increasingly valuable partners with time. Employees are important ambassadors for their organization and are likely to express a feeling of solidarity. Instruments of internal PR include newsletters, videos, company television, meetings, projects, staff parties and open days. Sports sponsorship programmes can have a motivating and uniting effect on the company's personnel distributed over regional branches and departments. When an organization's employees, through various forms of interaction, are selected as VIPs by the company in association with a sponsored sporting project, their commitment and emotional involvement can be increased.[12]

For example, an exhaustive study of the Bank of Ireland employees' perception of the bank's sponsorship programmes provides a number of additional insights.[13] It seems that the different categories of employees (management, staff) perceived the image transfer of human resources values from a sponsorship project in different ways. Employees felt that there was more than just its sponsorship projects that made the bank the desirable employer or 'winner'. The bank's 'winner' image seemed to be formed by a combination of all the strong points of the organization.

Sport and recruitment communication

In an age of labour shortages of well-educated people and specific professionals, the importance of recruitment communication increases. Every company wants to be on the shortlist of potential employers of recent graduates and experienced workers who are actively or potentially searching for a job.[14] The choice for a particular employer depends on its image among the general public. This is employment branding. Since the end of 1998, Ernst & Young in the Netherlands has sponsorsed the Dutch Olympic Committee and the Dutch Sport Federation (NOC*NSF). Creative recruitment communication is one of the objectives of the sponsorship of the Dutch umbrella sport federation. To place Ernst & Young higher on the shortlist of potential employers, the action 'Sign your contract in Sydney' was developed.[15] Accountants and tax specialists who had almost completed their training were stimulated through radio commercials to enter the Olympic contest. Among the almost 400 students who responded, eight signed an employment contract in the headquarters of Ernst & Young in Sydney. At the same time, they enjoyed the atmosphere of the Olympic Games.

Sport and merger communication

When the brand name of an organization changes as the result of a merger, the organization faces a significant challenge of corporate communication. Employees should be informed about the new brand name, which then must be made known to other stakeholders. The new brand name should incorporate positive image components. This implies that a strategy of merger communication is likely to remove all traces of the old brand name. A change of brand name usually implies a repositioning of the new brand, which does not make the communicative task easy. For example, the increase in scale in the European bank landscape from the mid-1990s was associated with many mergers and takeovers. New combinations, such as KBC, Dexia, Fortis and ING, were introduced forcefully into Belgium.

The timing of the brand-name change of the Belgische Gemeentekrediet, which merged with the Dexia group, was a result of its football sponsorship.[16] In 2000, the Gemeentekrediet sponsored Club Brugge and the Koninklijke Belgische Voetbalbond (Royal Belgian football league). Whereas in France the brand name Dexia had been introduced on 1 January 2000, this did not take place in Belgium until mid-May 2000. The marketing communication responsibilities of the Gemeentekrediet België led to a preference for launching the new brand name only after the end of the Belgian football competition (which Club Brugge got through with Gemeentekrediet as shirt sponsor). The sponsorship communications campaign in the run-up to and during Euro 2000 was used as a stepping stone to introduce the brand name Dexia in Belgium.

Sport and public affairs

Public affairs represents all activities of an organization aimed at influencing political pressure groups in a direction desired by the company. Lobbying is the key activity of public affairs and has far-reaching consequences for the future of organizations. Target groups of public affairs include the general public, the local community, government authorities, trading associations and pressure groups.[17] Organizations are dependent, after all, on subsidies and tax systems. In addition, they must deal with environmental and trade policies, establishment politics, and consumer and budgetary policy. Information provision, negotiations and influencing opinions and attitudes form the essence of lobbying. Informal meetings in the framework of sports sponsorship by a company, in which the opponent is interested, creates a basis for further negotiations.

Sport and financial public relations

Financial PR concerns the creation of goodwill and trust with (potential) shareholders, investors, bankers and the financial press. The instruments of financial PR are annual reports, financial newsletters and analysts' reports. An important component of financial PR is investor relationships.[18] This involves the nurturing of relations with current and potential financiers via roadshows, brochures, interviews and press conferences. Football clubs that are listed on the stock exchange are an excellent illustration of the increased interest in the financial PR of sport.[19]

Both the preparation of an application and the listing demand exemplary financial results, transparency, respect for regulations, and a professional approach to the financial press. Even for local sporting events, good relations with all financial stakeholders are essential. The economic press keeps close tabs on the financial quality of life of major sporting events. In the run-up to Euro 2000, for example, many critical remarks were made in Belgium about the inevitable financial costs and the uncertain benefits associated with the event.[20]

In addition, the integration of sport in the financial information of non-sports brands is becoming increasingly important. The 2001–03 annual reports of telecommunications company and tennis sponsor Siemens België were illustrated with photographs of the sponsored tennis stars Kim Clijsters and Justine Henin, decorated with the logo and the brand name of Siemens. By incorporating sporting illustrations in the annual report, the company wanted to convince institutional and private investors of its dynamism. In its commentaries, the financial press also referred to such dynamic brand developments. Sports photographs with mention of the brand name and the logo are rewarding eye-catchers for the financial press to lure the reader to a financial article that analyses the evolution of the share price of the sponsorship company.

Sport and marketing public relations

Marketing PR aims to create direct brand support and enhance the sale of products and services. In the case of a product launch or to support existing products or services, instruments of sports sponsorship are employed. Marketing PR is an integrated activity that shares more similarities with marketing communication than with corporate communication. The most important target groups of marketing PR are suppliers, distributors, wholesalers, retailers and competitors. Instruments of marketing PR in sport include meetings with the press and newsletters. With marketing PR through sport, a non-sports brand stimulates the interest of specialist and sports journalists in a creative manner.

For example, one key target group of sports brand Nike is teenagers between 12 and 19 years of age. During Euro 2000, Nike Parks were constructed for these teenagers in six European cities. In Amsterdam, Berlin, London, Madrid, Milan and Paris, football parks were erected for the kids.[21] The sports brand came into contact with young and assertive football players by presenting them with fun football exercise in different cages of the Nike Park. For example, the young players, to practise their kicking techniques, had to boot the ball through the open roof of a Fiat 500 instead of through the openings of a sealed goal. Between 10 June and 2 July 2000, approximately 200 000 children visited the Nike Park in Amsterdam.

3.3 Sports sponsorship and hospitality

Having discussed the most important forms of PR in sport, we will now examine the key activities of PR in sport. The techniques of PR vary widely. There are publications, press relationships, events, internal activities and advertising activities (see Table 3.1). Outline 3.3 provides an overview of these activities, which will be analysed further in this chapter.

Table 3.1 Techniques in public relationships

Publications	(= annual report, magazines, videos, brochures, books, website)
Press relationships	(= press releases, press conferences, press briefings, press receptions)
Internal	(= house journals, staff briefings)
Events	(= social events, factory tours, annual general meeting)
Advertising	(= corporate image)

Source: Brassington, F. and Pettit, S. (2003), *Principles of Marketing*, 3rd edn. Harlow: FT Prentice Hall.

Outline 3.3 Key activities of public relations in sport

- Sport as platform for relationship marketing (Section 3.3).
- Generation of positive publicity:
  - pull approach (Section 3.4);
  - push approach (Section 3.5).
- Crisis communication in sport (Section 3.6).

Corporate sports hospitality

Corporate sports hospitality involves the distinctive organization of relationship marketing activities in sport. Through the selection and exploitation of sporting activities, the organization supplies a tailored product, originality and quality. Sports hospitality offers distinctive and memorable experiences to sports viewers. The organization of sports hospitality sometimes assumes enormous proportions, as shown by the example of the Rabobank. During the cycling world championships of 1998, held in Valkenburg, the Rabobank welcomed about 5000 guests. These guests were mainly employees and customers of both Rabobank Nederland and various local branches of Rabobank.[22]

The selection of stakeholders for VIP packages in sport is a delicate balancing act. PR managers should first classify the public groups according to:[23]

- the dependence relationship between the public groups and the company;
- the perception by relationship groups of the company's image;
- the specific problem areas, disquiet or stability in the relationship;
- the demographic, socioeconomic, geographic and psychographic criteria;
- the public groups and the company;
- the communicative characteristics (reading and viewing behaviour, linguistic competency, etc.).

Achille Stabilo is the PR manager responsible for sports hospitality at a major multinational in Stockholm. He has to select the relationship groups for specific forms of active or passive sports hospitality. This demands the involvement of public groups in the sponsored sports project, which is the second step in the segmentation process.

Stabilo can make this step only after a thorough preliminary study of the empathy of the stakeholder or their partner for the selected sports project. The preparatory relationship research determines the quality of the VIP experience. This 'scanning of the terrain' should be conducted as discreetly as possible.[24] Stabilo has to classify the stakeholders into main groups and subgroups. This classifying of VIPs is the next important balancing act. The result of PR activities depends to an important extent on communication among the recipients. If regional business managers get to know each other better during a basketball game, then this forges particular links that can later support formal and informal processes in the company.

If Stabilo does not succeed, then corporate sports hospitality can lead to resentment, e.g. if he invites an important customer and his or her partner to a football game, only to discover at the game that the guests are not at all interested in football but are passionate opera buffs. In this way, relationship marketing can even be counterproductive.

A VIP experience is a promotional gift from the inviting company. If the size of the VIP package is considerable, then this could lead to integrity problems, because something enormous could be offered in return. Corporate sports hospitality is also likely to induce irritation in other relationship groups of the organization if they feel discriminated against compared with those who were invited. If this is the case, then the promotional event obviously loses its strength. Therefore, it is advisable to give sponsor's guests preferential treatment in the VIP village out of sight and sound of the paying public.[25]

Sport experiences

Typical of a sporting event are its unique features. Sport emotions can be classified into five experiences, which all work according to a certain emotional logic (Outline 3.4).[26]

Outline 3.4 Unique experiences in sport

- Adventure
- Friendship and solidarity
- Identification
- Care
- Serenity

The first experience in sport is the yearning for adventure. Sport has evolved from a weekend activity for leisure-time players to a large commercial adventure market. Adventure experiences provide a new dimension to sport. Computer manufacturer Compaq, for example, was the main sponsor of the polar expedition of Belgian adventurers Dixie Dansercour and Alain Hubert. Mountain climbers offer their adventurous stories to organizations that market products or services associated with the yearning for adventure. The sport of triathlon offers athletes large, middle and small adventures at various distances. Also, in terms of corporate sports hospitality, organizations provide unique adventure experiences to specific groups of stakeholders. During the Belgian and Dutch one-day cycling competitions in 2002, the Domo-Farm Frites team sold interested organizations a guest package. In the basic package, costing 195 euros, guests could follow the race at the best locations on the route and received a present. Around the start and arrival locations, and in the cyclists' hotel, 'meet-and-greet' opportunities had been provided. For an additional 125 euros, guests could circle in a helicopter over the cycling team for 20 minutes. Sport as an adventure experience is sold in a PR package. Top VIPs of the cycling team Deutsche Telekom were given an adventure in the Alps on the day of rest during the Tour de France. A mountain-bike trip offered them new challenges, and they could experience first-hand what the top cyclists went through, having to fight the elements every day.

Second, sport encourages friendship and solidarity. Brands look for ways to make interpersonal relationships such as friendship, love and solidarity accessible. In both team and individual sports, the friendship between athletes is tested. Team spirit and group dynamics stimulate the individual athletes to their finest performance. Competitors or team mates who practise sport together cultivate lifelong bonds of friendship. Even between fans, unique bonds are forged by the sporting experience. Both fans and practising athletes share sports emotions and experiences. During the après-ski they drink together and tell their stories. In a sporting environment, the sports consumer rises above the mundane.

Third, sport contains a unique identification experience. Through a sporting experience, consumers communicate who they are and what they find important. Sport allows a unique identification. Through the products and services that they buy, sports consumers emphasize who they are, what values they represent and what stories they can tell. At the who-am-I market, sports consumers can show who they differ from and who they are similar to. They may want to be like David Beckham and tell others who they are through football. This strong emotional attachment and personal identification with top sport make fans very loyal. Celebrity endorsement and merchandising, concepts that we shall consider in detail later, amplify this identification experience. Top footballers, for example, have grown into superstars, primarily due to this experience. The fact that many of them come from lowly backgrounds and have survived a difficult and tough climb to the top strengthens this identification. Whereas once pop-stars were the trendsetters in fashion and hairstyle, today it is the David Beckhams who carry out this function.[27] A sports consumer is poor in the who-am-I market if they cannot afford to buy goods, services or experiences with which they can identify. Singer Moby emphasizes the identification problem that develops when someone cannot afford to wear the sports gear that sends out the message they want to identify with: '... At home we were dirt poor. All my friends wore Adidas, while I was given sports shoes you could buy at the petrol station. With four stripes instead of three ...'

Fourth, there is the care experience in sport.[28] The care approach is included here under the heading 'sport experience'.[29] The need for care provision and social involvement is becoming an important submarket in the society of tomorrow. It is expected that corporate governance will continue to grow in significance and that sport will capitalize on this.[30] In a future integrated approach to corporate events, organizations will capitalize even more on the care experience associated with sport. Not only the recipient but also the provider fulfils a need, which leads to a positive interaction. The core values of Special Olympics Belgium, and of its sponsors, form a striking illustration of sport as a care experience. Special Olympics Belgium develops sports activities based on accessibility for all mentally handicapped people, competition, appreciation of all individual performances and celebration. The Special Olympics principles are also applicable to all training activities. To promote the integration of mentally handicapped people, the Special Olympics strives for the attendance and participation of the general public.

Mini-case study - Feyenoord supports Unicef

With the start of the new football season, Feyenoord Rotterdam will be supporting the Children's Fund Unicef for a period of three years. A gala dinner will be held for Unicef, a benefit match organized, and the youth members of Feyenoord informed about Unicef's work. Feyenoord guarantees revenue of at least 100 000 euros in the first year, which is destined for the Unicef project 'Every Adolescent Has the Right to Know' in Ghana. This worldwide Unicef programme targets providing information about HIV/Aids which is given by and for young people. Feyenoord supports this project not only financially but also by helping in Ghana with its implementation. The facilities of the Feyenoord Fetteh Football Academy Ghana have been made available to the project, and the pupils of the Academy will be providing Aids education. Currently, there are almost 60 children taking schooling and football training at the Football Academy.

Source: From www.sponsoronline.nl, accessed 8 February 2002.

Fifth, sport supports a serenity experience. In an unsafe and unsettled society, there is always a need for serenity and stability. People tend to glorify and romanticize the past. They want to cherish tradition and do things in the same manner as usual. For example, Wimbledon is one of the world's oldest sporting organizations, having existed since 1877. It is typical of this tennis tournament that the organizers try to do things as much as possible in the same manner as before. The Wimbledon organizers cling tightly to tradition: a small ceremony, a rule, the route you must follow or a product that is sold. It took years before the management of the All England Lawn Tennis Club agreed to allow players to wear tennis clothing that was not white. Wimbledon is also the only Grand Slam tournament played on grass. This is associated with wonderful stories full of tradition. The grass master, for example, starts to work on 'his' grass immediately after the end of the last doubles game, preparing it for next year's tournament.

Mini-case study - We innovate now

The participation of Belgian brothers Alain and Bruno Lewuillon in the Atlantic Rowing Race 2001 illustrates sport as an adventure, friendship and care experience. On 7 October 2001, 50 teams from around the world, consisting of two rowers each, started in Gran Canaria. The objective was to cross the Atlantic Ocean as quickly as possible, and 5400 km later (about

1.3 million strokes), to be the first team to reach the finish in Barbados.[31] Because of the distance and the dependence on weather conditions, this test had an unusually adventurous dimension. Not only their physical and mental condition, but also the friendship and the solidarity between the Lewuillon brothers were tested to an extreme. In addition, a humanitarian project was created. The Lewuillon brothers rowed under the flag of 'Keten van de Hoop België' ('chain of hope for Belgium').[32] This is an international association that brings sick children to Belgium for medical treatment that they cannot get in their own countries. The organization associated itself with this sporting adventure project to draw the attention of school children to their humanitarian projects. Through the Internet (www.winbelgium.org), students could follow the rowers' course. School children also became acquainted with maritime problems and humanitarian projects.

Telecom operator Win (We Innovate Now), the Belgian market leader and European forerunner in mutual network connections, was the main sponsor of the Belgian team in the Atlantic Rowing Race. Just like the rowing team, this telecom company considers the values of experience, trust, team spirit and speed to be important. The linking of the sporting adventure to the care project Keten van de Hoop provided Win with an additional important argument. Win wants to establish social roots partly through the development of pedagogic projects.

The aura of the sports environment

The emotional value of sports hospitality compared with that of cultural or leisure hospitality is seen primarily in the aura of the sports environment (sport atmospherics).[33] Permanent aspects of the aura of a sports stadium are listed in Outline 3.5. The jingles during the game, the stadium's architecture, a musical performance during half-time or fireworks after the game are several factors with an emotional surplus value for the guests. The relaxing spectacle, the unpredictability of the game and the uncertainty of the result can lead to a fun release and an escape from the mundane.[34]

Outline 3.5 The unique aura of the sports environment

Athletes	Michael Owen
Escape from the mundane	Paris–Dakar
Catharsis	Goal! Goal! Goal!
Social integration and community spirit	Ayrton Senna foundation
Music	'We are the Champions!'

Outline 3.5 continued

Set rituals and ceremony	Olympic torch
Personal identification	David Beckham merchandising
Mascot	Kinas, mascot of Portugal 2004
Aesthetic pleasure	Acro Gym
Uncertain result	Champions League final 1999: Manchester United–Bayern Munich: 2–1
Architecture	Ascott Venue
Presence of ex-athletes	John McEnroe
The public	Mexican wave
Fun sideline events	Fireworks
Top performances	Michaël Schumachter

Also typical of a sporting environment are the exaggerated fierce and aggressive emotions and reactions. A competition in a sports stadium can lead to harassment and frustrations and degenerate into supporter riots. In the 1980s and 1990s, problems with hooliganism were recorded regularly in and around European football stadiums. Violence on the field can produce a feeling of insecurity or aggression around the field.

Sport and culture experiences via city marketing

Around the sports stadium, organizers offer invited guests unique experiences. More and more, sports events exploit the historical surroundings of a city or region. In this way, the sponsor reaches not only the sports consumer but also the culture consumer. Usually, the guests or their partners are not interested exclusively in sport and appreciate the offer of cultural experiences as part of a VIP package. Still other guests enjoy gastronomic experiences set against a unique historical backdrop. The Ronde van Vlaanderen, for example, has started since 1998 in the historic centre of Bruges instead of in the regional city of Sint-Niklaas. The new starting point granted extra prestige to the race and to the VIP formulas. By offering complementary experiences, the VIP packages have become more commercially attractive for the organizer. Also, an organizer obtains an entrée into the city council and contact with local residents and workers.

Sport and city marketing is also a new municipal policy theme to attract more tourists. The growth in national and international tourism has always been an important exponent of the increasing leisure culture.[35] A city communicates distinctively via top sporting events. For example, the Giro d'Italia 2002 started in Groningen. The idea to bring the 'Euro-Giro' to Groningen developed from the special relationship that the city has both with bicycles and with Italy. Groningen is not only the first bicycle city in the Netherlands but, according to some sources, the first bicycling city in the world. Also Groningen, because of the Italian contribution to the renewal of the city centre and the Groninger Museum, presents itself as the most Italian city north of Milan. The Groningen project represented both tourism and sociocultural aspects. In the run-up to and during the weekend of this top sporting event, a number of additional Italian events were organized.

Barcelona, Athens, Turin and Rotterdam are other examples of places that attach great importance to top sport as an instrument of city marketing. Also, through sports clubs (Manchester United, Real Madrid) and sporting venues (Nou Camp Barcelona), a city positions itself as a strong brand on the tourist map.[36] For example, sports city Den Bosch feels that recreation and sport contribute to creating a lively and attractive place. Den Bosch was the starting point of the Grand Départ of the Tour de France in 1996 and of the Tour Féminin in 2002.

Experiential sports hospitality

Experiential sports hospitality involves offering stakeholders active sporting experiences. For the average sports consumer, active sports hospitality has a number of unique experience features. Specific groups are invited to participate actively in sport as part of a sports sponsorship project. For instance, Siemens Belgium sponsored not only the tennis stars Kim Clijsters and Justine Henin but also Nicolas Colsaerts, Belgium's best golfer. For Siemens Belgium, golf is the main sport with which to reach the CEOs of their business-to-business target groups. Once a year, Siemens invites these CEOs to go golfing with Nicolas, which has an enormous emotional value.

Sports consumers obtain surplus value in comparison with passive sports hospitality and certainly compared with cultural or leisure hospitality. There is a significant emotional surplus value for the active sports consumer if the activity meets the appropriate preconditions, enables an appropriate experience and leads to positive results (see Outline 3.6).

Outline 3.6 The unique features of an active sports experience

● Appropriate preconditions:

  – free choice

  – no obligations

  – take initiative oneself

● Appropriate experience:

  – self-expressive

- challenging

- rejuvenating

- stimulating

- playful

- qualitative

- relaxing

● Positive results

- physical wellbeing

- social wellbeing

- psychological wellbeing

Source: Based on Smith, A. and Westerbeek, H. (2002), *Sport Business in the Global Marketplace*. London: Macmillan.

3.4 Sports sponsorship and publicity

Sporting events are front-page news for both quality and popular newspapers. In the audiovisual media, sport plays an important role in the competition for viewers. An important objective of sports sponsorship is the written or auditory mention of the sponsor's brand name or of the sports organization in an editorial context. Whenever this is not accomplished through paid means such as advertisements, it is publicity. Shilbury and colleagues define publicity as '… the generation of news about a person, product, service [or organization] that appears in broadcast or print media [at no cost for the organisation] …'[37] In the description of publicity given by De Pelsmacker and colleagues, the emphasis is on the approach to the press to mention something in the media without having to pay: '… publicity is the term used to describe the free media coverage of news about the company or its products, often as a result of PR efforts …'[38] Publicity is a subset of PR, focused on generating media coverage at minimal cost to the organization. It happens when the media voluntarily decide to talk about the organization and its commercial activities.

Basically, a brand name gains 'access to the media' on the basis of freedom of expression and not on the basis of bought advertising space.[39] The free character of publicity produces confusion, however. A number of sources describe the citation in an editorial context as free publicity. The term 'free publicity' refers to publicity that did not have to be paid for. It is a free advertisement, as it were. However, if a brand obtains publicity through a sports sponsorship project, then this is usually associated with high costs. The approach to the press is also not free. Although an organization does not pay for it, free publicity takes an enormous amount of time (and personnel) to organize effectively.[40]

In contrast to advertising, publicity takes an indirect route. A disinterested party (journalist) found it worthwhile to report on the organization or the activity. What the newspaper prints in its editorial columns will sound more credible and trustworthy than what the organization claims in its advertising folders or television advertising spots.[41] Publicity in the media is financially attractive for a company because it saves on advertising costs. Nevertheless, an organization must be selective in its contact with the press.[42] This means that not every opportunity for publicity should be taken. An effective strategy consists of considering the interests of the press and the reactions that would be desirable.

A sporting issue is a performance, a result, a product, a service, a point of contention or an interest in sport. Whether a sporting issue leads to publicity depends primarily on how newsworthy the sports project is (see Outline 3.7). News is whatever differs from the usual and what many people find striking.[43] Whether sports news is newsworthy depends on the topicality, the other subjects on offer, the medium's field of special interest, the prominent image of the team or organization, the number of interested parties, the human-interest element, the source and the scope of the news, and the correlation of all of the above elements.[44] The number of newsworthy press releases is greater than the space reserved for reports in a newspaper. Is the submitted report big news? Is the news meant for a restricted number of readers or for a large group? Does the report have an independent news value, or is it purely advertising?

Outline 3.7 Determinants of publicity in sport

- Priming

- Major sport or minor sport

- (Inter)national or local reputation

- Importance of the sporting competition

- Duration of the sports sponsorship engagement

- Quality and originality of the approach to the press

- Established tradition of citing sponsor names

- Regulations concerning citing sponsor names

An important determinant of the newsworthiness, and thus of editorial attention for a sports item, is priming. This means that a (sports) organization is judged on sports issues that dominate the news.[45] There is disproportionately more attention paid to major sports, while minor sports receive much less – or even no – editorial attention. Associated factors include the local, national or international reputation, aura and importance of the particular sport. In sports reporting, there is typically excessive attention paid to (inter)national football competitions. Cycling events also enjoy extensive editorial coverage in key cycling countries such as the Netherlands, Belgium, France, Italy and Spain. For indoor sports, there is a continuous interest at a lower level. In Mediterranean countries such as Greece and Turkey, the interest in basketball is massive. 'Minor' sports such as judo, sailing and triathlon have a harder job drawing viewers' continuous attention and get into the limelight only during the Olympic Games and world or European championships. Press attention to these sports increases only during very big competitions. The chance of publicity in the media depends on the tradition followed by the media regarding sponsor citations and the local regulations. The quantity of publicity generated also depends on the quality and originality of the approach to the press, which we discuss further in Section 3.5.

Often, organizations invest large sums in marketing communication campaigns. The effect of these campaigns can be reinforced or destroyed by editorial reporting.[46] The tenor of publicity can be both positive and negative. The editorial attention for Anite's sponsorship of two Dutch women's bobsled teams is an example of positive publicity.[47] The company concluded a two-year contract with the bobsled teams through the Olympic Winter Games in 2002. Both teams qualified for Salt Lake City and finished in sixth and tenth place. During the preparations for the Olympic Winter Games, television, newspapers and magazines devoted considerable space to the women's bobsled performance. As the sponsorship was exclusive, Anite became involved directly in the sporting performances. The intensive support gave the publicity a positive undertone. The tenor was always that the success was attributable directly to Anite's support.

Bart Veldkamp, a Dutch skater with Belgian nationality, expresses clearly that negative publicity is also inherent in sports sponsorship: 'If you want only a good news story, then you musn't get involved with sports sponsorship. You should buy a painting and hang it on the wall. That is beautiful every day ...' In the reviews in the press concerning Paris-Roubaix 2002, for example, there was much negative publicity for tyre manufacturer Michelin. The cycling teams Mapei, Lotto and La Française des Jeux all have a contract with Michelin. These teams received new tyres for testing just three days before Paris–Roubaix. The tyres were tested straight away in a bone-dry 'Hell of the North', the sharp cobblestones that cyclists have to cope with during the race. During the race, however, the racers had to cycle through a mud puddle. The course was extremely slippery. Racers from teams using the new tyres had trouble keeping their balance and knocked roughly against the cobblestones of the 'Hell'. In the press, team managers and racers blamed the sponsor Michelin for not giving them enough time to test and evaluate the tyres, which clearly did not meet the standards required.

The mentioning of a brand name in an editorial context is a boost on both good and bad days. Therefore, it is important to cultivate good relationships with the press. This means that an organization is accessible to journalists and is consistent in its approach to the press. 'A good press can deliver more than an expensive advertising campaign. The other side of the coin is that a carefully constructed image can be destroyed even faster by bad press.'[48]

There are three ways to record an interview: by telephone (recorded live or not); during a journalist's visit (either in the office of the PR representative or on neutral ground); and recorded in the studio (live or pre-recorded). Outline 3.8 expresses this in a nutshell. The point of view taken in this paragraph is that of the PR officer of the sponsoring organization, who has to deal efficiently with the press.

Outline 3.8 Interviews: connections between channel, time and place

	Channel		'Place'	
	Print/radio/TV	Telephone	Visit by journalist	In studio
Time	In real time			
	Pre-recorded			

© J. Piet Verckens (2004).

The attention paid by the journalist to the content of the message depends on a number of factors. Along with the content of articles about the sport, there is the extent of support or criticism for a sport-sponsoring organization. This is associated with the question of whether the media perceive that a sponsor has been successful or failed with regard to a particular sporting issue. In the case of a bandwagon effect, fans might jump on board to support the winner. If, in contrast, there is an underdog effect, then the media may support the loser. The reaction to the information is the next step. This reaction is the result of a complex interaction of factors: the prior knowledge about a sporting issue, the existing image of the sponsor, and the skill to be able to process the information.

Publicity can be created in two ways. On the one hand, the press approaches a sponsor as a result of a particular performance of an athlete or a sporting organization because the target group of that medium is interested – positively or negatively – in their news. This is the pull approach to publicity. This means that sports consumers draw interesting sports news to themselves. Journalists and the media take note of this or create the need. Despite the fact that an athlete does not have to do anything for it, the moment of contact with the press must be prepared carefully.[49]

On the other hand, there is the push approach to publicity. The sports sponsor writes press releases, organizes press conferences and prepares its own reports or publications with the intention to generate positive publicity (see Section 3.5) or defuse negative publicity (see Section 3.6).

The media spontaneously approach a representative of a sponsor if there is interesting news to be had for their readers or viewers. The interest of a medium in an interview can be created by the interviewee (e.g. as sponsor of a good sporting performance) or by the medium itself (e.g. with a series on sport and the economy). In many cases the stimulus determines the tone of the interview: curious, sympathetic or investigative.

The media are also keen on sensational news. What often happens is that a journalist first approaches the sponsor by telephone and confronts the person who answers (hopefully, a PR officer) with a fact or rumour from another source.

The journalist wants a response on the telephone. The organization can respond only if it is well prepared. If the person answering feels overwhelmed, then he or she may not respond properly. The clumsy reply 'No comment' will not please the journalist and will lead to negative publicity for the organization. A sponsor prevents this by appointing an employee responsible for dealing with the press. Usually this is the spokesperson who is informed of all 'ins and outs' and has been authorized to make statements. One spokesperson must always be (easily) accessible to the press. Moreover, a plan with procedures that everyone is aware of and that people adhere to is no longer a luxury. Thus, the receptionist will know who is responsible for talking to the press regarding certain aspects and to whom journalists should be connected.

The spokesperson must not get ruffled, even when the telephone call is unexpected and conducted rapidly. It would be better to note down the questions and arrange to call back as soon as possible (and to do so). If the journalist cannot wait because of a deadline, then it is better not to respond than to give the wrong answer. If the journalist calls 'live' unexpectedly, then the spokesperson is not obliged to respond. The spokesperson can state that a response will be made after the facts have been checked. The spokesperson must exercise good self-control and always remain calm and friendly. Agitated people can be tricked into saying something that they later regret.

An interview is a unique opportunity to present a sporting project or sponsoring organization to the general public. Therefore, the interview must be well prepared. The attitude of the athlete, organization or sponsor is paramount. Understanding can soften a critical attitude if the interviewee succeeds in explaining an awkward situation; sympathy can change into grumpiness if the athlete turns out to be arrogant.[50]

Interviews can be conducted orally or in writing (even by email). An oral interview can be published in a newspaper or (sponsored) magazine, or it can be used as a testimony in a radio or television broadcast or a sponsored video. This testimony can be broadcast in real time or be pre-recorded. A written or emailed interview can find its way into newspapers and (sponsored) magazines; these are always pre-recorded (see Outline 3.9).

In general, it might be efficient to follow the items in the general checklist for an interview (shown in Outline 3.9).

Outline 3.9 General checklist for an interview

Preparation of the interview:

- What is the interviewer's knowledge of the subject?
- Are you acquainted with the medium and rubric/programme? Do you know the target group? Do you know the aim and context in which the interview will be placed?
- If not, inform yourself about the journalist/reporter, their channel, their aim, the context and the audience.

- Are other people being interviewed for the same programme/article? Who?
- Set conditions for the interview, e.g. go through the tenor of the article with the journalist beforehand.
- Discuss questions in advance.
- Agree what the first question will be.
- In consultation with the journalist/reporter, set a date, time and location for the interview (perhaps an environment where you feel relaxed).
- Know all the facts about the subject. If necessary, in consultation with the communication manager, prepare answers for likely questions.

During the interview:
- Remain calm and polite – even if the questions are irritating.
- Be brief and clear – avoid jargon and digressions.
- Use poignant metaphors, quotations, one-liners, etc.
- Answer snappily.
- Record the oral interview – with the interviewer's consent.

After the interview:
- Request to read/listen to/view the interview before publication/broadcasting.
- If factual mistakes or phrasing mistakes are detected, request a correction before publication/broadcasting.
- After publication/broadcasting, send a 'thankyou' note, letter or email.

The written interview

In a written interview, the sponsoring organization talks to the readers through the journalist about the sponsored sports activities. Because everything said in an interview can be used literally, there are dangers associated with an informal talk taking place before or after the interview. What the journalist thinks the spokesperson said is what is printed in the paper.

After the interview, the organizer of the sporting event or the sponsoring organization can offer the journalist some company merchandise. This must be a straightforward promotional gift for it to seem cordial; otherwise, it could be refused and have a counterproductive effect. After the article is printed, the company can send the journalist a letter with a compliment on their work.

The oral interview

Popular athletes and people with important positions in the sporting world are often interviewed on the radio or television. A checklist with tips for interviewees during such an interview is given in Outline 3.10.

Outline 3.10 Checklist for an oral interview

Environment:
- Your own organization:
  - face-to-face;
  - in a telephone call.
- On neutral ground (sporting venue/stadium, hotel, restaurant).
- Studio.

Time:
- Ask in advance what the time limit is.
- A programme lasting for 60 minutes or more gives the possibility for nuances.

Messages:
- Factuality:
  - place business card on table in front of reporter, with your correct name and function;
  - notes/sheet of paper on the table in front of you: be precise;
  - concrete, clear statements during interviews;
  - limit yourself to one or two key messages – repetition amplifies.
- (Non)verbal characteristics:
  - introduce inflections in your voice;
  - look at reporter during talk.

Keep results under control:
- Use personal cassette recorder/video recorder to record the interview.
- Say when you don't like a question.
- Don't say more than you want to.
- Listen to the tape afterwards.
- Do not pay attention to the atmosphere in the studio (it could intimidate you).

Specific to the medium of radio is the importance of the concise message, because people generally listen less attentively to radio than to television. In addition, radio reports are generally produced quickly and aired, at most, a few hours later. The location of the interview partly determines the success with which the right message is communicated. For a long interview, it is preferable for the reporter to visit the interviewee. A telephone call can be efficient for shorter replies.

If the interviewee succeeds in keeping to the allotted time, then the interview will be sent out unedited. For interviews on delicate themes, it is best to limit yourself to a number of key messages formulated in advance and written on a piece of paper, which you can consult during the interview.

In a television interview, the interviewee must take into account the importance of the visual. The media spectacle can distract attention from the real message. Media training for top athletes and PR officers who are overwhelmed at crisis moments by cameras can prevent problems. This is why media trainers emphasize that in a television interview, the non-verbal message (appearance, clothing, grooming) must be lively and persuasive.

3.5 A pull-push approach to press relationships

The active approach to the press – the push approach in publicity – is a complex balancing act. Tension exists between the press and the sporting world.[51] However, in principle, a journalist should be independent. That is why a strict separation is desirable between the editorial policy and the advertising exploitation of a medium. In addition, journalists insist on their autonomy and do not want any restrictions concerning the content. It can be counterproductive to give a sports journalist the task of mentioning a sponsor's name in the report. A journalist is also expected to produce critical comments on social developments. Despite the growing realization that elite sport is no longer possible without sponsorship, a journalist must still consider critically whether the sponsor's involvement undermines the sporting world. Through the journalist's critical attitude on the one hand and the desire for sensation on the other, the tenor of publicity about sponsorship can be negative. Therefore, an individual sports person, event or team has more credit a priori with the press than the sponsors.

Press release

The most common way for PR specialists to communicate is through a press release. This is a report of some event that an organization writes itself and sends to the media in the hope that it will be published for free. A newer version of this idea is a video news release (VNR), which tells the story in a film format instead.[52] A press release is an indirect means that is aimed directly at the media target group. Journalists and the media are intermediaries and not a target group for an organization. Launching a press release is opportune for an organization if there is sporting news to report, a sports event to announce, or an important sports meeting with background information to provide.

The relatively low cost and high return makes a press release an interesting marketing communication instrument.[53] If the press release is printed, the organization receives publicity. Also, the news comes from a more reliable editorial source than if announced by the company itself. Because of this objectivity, published press releases have a greater impact on the reader than does advertising.

One significant disadvantage is that a brand or sports manager has no influence over the content or the moment of publication or what the editor does with the press release.

What factors increase the chance of getting submitted press releases published? The higher the organization's turnover, the greater the chance of publication. The news value of large sporting events or organizations is considerably higher than that of small sporting events, regardless of the subject of the press release. Existing contacts in the media and knowledge of the policy with regard to press releases are other criteria that increase the chance of publication.[54]

Other direct mechanisms of influence are extra additions to press releases and the attention paid to the press releases (e.g. asking whether a press release has been received or asking whether the paper allows scoops).[55] However, goodwill can be nurtured in the journalist by providing him or her with extra information. Sometimes the number of advertisements or the sale of advertisements after publication forms an indirect selection criterion for press releases by editors. Tips about the content, form and layout of a press release are given in Outline 3.11.

Outline 3.11 Checklist for press releases

- A press notice, sometimes called a news release, is intended to be read not by newspaper readers but by people in the newspaper business.

- Tell them what the story is about in your title. It is a waste of time to write a headline: they'll do that.

- Put the date on it (the date they'll get it, not the date you wrote it).

- Tell them who you are in the organization.

- Tell them who to get hold of for further information, and how.

- Use white paper, A4 size, double-spaced, wide left-hand margin, one side only. If possible, try to adopt their house style.

- Number the pages. Type '/more ...' at the bottom of each page, except the last, where you should type 'end'. Repeat the title at the top of each continuation page.

- No underlining, because that is a printer's mark, meaning set in italics.

- Be brief. Be factual. Be accurate. Check everything at source.

- Encapsulate the whole of your story in the first paragraph – the intro – of your press notice. It may be all an editor can use or even has time to read.

- Add further qualifying and explanatory information in the next paragraph.

- If you have a genuine quote, which actually adds something to the story, use it. Get permission first! Identify clearly the name and relevance of the person being quoted.

- Bear in mind the needs of radio and television. They like brief 'sound bites' and 'screen bites'. If you can offer them someone to interview, a site to visit or a picture to take, then say so.

- Finish off with the practical data: where to send for the report/buy the widget/attend the event/sign up for membership, or whatever it may be.

- Details not intended for publication, such as phone numbers (day and night) of two contacts, help editorial staff. Notes to editors can include background facts, availability of interviewees and photographs, i.e. all the operational nuts and bolts.

- When to embargo? Don't, unless it will help the press or you have to for legal or other compelling reasons.

Source: Based on Stone, N. (1995), *The Management and Practice of Public Relations*. Basingstoke: Macmillan.

Press conference

A press conference is a meeting at which an organization announces important news to a group of invited journalists. A variation on the press conference is a visit by the press to the organization when there is news to report or as part of some special event.[56] Outline 3.12 provides various reasons, arranged from positive to negative, for why an organization would arrange a press conference in sport. For example, on 9 October 1999, one day before the practice international match of the Netherlands–Brazil, footballers E. Pélé and J. Cruyff were the main players at a press conference organized by Eurocard/Mastercard. The football stars presented their view of football in the coming century.[57]

Outline 3.12 Reasons for organizing a sports press conference

- A victory or a strong sporting performance
- Sports awards
- Announcement of sponsor agreement/partnership with a sponsor
- Name (or change) for a sports venue
- Important transfer, change of staff (owner, coach, etc.)
- Announcement of new sporting rules
- Announcement of breach of a rule
- State of affairs in a legal case (doping, bribery problems)

The rules of thumb for a press conference in sport are listed in Outline 3.13.

Outline 3.13 Checklist for a press conference in sport

Beforehand:

- Set theme of press conference
- Determine whether the theme merits a press conference
- Set date
- Check whether another press conference is being held concurrently
- Arrange location, paying attention to:
  - Reservation
  - Room layout
  - Accessibility (by car and public transport)
  - Parking options
  - Size
  - Catering
  - Telephone/fax connections
  - Signposting
  - Wardrobe
  - Sound equipment
  - Audiovisual facilities
  - Separate room for interviews
- Set programme, paying attention to:
  - Chairperson/management
  - Speakers
  - Demonstration/tour, etc.
- Prepare invitations, paying attention to:
  - List of press to invite
  - Text for invitation
  - Copying
  - Distribution
  - Reply card
  - Route description
- Deal with logistics, paying attention to:
  - Preparation of name tags for speakers
  - Press files
  - Attendance list

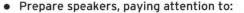

- Prepare speakers, paying attention to:
  - inventory of possible questions
  - media training

During the conference:

- Welcome journalists
- Sign attendance list
- Present press file
- Introduce speakers
- Supervise individual interviews

Afterwards:

- Send on documentation
- Collect press cuttings
- Be available for late questions
- Carry out evaluation

During the press conference, a press file is usually distributed. A press file contains relevant information and photographic material that could assist the journalists with the writing of their articles (see Outline 3.14).[58] It is also a useful instrument for absent journalists, as press files can be forwarded. This is why it is useful to keep an attendance list.

Outline 3.14 Checklist for sports press file and photos

Press file for sports sponsorship:

- Explanatory press release in sport
- Background information on the subject
- Texts of the speeches
- Copies of PowerPoint presentations
- Digital photo material
- Contacts with sport press photo agents
- Details about the speakers
- Background information about the sport and the company
- Recent annual report of the organization

Press photos for sports sponsorship:

- Print good-quality photos (no passport photos, vacation snapshots, etc.)
- Print photos on glossy paper and of a reasonable size (postcard)
- Put company's name and telephone number on the back of the photos
- Note whether the photos can be used without paying copyright fees

- Record the details (name, site, etc.) of the sports press photo agents
- Suggest captions for the photos
- Indicate whether the photos must be returned

However, there may be a conflict of interest between the sponsor and the media perspective, since an editor is likely to be interested in news, not obvious or disguised advertising messages meant for the advertising department. In contrast, for organizations, a press release or press conference is something that promotes without being an advertisement in the strictest sense of the word. Therefore, an organization must have something to report and the facts must speak for themselves. In general, organizations want to focus attention on a product or service or to show that business is going well.

Another conflict of interest may arise if the editor assumes that the sender is not objective. Therefore, a sponsorship manager should always act as an 'ideal' supplier of information. By providing exact information in a business-like manner, the PR manager may ensure that the editor has no further questions. Through references or quotations from neutral literature, the sports sponsor might establish a reputation for reliability in the long term. For instance, background material (e.g. press clippings, news reports, etc.) could be stored in an archive and used whenever the opportunity presents itself.

3.6 Sports sponsorship and crisis communications

Sport is not always in the headlines because of magnificent victories and brilliant performances. Doping problems, bribery scandals, financial difficulties and serious injuries are part of the reality of the sports world. This unpredictable and capricious nature of sport can put sporting organizations and sponsorship brands in a bad light. Typical of top sport is that athletes go to the limit of what is acceptable in medical and ethical terms. In addition, news of sporting incidents spreads rapidly to the various stakeholders of an organization. Both classic and new media play journalistic games to gather the latest news. In this case, we can talk of overshooting, i.e. more than a professional amount of attention being paid to sensational news.

Therefore, the tenor of publicity is negative in many cases, and the negative impact of crisis news on the company image persists for a long time.[59] Sport is exaggerated not only for its very best achievements but also for its worst. Because the negative news spiral can seriously damage the organizing or sponsoring brand, proactive or reactive crisis communication in sport has grown into an important theme. Common features of problems arising in sport are an environment full of passion and emotions, the threatening character, rapid decision-making, and the high level of uncertainty.[60] In such situations, the perception of the facts is very important. Unpredictable sporting events lead to crisis communication. The objective of crisis communication is to eliminate or control the negative perception of stakeholders. Proactive crisis communication, or pre-crisis communication, anticipates a sporting crisis. Therefore, it is essential to elaborate the rules and procedures to be followed when a problem does occur. Preventive crisis communication rules in sport are listed in Outline 3.15. It is important for a brand to be able to depend on an existing reservoir of trust and goodwill with the press in a crisis situation.

Outline 3.15 Preventive crisis communication rules in sport

- Anticipate crises in sport via 'what-if' scenarios
- Build up goodwill, trust and brand value
- Do not deny sports problems
- Communicate sports problems with the sports team
- Work preventively with authorities
- Be accessible to the press

Mini-case study – Anti-doping plan of the Tour de France

Both sporting organizations and sponsors have a vested interest in controlling the doping problem. This is why Amoury Sport Organisation (ASO), the organizer of the Tour de France, produced an anti-doping plan from 1999 onwards. This was produced in collaboration with the Union Cycliste International. In the ten-point plan, there are four main themes: ethics, testing, research and prevention. First, a code regarding doping use is highlighted in the ethical part of the anti-doping plan. Racers, team leaders and doctors have to agree to it. Under pressure from the non-sport sponsors, an agreement was reached with the participating teams that a racer would voluntarily leave the Tour if found to be 'not negative'. The cycling teams also concluded an anti-doping charter with their racers when signing their contracts. Second, the number of tests performed outside of competitions was increased. Third, a committee of medical experts is checking whether the massive number of therapeutic regulations can be justified. Fourth, the tour management invests in making young racers aware of the risks of doping and of doping prevention.

The ten measures are:

1. Establish an ethical code that stresses the sporting spirit of the Tour.
2. Cycling teams sign the ethical code and the Tour regulations.

3. The racers promise to do the same. The youngest participant in the Tour 2002 (a 22-year-old Frenchman, Jérôme Pineau) led the 'oath'.

4. Create a committee of eight medical experts.

5. Conduct blood tests two days before the start of the Tour.

6. Conduct announced and unannounced doping tests before and during the Tour.

7. Elaborate a better logistical apparatus for good and rapid handling of the tests.

8. Elaborate a three-year research programme together with a scientific centre.

9. Inform racers before the start of the Tour about the risks of doping use.

10. Propose an educational project to prevent the use of doping among young racers.

Source: Based on *De Standaard* (2002), Ik geloof echt dat we het dopinggebruik terugdringen, *De Standaard*, 8 July 2002

Mini-case study – Deutsche Telekom and crisis communication in sport

Sometimes preventive crisis communication in sport has the unwanted effect of causing a genuine crisis. To demonstrate that Deutsche Telekom was serious about the anti-doping campaign for its cycling team, it not only had anti-doping clauses inserted in the cyclists' contracts and preached 'zero tolerance' but also organized unannounced tests of the racers outside of competitions. By forcefully preventing doping use, the Telekom management wanted to create a solid reputation and work on the team's credibility. Racers in the Telekom team had already been tested for years and followed up medically at the University of Fribourg. After the Festina drugs scandal of 1998, Telekom invested a great deal of money in the fight against the use of doping. It communicated proactively about this preventive approach to generate goodwill in the specialist press. The Telekom management was dismayed to discover that in July 2002, its financing of out-of-competition doping tests had led to problems for Jan Ullrich, ex-Tour winner and the star of the Telekom team. During a visit to a discotheque, Ullrich had taken forbidden amphetamines. Ullrich admitted this in Germany during a press conference, which was broadcast live on the day of the start of the Tour de France 2002 by the German station ARD (secondary sponsor of the Telekom cycling team). The German Cycling League decided several weeks later to suspend Jan Ullrich until 23 March 2003.

Unhappy with this measure, Ullrich left the Telekom team several weeks later for the team of bicycle manufacturer Bianchi. Coming second in the Tour de France in 2003, Ullrich gave a splendid performance. The management of the Telekom team became interested again in top German racers. From 2004, Ullrich was again under contract to the German team, which was now going under the brand name t-online.

A crisis is an acute phenomenon that raises a lot of questions. During a sporting crisis, people often lose control over the problems involved. The rapid decisions that must be made during a crisis tend towards improvisation instead of well-considered decisions. The uncertainty and the lack of information during a sporting crisis are breeding grounds for rumours. In addition, the media places a sporting crisis in the spotlight, which makes management of the crisis even more difficult. Because crisis communication is an aspect of the global (active) press approach in sport, the same rules apply here as in the push and pull approach. Outline 3.16 lists a number of reactive procedures that an organization must follow when a crisis breaks. It is very important for a sports team or sponsor not to panic when the media exaggerate a sporting crisis. Sometimes the pressure the media exert is so great that an athlete is immediately fired or a sponsor issues impulsive or scathing statements. Once the mist around the crisis file has lifted, it sometimes seems that the accused party communicated too impulsively.

Outline 3.16 Curative rules for crisis communication in sport

- Test procedures in 'peace time'
- Appoint a management team to handle sporting crises
- Appoint one – trained – spokesperson
- Simulate, with role-playing, the reactions to the spokesperson's announcements
- Bolster the spokesperson's announcements with all possible alternative explanations by company management
- (Parallel) communication with internal and external relations groups
- Do not take impulsive decisions under pressure from the press

3.7 Summary

The demanding environment in which sports sponsors work forces them to take every measure to achieve the desired identity and project a good image. As part of integrated sports marketing communication, PR activities are essential because they form the core of corporate communication and simultaneously bridge the gap to marketing communication. On the one hand, PR in sport involves relationship marketing. Since various public groups shape, or are influenced by, company decisions, the allocation of PR activities is done subsequent to classifying stakeholders into main groups and subgroups. Various public groups shape, or are influenced by, company decisions.

On the other hand, PR in sport aims at good press relations. In a pull approach to publicity (e.g. an organization is mentioned in an editorial context for free), the media might also be interested in the sponsoring organization. Certainly for major sports such as football and tennis, and during major sports events, the press may come to the sponsors of the athlete or sports event. Therefore, sponsoring organizations should prepare professionally for written, radio and television interviews. In a push approach, a sponsor must employ press releases, press conferences or its own media. Overall, the main objective of a push or pull approach is generating publicity. However, due to the editorial independence of journalists, it is difficult to control the timing and content of news processing. Therefore, an organization will try to gain control over reporting primarily via press releases, press conferences and employing its own media. Sport is not always presented in a positive light, though, and when a sports crisis breaks, the sponsor could be even more in the limelight. In this case, preventive and curative crisis communication are essential steps that should be taken to manage and solve the crisis.

Key terms

Corporate communication
Corporate sport hospitality
Crisis communication
Curative crisis communication
Experiential sport hospitality
Financial public relations
Interview
Marketing public relations
Media public relations
Merger communication

Press conference
Press release
Preventive crisis communication
Priming
Public affairs
Publicity
Public relations form
Pull approach to press
Push approach to press
Recruitment communication
Relationship marketing
Retention communication
Sports aura
Sport experiences
Sport and city marketing
Sports issue
Stakeholders
Traditional sports hospitality
VIP segmentation

Questions

1. Assume that you are a sponsorship manager of a shirt sponsor of an England Premier League football club. Identify the various publics with whom you should communicate on a regular basis.

2. Discuss, with examples, how sports sponsorship may enhance hospitality.

3. How is relationship marketing in sports sponsorship different from other forms of relationship marketing?

4. Discuss the effects of publicity on the image of a financial institution sponsoring a golfer or a rugby club.

5. Under what conditions is it opportune for a sports sponsor to issue a press release or call a press conference?

6. Discuss and compare, with recent examples, the preventive and curative rules of crisis communication in sports sponsorship.

Endnotes

1 Heil, P. (1983), II.4.b.4 pressmededelingen. In: Kolkhuis Tanke, J., Korswagen, C. and Verrept, S. (eds), *Handboek Taalhantering. Praktische communicatiegids voor bedrijf, instelling en overheid.* Deventer: Van Loghum Slaterus, pp. 1–21.

2 Floor, J.M. and van Raaij, W.F. (1998), *Marketing-communicatiestrategie.* Groningen: Stenfert Kroese.

3 Fauconnier, G. (2002), De ondergang van public relations, *Ad Rem, Tijdschrift voor zakelijke communicatie,* 16(3), 1.

4 Shank, M.D. (2002), *Sports Marketing: A Strategic Perspective.* Upper Saddle River, NJ: Prentice Hall.

5 Mullin, B.J., Hardy, S. and Sutton, A. (2000), *Sports Marketing.* Champaign, IL: Human Kinetics.

6 De Pelsmacker, P., Geuens, M. and Van den Bergh, J. (2001), *Marketing Communications.* Harlow: Pearson Education.

7 Peeters, L. (2002), Naar stakeholder synergie, Vlaams Wetenschappelijk Economisch Congres. In: Peeters, L., Matthijssen, P. and Vereeck, L. (eds). *Stakeholder synergie.* Antwerp: Garant, pp. 15–21.

8 Floor and van Raaij (1998), op cit.

9 Fauconnier (2002), op cit.

10 Argenti, P.A. (1996), Corporate communication as a discipline toward a definition, *Management Communication Quarterly,* 10(1), 73–97.

11 De Pelsmacker *et al.* (2001), op cit.

12 Michiels, W. and Notten, W. (1990), *Pr in Hoofdlijnen.* Groningen: Wolters-Noordhoff.

13 Grimes, E. and Meenaghan, T. (1998), Focusing commercial sponsorship on the internal corporate audience, *International Journal of Advertising,* 17(1), 51–74.

14 De Bruyn, B. (2000), Werven op een krappe arbeidsmarkt. Naar een marketingbenadering van de arbeidsmarkt. In: Duyck, R. and Van Tilborgh, C. (eds), *Marketing Jaarboek 2000.* Zellik: Roularta Books, pp. 204–10.

15 Adfo Specialists Group (2002), Ernst & Young, partner in sport van NOC*NSF. Via Sydney naar Salt Lake City en verder naar Athene – een route richting rendement. In: *Adfo Sponsorship Cases,* no. 8. Alphen aan den Rijn: Samsom, pp. 7–40.

16 Borghs, H. and Lietaer, L. (2002), Case: Dexia in de sport. Presented at Vlekho Business School, Brussels, 23 May 2002.

17 De Pelsmacker *et al.* (2001), op cit.

18 Van der Meiden, A (1993), Public relations: een fenomeen in 12 paragrafen. In: Roomer, J. and Van Tilborgh, C. (eds), *Intern/Extern. Communicatie voor bedrijven, organisaties en instellingen.* Deventer: Kluwer Bedrijfswetenschappen, p. 3.8.1.

19 Lagae, W. (2000), Europese voetbalclubs bekampen elkaar met ongelijke wapens. *Praktijkgids Sportmanagement,* 20, 119–28.

20 Despiegelaere, G. (2000), Les in voetbaleconomie, *Knack,* 7 June, 76–8; Demets, F. and Killemaes, D. (2000), Euro 2000: Het gouden bal, *Trends,* 1 June, 22–6.

21 Adfo Specialists Group (2000), Nike, de kledingsponsor van de KNVB. Een warm gevoel weegt zwaarder dan kille cijfers. In: *Adfo Sponsorship Cases,* no. 7. Alphen aan den Rijn: Samsom, pp. 35–49.

22 Adfo Specialists Group (1999), Rabobank wielerplan. In: *Adfo Sponsorship Cases*, no. 2. Alphen aan den Rijn: Samsom, pp. 23–35.

23 Van Ommen, H., Sterk, R. and van Kuppenveld, E. (1990), *De Pr-methode. Een inleiding in de pr.* Groningen: Wolters-Noordhoff.

24 Lagae, W. (1997), Vips en klanten op pr-evenementen: succesvolle marketingcommunicatie. In: Roomer, J. and Van Tilborgh, C. (eds), *Intern/extern. Het integreren van communicatie in bedrijven, organisaties en instellingen.* Deventer: Kluwer Bedrijfswetenschappen, 24, 3.8.9 p. 12.

25 Lokerman, J.W. and Westermann, M. (1999), Sponsoring als communicatie-instrument. In: *Communicatie-memo*, no. 15. Alphen aan den Rijn: Samsom.

26 Jensen, R. (1999), *De droommaatschappij.* Rijswijk: Elmar.

27   Green, G. (2002), *Popstar United.* Amsterdam: British Readershouse.

28 Pine, B. J. and Gilmore, J. H. (2000), *De beleveniseconomie.* Schoonhoven: Academic Service.

29 Jensen, R. (1999), op cit.

30 Peeters, L. (2002), op cit. Smith, A. and Westerbeek, H. (2002), *Sports in the Global Marketplace.* London: Macmillan.

31 Sport Fun Events (2001), Atlantic Rowing Race 2001. Een ultieme belevenis van menselijke kracht en weerstand, Brussels, press release 7 September 2001; Win News (2001), Win. Belgium. La traversée de l'Atlantique à la rame. Un défi ambitieux.

32 De Keten van de Hoop (2001), 1.300.000 roeislagen voor de 'Keten van de hoop'. Om niet dwaas te roeien, press release September 2001; De Keten van de Hoop België (2001), internal memo.

33 Irwin, R., Sutton, W.A. and McCarthy, L. (2002), *Sport Promotion and Sales Management*, Champaign, IL: Human Kinetics.

34 Smith, A. and Westerbeek, H. (2002), *Sports in the Global Marketplace*, London: Macmillan.

35 Hemelaar, M. (2000), *Let the games begin … Een sociaal-geografisch onderzoek naar topsportevenementen in Nederland*, thesis. Utrecht: University of Utrecht.

36 Braun, E. (2002), *Sport & stedelijke economie.* Rotterdam: Rotterdam sportstad.

37 Shilbury, D., Quick, S. and Westerbeek, H. (1998), *Strategic Sport Marketing.* St Leonards: Allen & Unwin.

38 De Pelsmacker, P., Geuens, M. and Van den Bergh, J. (2004), *Marketing Communications. A European Perspective*, Harlow: FT Prentice Hall.

39 Heil, P. (1983), op cit.

40 Baverstock, Alison (2002) *Publicity, Newsletters and Press Releases.* Oxford: Oxford University Press.

41 Palmer, A. (2001) *Principles of Services Marketing*, 3rd edn. London: McGraw-Hill.

42 Manshanden, M. (2001), Uw organisatie in het nieuws, *Management en Communicatie Dossier* 9, September, 5–16.

43 Heil, P. (1983), op cit.

44 Waardenburg, M. (2000), *Praktisch pressbeleid. Het organiseren van presscontacten.* Alphen aan den Rijn: Samsom.

45 Oegema, D., Meijer, M.-M. and Kleinnijenhuis, J. (2001), Naar een mediamonitor. Effecten van nieuws op imago's, *Management en Communicatie Dossier 9*, September, 5–16.

46 Oegema, D., Meijer, M.-M. and Kleinnijenhuis, J. (2001), Naar een mediamonitor. Effecten van nieuws op imago's, *Management en Communicatie Dossier 10*, December, 29–44.

47 Adformatie group (2002), Anite en dames bobslee. In: *Adfo Sponsorship Cases*, no. 11. Alphen aan den Rijn: Kluwer, pp. 7–28.

48 Hunt, T., Grunig, J.E. (1994), *Public Relations Techniques*. Fort Worth, TX: Harcourt Brace College Publishers.

49 Manshanden, M. (2001), op cit.

50 Hunt and Grunig (1994), op cit.

51 Seitel, F. (1995), *Practice of Public Relations*, 6th edn. Englewood Cliffs, NJ: Prentice Hall.

52 Solomon, M.R. and Stuart, E.W. (2003), *Real People, Real Choices*, 3rd edn. Upper Saddle River, NJ: Prentice Hall.

53 Maitland, I. (1996), *How to Organize a Conference*. Aldershot: Gower.

54 Van Sande, N. (2002), Geen nieuws, geen pressbericht, *Ad Rem*, 16(1), 8–9.

55 Jansen, I. and Bouwman, H. (1991), Randvoorwaarden voor de plaatsing van pressberichten, *Communicatief*, 4(1), 31–40.

56 Lagae, W. (1997), Open bedrijvendag Vlaanderen: creatief instrument voor interne en externe pr. In: Roomer, J. and Van Tilborgh, C. (eds), *Intern/Extern. Communicatie voor bedrijven, organisaties en instellingen*. Deventer: Kluwer Bedrijfswetenschappen, p. 6.

57 Adfo Specialists Group (2002), Eurocard/Mastercard en het onbetaalbare voetbalmoment. In: *Afdo Sponsorship Cases*, no. 7. Alphen aan den Rijn: Samsom, pp. 73–91.

58 Penrose, J.M., Rasberry, R.W. and Myers, R.J. (2001), *Advanced Business Communication*, 4th edn. Cincinatti, OH: South-Western College Publishing.

59 Renkema, J. and Hoeken, H. (1998), The influence of negative newspaper publicity on corporate image in the Netherlands, *Journal of Business Communication*, 35(4), 521–35.

60 De Vlaminck, D. (2000), *Crisiscommunicatie in de sport. Een theoretische benadering met voorbeelden uit de Belgische sport*, Master of Sports Management dissertation. Brussels: Vlekho Business School.

Case 3 Elite sporting events and hospitality: the skybox is the limit

Key learning points

After studying this case, you will be able to:

● understand the synergy between event and player hospitality;

● illustrate why sports sponsorship is a platform for relationship marketing;

● discuss the (monetary and emotional) value of different VIP packages.

Introduction

Who can still imagine a top sporting event without VIPs and an associated hospitality programme? In the cycling race Ronde van Vlaanderen at the start of the 1970s, important guests were received in the home of the mayor of Meerbeke, a small Belgian municipality where the cycling classic finished at that time. Thirty years later, thousands of VIPs follow the race, while another thousand people attend the reception afterwards. For the arrival of a stage of the Tour de France, Antwerp kept open house for about 3000 'important' people. But the World Championship Road Racing for professionals in 2002 in Zolder, Belgium, topped the record with 12 000 VIPs.

Three Belgian hospitality events run as themes through this case:

● World Open Squash Flanders 2002, the conclusion of the PSA World Tour in Antwerp's Commodity Exchange.

● World Championships Road Racing 2002, an organization of the Union Cycliste International (UCI) cycled on and around the Circuit Zolder.

● Proximus Diamond Games Antwerp 2004, a WTA Level II tournament organized in the Sportpaleis in Antwerp.

Event hospitality and sports facilities

Corporate sports hospitality has become a cornerstone in the public relations leverage of sports sponsorship, because sport seems to be a very strong emotional medium in the relationship marketing of organizations. Indeed, it is the dream of every PR manager to supply a tailored hospitality product that is original and creative. Through professional selection and leverage of sport activities, an organization wants to offer its core stakeholders distinctive and memorable experiences that money cannot buy.

Event hospitality sets great store by the choice of the tournament site and the hospitality services for the athletes and the spectators of the event.

Satisfied athletes produce top performances and attract other athletes. They guarantee the continuation of the sporting event. Satisfied enthusiastic spectators create a unique sporting atmosphere, contribute to the positive image of the hospitality event, and encourage the athletes to do their best.

The choice of the tournament site depends primarily on the sport being presented and the anticipated number of spectators. The organization of the World Open Squash Flanders had a wide range of options regarding the glass court in which the squash players complete their games. The final choice was the Commodity Exchange in the historic centre of Antwerp. At this location, the main sponsors Esso and the city of Antwerp reached both the sports consumer and the culture consumer. Usually, the guests and their partners are not interested exclusively in sport and appreciate the offer of cultural experiences as part of a VIP package.

For the spectator, the event starts the moment that he or she begins travelling to the event. It is important to facilitate this journey. Accessibility and experience in welcoming sports fans are key words, but despite a good mobility plan, a lot can still go wrong, and traffic jams and other delays cannot always be prevented. The World Championships Road Racing 2002 welcomed 100 000 spectators, including 12 000 VIPs, without difficulty, but the organizers were attacked in the press for problems with mobility. One approach route was filled with motionless cars displaying VIP stickers and hundreds of strolling people moving towards the track. Under newspaper headlines like 'Zolder buried under VIPs' (*De Standaard*, 14 October 2002) the logistics were criticized.

When organizing a hospitality event, the existing hospitality infrastructure is evaluated during the selection of a tournament site. Sites such as the Circuit Zolder, the Sportpaleis and the Koning Boudewijn Stadium have hospitality infrastructure in the form of skyboxes. The Circuit Zolder would do well to construct more skyboxes and add an extra campsite covering at least 17 000 m^2. The Antwerp Commodity Exchange did not have skyboxes, but it could provide a temporary hospitality structure. Sports competitions, like the Tour de France, that do not have a permanent infrastructure utilize mobile hospitality units. In 2001, 11 such trucks accompanied the Tour. First thing every day, three trucks would be transformed into VIP villages: one for the main sponsors, one for the subsponsors and one in which cycling teams such as Quick. Step and Rabobank could receive five guests. The remaining units were destined for radio and TV journalists, the Tour management, etc.

Player hospitality

The presence of top athletes, for example Kim Clijsters, Justine Henin, Venus Williams and Daniela Hantuchova, is the cornerstone of the Proximus

Diamond Games. An attractive field of participants draws other athletes, which in turn increases the size of the viewing public and the events' commercial attractiveness. The Proximus Diamond Games form part of the WTA Tour and are among the Level II organizations. The WTA rules, as stated in *The 2003 WTA Tour Official Rulebook*, must be followed. In total, there are 17 Level II tournaments. For each organization, the trick is to grab the limelight and the players' attention while staying within the standard rules that apply to every tournament. Player hospitality plays an important role in this.

From the WTA factsheets, the players become acquainted with the Proximus Diamond Games and can consult them for all practical information. This information is announced by the organizers during the WTA and is an important form of pre-event communication. In this way, players and their delegations can plan their WTA Tour, and they have a better impression of the nature of the event. The tournament website www.proximusdiamondgames.be is also valuable in pre-event communication. Practical information can be consulted, first impressions can be made and the players can find information on the website.

Upon arrival of the participating delegation, a host is assigned to answer their questions and deal with their needs. The host is their guide during the event and will ensure that the players arrive on time for every appointment. The host speaks the language of the full delegation or at least the language of one person in the delegation. The host is acquainted thoroughly with the event and can answer all questions, from tournament to transport information. The host will therefore remain in contact with the organizing committee in order to be informed of any changes in the tournament. The host is the players' contact person and also has a social function. For example, Venus Williams' host took her to the diamond district and the more exclusive clothing stores in Antwerp.

Aside from the trophy and the prestige, athletes are looking for that extra touch that makes participation in an event an unusual experience and that makes them come back year after year. Upon arrival at the Proximus Diamond Games, the players receive a Players' Guide. This guide lists the services that the athletes can use during the tournament: this is a must for every tournament that portrays itself as 'player-friendly' and an example of player hospitality. The Players' Guide contains the opening hours of the training areas and details of the supply of balls and towels. Players are requested to reserve the court and the training period a day beforehand at the Players' Relations Desk in the Players' Lounge. The WTA rules prescribe that a fitness centre must be available within a reasonable distance of the tournament site or in the hotel.

The Proximus Diamond Games offer the players a separate room where they can relax without being disturbed and get away from the crowd for a while. In this room, they can read, play computer games, surf the Internet, watch television, etc. One hundred security agents are on duty in the Sportpaleis to guard the players and the public. Although tennis is not a sport associated with hooligans, the organization still watches out for stalkers. Top athletes are accompanied to and from the hotel by federal police agents. The most difficult time for the security personnel is usually autograph sessions, when players can be thronged by a mass of people.

As a Level II tournament, the Proximus Diamond Games awarded a prize of 585 000 US dollars in 2003. However, it is another trophy that is associated with the Proximus Diamond Games: a racquet made of gold and set with 1500 diamonds. The racquet, which has normal dimensions, weighs about four kilograms and is valued at one million euros. This trophy will be awarded to the player who wins the Proximus Diamond Games Award three times within a five-year period. The racquet is an attraction to draw the best players to the tournament in Antwerp.

Ticket organization

The World Championships Road Racing 2002 sold tickets in advance only through the ticket shop of the main sponsor bank or on the website www.2x2002.com. On the day of the game itself, the ticket office was open at 7:30 a.m. The time when the ticket office closes must be communicated clearly to the public. Entering the site must be a smooth process without having to stand in a long queue. Having several entrances and ticket checkpoints helps to deal with this potential problem and spreads out the spectators. For most events with a large number of spectators, coloured tickets are used, each colour corresponding to only one entrance with the same colour. VIPs are provided with a separate entrance. The Circuit Zolder had no fewer than 12 entrances, which also served as checkpoints. Extra entrances were reserved for the residents of Hasselt and Heusden–Zolder, who were allowed free entrance upon showing their identity card.

Once the spectators have entered the site, they must have all the information they need, including site maps showing where the spectators are standing and where the different activities and facilities can be found, and information stands attended by well-informed staff and supplied with documents that answer all possible questions. A customer service centre can help the spectators with complaints of poor seats, lost property, theft or assault, etc.

The World Championships Road Racing 2002 had eight different public zones in the most important parts of the circuit. Each public zone was provided with a sound system and video screens so that the public could follow the race. In addition, these zones also included catering and sanitary facilities. At various other locations, 16 smaller public zones were created, also containing catering facilities. On the Circuit Zolder itself, the grandstand was reserved for VIPs and officials; the general public had to be satisfied with standing room only. This is not unusual in cycling races, but it does lead to a risk of crowding.

VIP packages

Tables 3.2, 3.3, and 3.4 present the different VIP formulas offered by the event organizers. For instance, five different formulas were proposed for VIPs during the World Championships Road Racing 2002. The simplest package was the Cycling Café. Guests received an admission ticket, VIP parking with shuttle, a programme booklet, a mobile buffet, expert commentary and a reception upon arrival. The most exclusive package was the Cruise, Sports and Leisure. For this, two boats were fully booked with 200 guests each. Such a boat costs 625 000 euros without extras such as live music. Guests spent the night before the World Championships in a hotel near the Albert Canal. Embarkation was scheduled for 8.30 a.m., followed by a champagne breakfast, and the guests could watch the start of the game on a large screen. While the boat sailed slowly down the canal, lunch was served. After about two and a half hours, they reached the mooring at the circuit. Hosts took the guests to the Cycling Café and then to the grandstand. There was a reception upon arrival and dinner was served during the return trip.

Table 3.2 VIP formulas for the World Open Squash Flanders 2002

VIP Box

Box with eight seats alongside the court during the four last days (quarter-finals, semi-finals and final)

Full first-quality catering (dinner and free drinks) for 32 people

Two bottles of champagne each day per box

Your company logo clearly visible on the box

Free parking and shuttle service

Fee: €6200

VIP Business seats

Full first-class catering and free drinks

Free parking and shuttle service

Quarter-finals: €125

Semi-finals: €150

Finals day: €200

Source: flyer, World Open Squash Flanders 2002.

Table 3.3 VIP formulas for the Proximus Diamond Games 2004

Proximus Diamond Games VIP village			
Formulas:			
1. Clubhouse	2. Reception lounge	3. Central lounge	4. Company village
• For all seven sessions • At least 30 people	• Per session • At least 30 people	• Per session • At least 10 people	During the first six days of the tournament, the entire VIP village can be hired by a firm
• Reserved VIP places • Entry permits to VIP village • Programme brochure • Access to VIP village after tennis sessions		• Shuttle service to and from the VIP village • Reserved cloakroom • Entry permits to VIP seats	
Prices: • Single clubhouse (30 VIPs): €25 000 • Double clubhouse (64 VIPs): €50 000 • Triple clubhouse (100 VIPs): €75 000 • Quadruple clubhouse (140 VIPs): €100 000	Prices: • 1/8 finals (30 VIPs): €150 • 1/4 finals (30 VIPs): €175 • 1/2 finals (30 VIPs): €200 • final (30 VIPs): €225	Prices: • €150 per person, including open bar	Prices: • €100 000 per day • €50.000 per session • These prices do not include shuttle service, catering or VIP game seats
Catering formulas: • Open bar: €25 per person • Open bar and sandwich buffet: €35 per person • Open bar and buffet dinner: €50 per person • Option: dinner in the VIP restaurant*		• Option: dinner in the VIP restaurant*	
*Restaurant:			
Formula 1 (€45 per person): • Cold starter buffet • Choice of two hot main courses • Dessert of the day (choice of two desserts) • Unlimited Australian wine (Penfolds) and water	Formula 2 (€35 per person): • One main course (from the buffet or a hot dish) • Dessert of the day • Unlimited Australian wine (Penfolds) and water	Formula 3 (€25 per person): • Main course only (from the buffet or a hot dish) • Unlimited Australian wine (Penfolds) and water	

All prices are VAT-exclusive.
Source: www.sport.be/proximusdiamondgames/2004/eng/hospitality/

Table 3.4 VIP formulas for the World Championships Road Racing 2002

Business Seats				
Formulas:				
1. Champions house	2. Cyclo-lounge	3. Sprinters Club	4. Cycling Café	5. Cruise, Sports and Leisure
• Saturday • Sunday	• Saturday • Sunday	• Friday • Saturday • Sunday	• Friday • Saturday • Sunday	• Sunday
• Gastronomic menu and free drinks • Seat in VIP stand • Access to closing ceremony in the Cycling Café	• Gastronomic menu and free drinks • Seat in VIP stand • Access to closing ceremony in the Cycling Café	• Buffet with free drinks • Permit to follow the race along the track • Access to closing ceremony In the VIP tent	• Mobile buffet with free drinks • Access to closing ceremony in the Cycling Café	• Reserved private parking at Albert Canal • Embarkation in Antwerp or Luik • Breakfast on boat • Screen to follow the race
• Aperitif • VIP parking and shuttle service • Entry ticket • Expert commentary • Screens to follow the race • Presence of stars commenting on the race				• Arrival next to track • Reserved tickets to stand • Access to the Cycling Café • Access to the ceremony honouring the winner • Return to boat • Champagne and gastronomic dinner Access to casino
• €300	• €400	• Friday: €200 • Saturday: €200 • Sunday: €250	• Friday: €125 • Saturday: €125 • Sunday: €150	• Budget specifications on demand
Company skyboxes				
Formulas:				
1. Skybox in VIP tent		2. Fixed skybox		

• Open from Tuesday to Sunday
• Restaurant in VIP tent for invitations
• From 80 m^2
• Catering and services by Circuit Zolder
		• Open from Tuesday to Sunday
		• Tour VIP:
		  Skybox 1 (100 m^2): €7500
		  Skybox 2 (100 m^2): €8500		

• Specifications on demand	Skybox 3 (100 m²): €8700
	Skybox 4 (100 m²) + terrace: €12 500
	• Pitlane building:
	Skybox (48 m²): €4700
	Skybox (96 m²): €9900
	Racing Center (126 m²): €4700
	Skybox at start/arrival (130 m²): €9900
	Skybox Stand (85 m²): €4700
	Club (350 m²): €22 400

All prices are VAT-exclusive.
This case is based on Pinxteren, K. (2003), Sport events and hospitality: zin en onzin [Sports events and hospitality: does it make sense?], research paper. Brussels: VLEKHO Business School.
Source: World Championships Road Racing 2002 flyers

Proximus, presenting sponsor of the Proximus Diamond Games, has a ProxiClub, consisting of loyal clients. These receive benefits all year round in the form of free tickets to sporting and cultural events. Proximus invites the 'ProxiClubbers' to the Proximus Diamond Games to thank them for their loyalty. Other guests include the top sales people, business partners, politicians and companies that have a Proximus subscription for professional use. As title sponsor, Proximus has a powerful platform in the Diamond Games with which to invite guests. The entire tournament site was decorated with its purple logo. This gave Proximus a strong brand association.

Esso invited guests to the World Open Squash Flanders 2002, an example of traditional hospitality. Although such hospitality clearly has a certain value, clients may already have received a dozen invitations to other sports events. Thus there is the risk that clients no longer remember at the end of the year who invited them to the World Open Squash Flanders 2002. With another distinctive approach, with experiential hospitality, the experience gains its own identity and the client will remember this unique experience for longer.

The hospitality supplier (the organizer) would do well to present the different packages early to the potential customers, the inviting companies. These companies in turn will want to issue early invitations to their guests. For example, the clients of Octagon-cis received tickets one month before the Proximus Diamond Games. Together with the tickets, Octagon-cis provided standard invitations that their guests could print on their own stationery. The invitation also included a fax number, which the guests of the clients were requested to use to indicate whether they would or would not attend the Games. If a guest responded positively to an invitation to an event, the admission tickets, a travel plan and the VIP tickets were sent out at the latest two weeks before the event.

Questions for discussion

1. Discuss and compare the potential of VIP segmentation in the different packages offered.

2. Compare the possibilities for experiential hospitality in the three cases presented.

3. What crises could occur during the WTA event? How should an event organizer handle a crisis, starting from the theory of preventive and curative crisis communications?

4. Propose new mini-events before, during or after the world squash championships that could generate positive publicity.

References and further reading

Ammon, R. and Stotlar, D. (2001), Sport facility and event management. In: Parks, J. and Quarterman, J. (eds). *Contemporary Sport Management*, 2nd edn. Champaign: Human Kinetics, pp. 255–70.

Anderson, K. and Kerr, C. (2002), *Customer Relationship Management*. New York, McGraw-Hill.

Huyghe, P. (2003), Siemens: sponsorship strategie. Presented at VLEKHO-seminar, Brussels, 15 May.

Kolah, A. (2001), *How to Develop Effective Hospitality Programmes*. London: SportBusiness Group.

Solomon, J. (2002), *An Insider's Guide to Managing Sporting Events*. Champaign: Human Kinetics.

Wilkinson, D.G. (1988), *The Event Management and Marketing Institute*. Willowdale, Canada: The Wilkinson Group.

Interesting websites

www.circuit-zolder.be
www.kbc.be
www.octagon.com
www.proximusdiamondgames.be
www.siemens.be
www.verhulst.be
www.worldopensquash.com

4

SPORTS SPONSORSHIP AND ADVERTISING

'Hi! I'm Phil Knight, and I hate advertising ...' (Nike founder *Phil Knight* shaking hands with his advertising executive Dan Wieden for the first time)

Overview

Characteristics of advertising

Advertising strategies in sport

Communication carriers in sport

The creative strategy

Media selection for advertisement in sport

Aims

After studying this chapter you will be able to:

● classify sponsorship-related advertising campaigns into standard formats;

● describe the development of sponsorship-related advertisement strategies;

● provide examples of the different categories of communication carriers in sport;

● gain insight into the advantages and disadvantages of the forms of mass media employed in the communication of sponsorship.

4.0 Introduction

The development of sports sponsorship via advertising is the foundation of every sports marketing communication strategy, since advertising is one of the oldest, most visible and most popular promotion tools. Large sums of money are committed to ad campaigns because advertising is perceived to be an efficient marketing communication tool. Despite the fact that the growth curve for sponsorship has been climbing more sharply than that for advertising decline since the mid-1980s, advertising is a very mature communications tool and remains the cornerstone of a marketing communications portfolio. For instance, in 2000, European sponsorship rights only amounted to 8% of advertising expenditure (see Table 4.1).[1]

Table 4.1 Advertising expenditure and value of sponsorship rights in Europe, 2000

	Value of sponsorship rights, 2000, in $m (€m)*	% of Europe	Total advertising expenditure, 2000, in $m (€m)	Sponsorship as % of advertising expenditure
Europe	7778 (8361)	100	97702 (105030)	8
Denmark	115 (124)	1.48	1673 (1798)	6.9
Finland	72 (77)	0.93	1250 (1344)	5.8
France	1042 (1120)	13.4	10967 (11790)	9.5
Germany	2317 (2491)	29.79	24173 (25986)	9.6
Ireland	53 (57)	0.68	781 (840)	6.8
Italy	510 (548)	6.56	7980 (8579)	6.4
Netherlands	567 (610)	7.29	4189 (4503)	13.5
Spain	516 (555)	6.63	5624 (6046)	9.2
Sweden	197 (212)	2.53	2047 (2201)	9.6

Table 4.1 continued

	Value of sponsorship rights, 2000, in $m (€m)*	% of Europe	Total advertising expenditure, 2000, in $m (€m)	Sponsorship as % of advertising expenditure
Switzerland	254 (273)	3.27	2890 (3107)	8.8
UK	1261 (1356)	16.21	20231 (21748)	6.2
Others	874 (940)	11.24	15897 (17089)	5.5

Source: Based on Sponsorship Research International (2001), *Worldwide Sponsorship Market Values Report*. London: Sponsorship Research International, SportBusiness Information Resources. *Conversion rate: $1=€0.75.

Advertising plays an important role in the creation and maintenance of the brand value, not only for sports brands (advertising of sport) but also for non-sports brands (advertising through sport) (Section 4.1). A number of steps can be distinguished in the development of an advertising campaign in a sports sponsorship project. Advertising must first and foremost be integrated clearly in the global strategy of sports sponsorship communication (Section 4.2). The next step is the selection of signage. These communication carriers either form part of, or supplement, the negotiated package of sports sponsorship (Section 4.3). Next, distinctive advertising works around set advertising formats, or combinations of them (Section 4.4). Media selection, timing of the campaign and insertion frequency are the next steps in the development process (Section 4.5).

Case 4 concerns virtual television advertising in sport. Since the mid-1990s, virtual advertising techniques have been employed, primarily in North America. It is expected that further advances in, for example, the Internet, interactive television and pay-television will come to Europe, bringing more and new virtual advertising techniques.

4.1 Characteristics of advertising

Advertising can be defined as any paid, non-personal communication through various media by organizations that hope to inform and/or persuade a particular target group.[2] Not surprisingly, advertising is a commonly used tool to promote products (Adidas: 'Impossible is Nothing'), services (Passage Fitness First: 'A Strong Mind Starts with a Fit Body') and ideas (Sport for All).

It is characteristic of advertising via the mass media that a message may be directed towards a number of receivers who cannot be identified.[3] In addition, paid information in the mass media aims to increase market share by influencing the cognitive, affective and behaviour-oriented attitude of the consumer towards the advertised brand. The deployment of direct media, in contrast, is geared to increasing the returns per customer. There are also great differences between advertising and publicity (Outline 4.1). An advertiser pays for the message and controls what, how and to whom it is said. The advertiser also controls frequency of use and media selection.

Outline 4.1 Differences between advertising and publicity

- You pay for it
- You control what is said
- You control how it is said
- You control to whom it is said
- You control the frequency of its use
- To a degree, you control where it is put in a publication or on the air

Source: Seitel, F. (1995), *Practice of Public Relations*, 6th edn. Englewood Cliffs, NJ: Prentice Hall.

Surrounding sports sponsorship projects with advertising campaigns might be very efficient in terms of reaching target groups. For instance, the manner in which Guinness employed its sponsorship of hurling in advertising forms a good illustration of sports sponsorship-related advertising (see the mini-case below).

Mini-case study – Sports sponsorship-related advertising

In 2002, brewery and transnational brand Guinness developed a single key brand benefit (KBB): 'Guinness brings out your inner strength'.[4] Sports sponsorship plays an important role in delivering the KBB to consumers in a locally sensitive and male-oriented way. Guinness sponsors different properties in its main markets. In Africa, this revolves mainly around football, such as the local Guinness marketing team in Cameroon sponsoring the national team in the African Cup of Nations, a tournament that the team won. Each local marketing team was encouraged to develop a football sponsorship programme that supported their national teams, particularly those that qualified for the 2002 World Cup Finals in Japan and Korea.

In Great Britain, Guinness currently sponsors, among others, London Irish Rugby Football Club, a professional team that plays in the highest division of professional rugby in England. It also sponsors the Cheltenham Horse Racing Festival, noted for its prominent Irish theme and the fact that thousands of Irish racing supporters travel from Ireland to attend the week's races. In Ireland, among the multitude of sponsorships, which include golf and horse racing, the most notable is the Guinness All-Ireland Hurling Championship. This event has been supported by Guinness for over eight years and is seen as being a flagship sponsorship by the Irish brand team.

The development of the KBB has been accompanied by the creation of the global 'Believe!' advertising campaign. The first advertisement created in this campaign, 'Free In', is set at the end of a hurling match and was thus seen, particularly by the Irish brand team, as being a natural progression from the sponsorship in Ireland of the Guinness All-Ireland Hurling Championship. This sponsorship has been described as the most effective sports sponsorship in Ireland. The main reason for this is the close match between the values that underpin the Guinness brand and the sport.

Hurling is a little-known Irish sport that appears to be a combination of field hockey and lacrosse and is played on a field that is approximately the size of a football pitch with hybrid football/rugby goals at either end. During trials, the advertisement's storyline of Guinness was consumer-tested using football and rugby scenarios. It was found that football was not seen as a good fit for Guinness in the highly important British market, and that although rugby was seen as fitting well with the Guinness brand, it held no appeal for those consumers who did not like rugby. The point that hurling was perceived as a generic sport was reinforced further by the decision to utilize a nameless unknown figure as the central character, because the desire was clearly that the KBB should not be overshadowed by the sport or the characters within it.

4.2 Advertising strategies in sport

As is the case with other communication tools, special attention has to be devoted to the different steps in sports advertising campaign development. Outline 4.2 shows a number of successive steps to be elaborated in an advertising plan in sport.

Outline 4.2: Phases of an advertising campaign in sport[5]

Step 1: Outline the sports advertising strategy (Section 4.2):

- integrate into the strategy of sports marketing communication
- determine advertising target groups
- set budgets
- set advertising goals

Step 2: Select signage (Section 4.3):

- within the sports sponsorship package
- in addition to the sports sponsorship package

Step 3: Elaborate the creative strategy (Section 4.4):

- strengthen the brand promise

- work around advertising formats in sport

Step 4: Elaborate the sporting media strategy (Section 4.5):

- selection of advertising media

- frequency of advertising blocks/print inserts

Step 5: Evaluate the sports advertising campaign (Chapter 7)

The first phase of an advertising campaign in sport is outlining a strategy, which must fit naturally with the strategic marketing plan. Further strategic steps include determining the advertising target group, setting the goals and establishing the budget.

Integration in sports marketing communication

The integration of sports advertising in the global strategy of marketing communication is a professional starting point. The brand manager must ensure that the brand is expressed uniformly in all forms of advertising communication. The relationship between sports advertising and sports sponsorship therefore is essential. In addition, a coherent integration of advertising and sponsorship may lead to synergetic marketing. For instance, an advertising campaign in sport that anticipates an expected victory by a marathon runner must be able to assess the sporting capacities of the runner. The athlete also must not feel pressured by the expectations created by the advertisement or commercial. In addition, one cannot snub the athlete or present their sporting achievements incorrectly. Carelessness or a lack of sporting knowledge can sabotage an advertising campaign in sport. For example, VISA-Belgium, the main sponsor of the Belgian mountain bike team, claimed in one of its forms of advertising that Filip Meirhaeghe had won an Olympic gold medal in Sydney. However, in reality, he had only won a silver medal.

The timing of a sports advertising campaign must be considered carefully. The layout of an advertisement demands the necessary organization in the weeks or days preceding the sports event. In the trailer, the brand manager anticipates a number of 'what-if?' sporting scenarios. Immediately after the game, the manager must communicate to the advertising department whether the advertisement can be published effectively. It is also important that the advertiser is aware of the publicity effect of the sponsored sporting object. An analysis of the contents and the quantity of sponsored publicity will reveal which additional advertising message is required. Thus, sports advertising that explains what the brand name stands for is less expedient if the editorial context already contains this information, for instance as a consequence of a remarkable sporting achievement by the sponsored athlete.

Determining the advertising target group

Based on the market structure, the brand positioning and the brand target group, the advertising target group should be determined. The more precise the description of the advertising target group (e.g. teenagers between the ages of 12 and 15 years), the more effective the advertising campaign potentially can be. To reach this target group, different instruments of the communication mix can be employed successively. The advertising target group can be associated with the target groups reached by other communication instruments, e.g. if the sponsorship appeals mostly to boys, then the advertising should target girls in the same age category.

Setting budgets

The traditional techniques of budgeting for advertising are similar to those for sports sponsorship, introduced in Chapter 2. The budgeting of advertising campaigns in sport involves an even more difficult balancing act because of the problems of image rights on the one hand and of commercial signage (see Section 4.3) on the other. Portrait rights specify that the creator of a portrait may not sell a representation without the permission of the person portrayed if the latter feels that his or her personal interests are affected.[6] Also, the commercial interests derived from the value of the person's popularity must be considered. Portrait rights apply to all sorts of representations in which the athlete's face is recognizable and is being used by the company as a form of advertising. When planning an advertising campaign, it is essential to budget the costs of the portrait rights. The transfer of image rights to a federation, team or sponsor is a complex balancing act that could lead to conflict. When sponsoring a team or federation the topic of portrait rights that are bound exclusively to a top athlete usually surfaces quickly in discussions.

Setting advertising goals

Before the start of an advertising campaign, the advertising goals must be determined precisely. In this context, a distinction should be made between process and effect goals. Process goals determine the conditions that must be met by advertising to achieve the ultimate effect goals. Advertising goals are created after a complex interaction of the process and effect goals.

Process goals

Process goals aim at a direct reaction from a consumer to a form of advertising. A brand aims to contact the consumer directly via advertisements. Because the consumer is bombarded constantly with innumerable stimuli, the brand must attract the consumer's attention in a sympathetic manner. Process objectives are an essential but insufficient precondition for successful advertising. Process goals involve spontaneous reactions from the recipient of the advertising stimulus, such as attention, sympathy, and processing of the information contained in the form of advertising (see Outline 4.3).

Outline 4.3 Process goals in sport advertising

- Attracting attention
- Creating acceptance and sympathy
- Stimulating information processing

Attracting attention

Among the profusion of advertising stimuli, the challenge for an advertiser consists first and foremost of attracting the attention of the target group. First, the attention paid to an advertisement depends on the involvement with the brand. A consumer who intends to buy a snowboard is more likely to see or read advertising about snowboards. This is the 'perceptual vigilance' or alertness of the consumer.[7] Second, the environment of the form of advertising determines the attention paid to it. This is the extent to which one is successful in advertising distinctively in terms of, for example, colour, layout, text or music. Third, attention is determined by the reader's or viewer's interest in the medium in which the advertisement or commercial appears. For example, a recreational cyclist is more likely to pay attention to the advertisements printed in cycling magazines.

Creating acceptance and sympathy

An advertisement must not only attract the attention of the consumer but also give the consumer a good feeling. By advertising in a positive manner, the brand also obtains a positive association. This is the 'likeability' of an advertising message.

Stimulating information processing

Attention paid to and sympathy for the advertisement benefit the provision of information. However, consumers can process advertising messages in different ways, as explained by the elaboration likelihood model.[8] If consumers feel strongly involved with the brand, then they process the information via the 'central route'. For example, a snowboard fanatic will study exhaustively the advantages and disadvantages mentioned in the advertising message. Typical of information in the sport hobby field is that it is stored firmly in short-term memory, so in a shop or during a visit to a trade fair, this information can be recalled quickly.

In the case of low involvement of the consumer with the brand, the information is processed peripherally or not at all. Because the consumer's processing is limited, it would be better if the advertiser did not use contextual arguments. What are effective in the communication are cues, familiar symbols with a certain meaning that draw the consumer's attention. Communication cues in sport include the expert (a tennis star in a sports outfit recommends a new type of tennis racquet), the model (an attractive athlete recommends body-care products) and the price (a more expensive bicycle frame is better than a cheaper one).

Effect goals

Advertising can become effective only when the process goals are realized. The effect goals are the ultimate marketing communication goals that an advertiser wants to realize. Effect goals of advertising refer to the effect of the advertising on the ultimate change produced in the consumer's knowledge and attitude with respect to the brand. Outline 4.4 lists some of the successive effect goals that a brand manager may want to achieve with advertising. Normally, the consumer will go through several steps, as explained in the hierarchy-of-effects model.

Outline 4.4 Effect goals in sport advertising

Effect goal

Stimulate need for a product category

Increase brand familiarity

Supplement passive or active brand knowledge

Accentuate brand attitude

Stimulate behavioural intention

Stimulate behavioural facilitation

Stimulate behaviour

4.3 Communication carriers in sport

Because signage provides a limited message, sponsorship is usually supported by an advertising campaign. In this case, supplementary communication carriers are employed to achieve advertising goals. On the one hand, sports advertising contains the development of sports sponsorship via advertising as part of a sports sponsorship contract. On the other hand, sports advertising concerns all advertising of and through sport, independent of a sports sponsorship contract. Increasingly frequently nowadays, team and federation sponsors have to invest extra money to use photographs, an athlete's name or the logo of the sponsored object in further advertising activities.

Outline 4.5 Categories of communication carriers in sport

- Brand name and logo representation on:
  - clothing of a sport cell
  - sport-linked outside media
  - materials that can be used directly or indirectly when practising the sport
  - all additional communication expressions of a sport cell
- Linking of a brand name to a sport object
- Virtual advertising carriers
- Speciality media in sport

Outline 4.5 lists the most important categories of communication carriers. A traditional communication carrier is the printing of the brand name, logo or other advertising text of the sponsor on the competition, training and leisure clothing of top athletes and their trainers. Furthermore, sports brands provide material that the sponsored athletes can use directly or indirectly. Sports drinks, sports supplements, training materials and services (e.g. a personal trainer or the accommodation of a fitness centre) are the most important categories of communication carriers. The brand name and the logo also can be introduced into all remaining communications from a sponsored object. We can distinguish here between classical printed media (e.g. all communication carriers of TCB, elaborated in Case 2) and new media (e.g. the website of the sporting organization).

In and around sports venues and their arrival areas, various sport-linked outside media have been developed. 'Outside media' is an umbrella term for media other than the audiovisual and printed forms. Despite what the term suggests, outside media usually do not have a contextual relationship with the place where they are established. The concept of outside media refers to the fact that these mass media are separate from TV, radio and the printed press. A distinction can be made between sport-linked and non-sport-linked outside media. Sport-linked outside media are negotiated in a sports sponsorship package and are static or moving. Static outside media are established at a fixed location and can be mobile, such as a rotating advertising hoarding. Outline 4.6 provides examples of sport-linked outside media. An important category of static outside media, city dressing, is described below.

Outline 4.6 Examples of sport-linked outside media

- Static outside media in sport:
  - boards in an athletics stadium
  - floor stickers (sports hall, surface of passage)
  - video screen in football stadium

- Moving outside media in sport:
  - basketballs
  - skating suits, football outfits
  - following cars

City dressing is an important category of static outside media.[9] It may include poster displays on bus and tram stops, large advertising boards alongside busy roads (billboards), electronic messaging display signs and large video screens. Examples of moving outside media include mobile billboards (cars with large side panels) and transportation advertising (external advertising objects on vehicles and on and in public transport).

Mini-case study – Edgar Davids and Euro 2000: striking outside media

The most daring and striking example of sport-linked outside media was the immense picture of Edgar Davids placed on the 150-metre-high Nationale Nederlanden building during Euro 2000.[10] A portrait of Davids was created that appeared to smash through the glass walls on one side. On the other side, Davids reappeared as if by magic, with the ball and broken glass at his feet. In many previews, reporters chose this building, which literally coloured the skyline of Rotterdam, as their background. The subject covered over 4500 panels. The Nike and Nationale Nederlanden logos were incorporated into the approximately eight kilometres of metre-wide artwork. Sports brand Nike had come up with the idea. The striking aspect of this outside media campaign is that a similar campaign in a post-11 September 2001 context could bring to mind undesirable associations. Mid-2000, however, the portrayal of Davids was seen around the world and was the promotional stunt of Euro 2000.

A powerful communication carrier in sport is coupling the sponsor's name to the sporting object. The brand name is written or amplified by references to the sporting event or team. An active press approach increases the chance of publicity references. In the advertising activities of sports sponsorship, advertisers utilize speciality media in many cases. These are usually small objects on which the advertising messages are printed.[11] Some examples of advertising articles include diaries, blotting pads, calendars, ties, pins, sport bags, key chains and T-shirts. Usually, the brand name and/or logo and perhaps abbreviated information (telephone number, website, etc.) are mentioned on the article.

A third category includes virtual advertising carriers in sport. With the introduction of new digital techniques in television advertising, advertising carriers have been qualitatively improved and quantitatively expanded, as will be discussed in Case 4.[12]

Another issue concerns the categorizing of communication carriers in sport (see Outline 4.7). First, communication carriers in sport are either part of, or not part of, a sports sponsorship agreement. Second, communication carriers in sport are employed for publicity or advertising goals, on a case-by-case basis.

Outline 4.7 Positioning of communication carriers in sport

- Positioning of communication carriers with regard to sports sponsorship

  - communication carriers as part of a sports sponsorship package

  - communication carriers in addition to a sports sponsorship package

- Effect of communication carriers

  - spontaneous reporting in editorial contact with mass media = publicity
    (no control over content of the message)

  - complete control over the content of the advertising message = advertising

The specification of the communication carriers is a very important element in the negotiation of a sports sponsorship contract. The sponsorship contract specifies the permitted advertising carriers for sponsors. How many banners, posters, panels or flags can the sponsor use? What are the dimensions of the sport-linked outside media? Where can banners be hung, and what text can they carry? Also, contractual agreements are made about the responsibility for the production, payment and placing of the material at the location. Under what conditions can the sponsor use the logo of the sports organization? Who owns the copyright on specially designed logos? Can the sponsor use the logo to promote its own products?

Sports sponsorship packages also increase in value through media-exchange agreements. It is possible to conclude certain agreements with the media for guaranteed mention in the mass media in exchange for payment, goods, certain privileges, etc. This is advertising, not publicity, because the advertiser has control over the content of the message. A very special relationship arises between sponsors and a medium when a mass medium actively sponsors an event or organization. In most cases, some or all of the return provided by the sponsorship medium consists of promoting the sponsored organization or event and/or the other sponsors of the project. For example, a newspaper sponsors an athletics event as part of a recruitment drive for new subscribers and to improve their relationship with the advertisers (business-to-business). On the sports results page, advertisements are placed for the other sponsors, while the names of the sponsors appear regularly in articles about and photos of the event. The organizers of the event are thereby guaranteed advertising and can offer the other sponsors an attractive return. Due to the rapidly increasing competition between the mass media and the further commercialization of these media, the possibilities in this area will continue to grow. Almost all large events currently have a mass medium as one sponsor. Top sporting events usually have a television station, a radio station, a newspaper, a magazine and a sporting website as media partners.

Mini-case study – Wimbledon is more important than the sponsors

People watching the Wimbledon tennis tournament on television will never see advertising boards lining the courts. In the entire Wimbledon complex, there is no promotional signage to be seen. Only flowers. Is the prestigious tournament the sole sports event that can manage without sponsorship and commerce? Not by a long shot. It's just that Wimbledon is more important than the sponsors. Wimbledon exudes tradition and aristocratic refinement. It is the oldest of the four Grand Slam tournaments and the only one organized and played in a private club: the All England Lawn Tennis and Croquet Club. This was established on 23 July 1868 as the All England Croquet Club. From 1875, in addition to croquet tennis was played, and therefore the name was extended in 1899 to include tennis.

The club has 375 official members, plus honorary members including former champions who have rendered great services to the game. These are the members who determine the rules of the organization, and they are particularly fierce on tradition and exclusivity. They would never call Wimbledon 'the British Open', as Flushing Meadow is known as 'the US Open'.

The advertising-free courts also belong to this atmosphere of exclusivity. It gives more of an aura of class and prestige than do courts covered with advertising panels. Only on the dark-green clothes can the careful observer note the black letters of the ball manufacturer Slazenger, but this company has been the house supplier for over 100 years. Does the club keep its distance from all matters of money? Of course not. The tournament and the club form a particularly lucrative business. The annual income of the All England Club is estimated at 71 million pounds (100 million euros). Most of this money derives from TV rights, ticket sales and agreements with sponsors. Because there definitely are sponsors, only they are not called sponsors, but official suppliers. There are 13 of them, ranging from Rolex (the official time-keeper) through Hertz, Philips and IBM, to Coca-Cola and Slazenger.

However, the sponsors are not permitted to put up advertising boards. They must be satisfied with media campaigns preceding Wimbledon in which they stress their association with Wimbledon. The sponsors are satisfied with this; after all, this is Wimbledon, and everybody wants to be a part of it.

In addition, the official suppliers are particularly well protected. During a semi-final between Tim Henman and Lleyton Hewitt, supporters had to leave their British flags outside, because the flags were printed with the prominent logo of a sports manufacturer. One woman even had to leave her raincoat behind because it was decorated with the logo of a car manufacturer other than the official car supplier for the tournament (Ford via Hertz).

Source: Based on Minten, D. (2003), Wimbledon is belangrijker dan de sponsors, *De Standaard*, 4 July 2003.

4.4 The creative strategy

Because consumers are bombarded daily with an enormous number of promotional stimuli, they often develop an immunity to advertising messages. This can reduce the effect of an advertising campaign. In addition, media and amusement are increasingly distracting attention away from the advertising presented.[13] Therefore, advertisers have developed creative formulas to generate visibility for their brand names and logos. Advertising agencies take care of the development of the brand message and the packaging of the message. A copywriter and an art director try to invent and consider different advertising concepts, which should express well-determined strategic choices. Ultimately, they arrive at a definitive choice for an advertising concept, which is then developed.

Consumers may feel attracted to brands because the image radiates a number of values that they identify with or agree with. Various approaches may be taken to stress the range of the brand's qualities. Despite the excess of communication messages, consumers can absorb, process and remember only a limited amount of information. Therefore, a brand must restrict itself to one main message. Ideally, this brand promise should fulfil the following four criteria:[14]

- corresponds to the real brand qualities (product quality, service provision, etc.);
- corresponds to the consumer's brand perception;
- is distinctive from the brand promises of competing brands;
- reflects the current relevant trends in society.

The strongest brands summarize their messages in a core sentence or even a concept. If the brand promise refers to a functional advantage, then this is called the unique selling proposition (USP). In the case of a referral to a non-functional advantage or a unique emotional advantage, the term is emotional selling proposition (ESP).[15] Cycling-helmet brand Giro replaced its key slogan 'Impact Is Everything' (a USP) with 'Winners wear it' (an ESP).

Sports brand Nike communicated its brand name in the 1990s first with the slogan 'Just do it' and from 1996 only with the 'swoosh', the logo of Nike. The 'swoosh' symbolizes the stylized wing of the Greek goddess of victory, Nike. Because the brand name Nike is no longer visible and yet the 'swoosh' is reconized instantly, it might be suggested that this sports brand has reached the pinnacle of communication.

Advertising formats in sport

To communicate distinctively in the 'advertising clutter', brands have to utilize strong emotions. Otherwise, the advertising will neither have impact nor be memorable. The danger of disappearing into anonymity amid the media clutter is real for overly polite and proper advertising. Conducting an advertising campaign that is not striking enough can therefore carry an equally great if not greater risk than a shocking campaign. Advertising in sport usually deploys strong emotions via a number of set formats (see Outline 4.8), which are elaborated upon briefly below.

Outline 4.8 Advertising formats in sport

- Celebrity endorsement

- Association with sport features and experiences

- Association with sport competencies

- Sport and

  - daily life

  - humour

  - erotic

  - fear

  - music

Celebrity endorsement in sport

A very important format in sports advertising is celebrity endorsement.[16] Endorsement signifies approval, support or affirmation or might be considered as providing a guarantee. With celebrity endorsement in sport, the popular athlete acts as the 'endorser'. The athlete transfers his or her name and image to the brand. To achieve the desired brand associations, the endorser must be well known and have a relevant meaning for a brand. To increase the brand's familiarity and to support or change the brand image, brands attract the attention of their target groups via popular athletes. Brand managers choose athletes who can help to produce a sporting, sympathetic, dynamic or successful association with the brand. Celebrity endorsement involves the perception by the target group of the values that the top athlete upholds. In times of an excess of advertising stimuli, and when the variations in quality between products and services are small, the ambassador function of a popular athlete for a brand can make all the difference. The target group's perception of the brand of the athlete involved is determined partly by the athlete's image created in the media.[17]

However, binding a brand to an athlete carries certain risks. The association with an athlete can result in brand damage. This is the reason why Jim Davis, owner of an American sports shoe brand, New Balance, does not want to base advertising campaigns on individual top athletes. We can see that involving modern sports idols is not risk-free from the examples of the sudden termination of the campaigns conducted by a pasta brand and a breakfast cereal brand involving, respectively, the Festina cyclists Richard Virenque and Alex Zülle. The doping scandal that plagued these cyclists during and after the Tour de France in 1998 brought the advertising brands into discredit. Only in exceptional cases can a top athlete's misconduct be transformed by a sponsorship brand into a communicative opportunity. For example, top French football player Eric Cantona was under contract to Nike when he kicked a supporter in a British competition. Nike managed this sports crisis by printing T-shirts with the word 'punished'. Young people who admire rebels and the footballing of Cantona bought this T-shirt in droves. In the end, Nike confirmed its image as a rebel in this way.[18]

Another danger associated with celebrity endorsement in sport is that the sporting hero may retire unexpectedly. For example, Belgian swimmer Fred Deburggraeve, the Olympic champion of the 100-m breaststroke in Atlanta, was the standard-bearer of the campaign of the Belgian Olympic and Interfederal Committee (BOIC). In the run-up to Sydney 2000, the BOIC prepared a campaign in which the central image was Deburggaeve reaching the shore as the winner after a strenuous journey through a turbulent sea. The swimmer symbolized all Belgian athletes who would give their utmost. Several commercial partners of the BOIC were mentioned in every advertising spot. The 'Sydney here we come' campaign was awarded a Belgian distinction in 2000 for creativity in advertising campaigns. Nevertheless, this creative advertising campaign came to grief later. Deburggraeve retired suddenly from swimming after he was unable to reach the Olympic limit. Also, the brand Ocean Underwear, which was to capitalize on the popularity of the Olympic champion, suffered a rude shock. The text of the print advertising 'Will it be silver or gold this summer?' was completely misplaced once it was announced that Deburggraeve was retiring.

Association with sports features and experiences

A second advertising format in sport is the association with sporting features on the one hand and sporting experiences on the other. It is primarily sports brands that communicate through these attributes, which are listed in Outline 4.9. Even in the sporting world, the strong brand is gaining ground. A sports club aims to establish a strong link with the fans. Along with sporting results, a well-balanced brand strategy is also crucial. The recognition of this brand policy is expressed through advertising campaigns. Both in audiovisual and in printed media, the top football clubs and large athletic events can improve the attractiveness of their brand.

Outline 4.9 Association with sports features and experiences

- Sports features:
  - Star players
  - Stadium
  - Logo design
  - Product quality

- Sports experiences
  - Winning
  - Breaking records
  - Escaping the daily routine
  - Accepted by the peer group
  - Arousing feelings of nostalgia
  - Creating pride

These sports features and experiences were utilized in Nike's 2003 campaign (see mini-case below).

Mini-case study – Nike, Ronaldinho and 'Stickman'

Paris was the background for Nike's advertising campaign which ran at the start of 2003 in Europe, Africa and the Middle East.[19] Via animation between 'Stickman' and top Brazilian football player G. Ronaldinho, the association was evoked that football contains many creative, amusing and provocative emotions. Stickman, created with a computer, symbolized everyone who loves football and wants to escape anonymity. The boundary between the real and the virtual world is vague in Nike's advertising spot. For many teenagers adept at television and video games, the virtual and the real worlds are linked inextricably. This advertising campaign was elaborated by the communication agency Wieden Kennedy in Amsterdam. The advertising spot ran in TV and cinema campaigns.

In April 2003, a Nike advertisement featured the interaction between Stickman and kids playing with a frisbee. This 'cool' outdoor sport demands creativity and daring, talents that Stickman possesses.

Association with sports competencies

The transferral of sports competencies is a third advertising format along with celebrity endorsement and association with sports experiences. The Volvo campaign that ran in 1992 in Belgium and, subsequently, due to its great success, also in the Netherlands and Luxembourg, is a salient illustration of advertising through sport.[20] At this time, Volvo had two difficult image problems. First, the design of the V740 and V940 had not evolved in parallel with the design of new models by Volvo's competitors. Second, the Volvo association with safety appeared to have negative associations ('a Volvo is for someone who cannot drive "sportily"'; 'driving a Volvo gives the chauffeur an overprotected "armoured-tank" feeling'). The association with safety seemed to be too passive or not dynamic enough.

Therefore, when launching the V850, Volvo wanted to present the model as more elegant. The traditional Volvo values of safety and durability (anti-corrosion) were expressed in a revamped way. At the same time, the car manufacturer wanted to communicate the reliable road-holding and the power of the motor. Volvo was looking especially for a warmer image. To play on the feelings of the consumer, who is strongly emotionally involved with 'his or her' car, communication centred around strong sport emotions.

The traditional building blocks of safety and anti-corrosion were communicated via impressive black and white portraits of a fencer and a swimmer. In addition, a skater illustrated the road-holding, while a runner demonstrated the power of the motor. In the accompanying text, the association between the athlete and the features of a Volvo were expressed:

● Swimmer: hardened against water

All Volvos come with an 8-year guarantee against corrosion: the result of a tough programme that renders the bodywork invulnerable and raises the average life expectancy of a Volvo to 20.8 years.

- Fencer: the art of protection

  The famous Volvo safety cage – with steel bars in the doors – is a feature of all Volvos. And for extra protection on the sides, the Side Impact Protection System is built into the 850 and the 900 series.

- Skater: master of the curves

  Along with the exceptional qualities of the front-wheel drive in the 400 and the 850 series, the patented Delta-link suspension of the Volvo 850 ensures unprecedented road-hugging in the curves.

- Runner: a heart with 20 valves

  Under the hood sits the heart of the Volvo 850 GLT: a compact, transversely positioned power source with 5 cylinders, 20 valves and 170 horse-power, with which it can go from 0 to 100 in 9.2 seconds.

This campaign also was very successful because of the impressive size of the sporting photographs used for the presentation. The full-page advertisement in newspapers and magazines, illuminated tour buses and the large posters at dealers were eye-catching. In addition, selection of the environment for the shooting of the photography sessions was done with care. The runner, for example, displayed his sporting efforts against the background of several windmills. These windmills evoke an unpolluted or clean dynamic, with which Volvo wants to be associated. Also, because of the strong sporting emotions utilized, the campaign was very memorable.

Other sponsorship-related advertising formats

There are other advertising formats in sport. Advertisers work with the normal aspects of life, humour, eroticism, fear and sounds generated by sport. Slice-of-life advertisements usually start with the everyday family situation. Examples of daily sport-related situations in advertising include washing the clothes of a young football player with the 'best' washing powder, taking the children to their tennis lessons in a spacious car, or frying a top athlete's chips in a particular brand of oil. The advertising campaign of Flemish newspaper *Het Nieuwsblad* capitalized on these ordinary situations. The focus of the advertisement was a father who wanted to play football with his son late in the evening in the garden. The light towers are switched on, and the ordinary garden is transformed into a real football stadium, while the public enthusiastically chants the name of the advertising newspaper.

Belgian banker Dexia, shirt sponsor of Club Brugge, created a humorous sports advertising campaign in 2002. Captain Gert Verheyen is lying on the ground moaning with pain. However, instead of taking care of the injured knee, the attendant rushes over to clean the mud from his shirt, making the Dexia brand name and logo visible again. Mild forms of eroticism also are used as a format in sports advertising, e.g. the blown-up skirt of Anna Kournikova, in a Marilyn

Monroe pose, at the side of a swimming pool. Sports shoe brand Reebok produced an advertising campaign starring Mario Cipollini, world champion cyclist in 2002, naked apart from his Reebok shoes. Cheerleaders also are sometimes used as attention-getters for sports advertising campaigns.

Other sports advertising takes advantage of the consumer's fear or feeling of insecurity. The 'Impact Is Everything' campaign of cycling helmet manufacturer Giro showed the wall into which the lead cyclist Chris Boardman smashed at a speed of 55 km/h during the opening weekend of the 1998 Tour de France. The message is that the Giro Boreas crash helmet, also shown in the advertisement, saved him from a possibly fatal accident.

Finally, sounds, voices and music from the sports world regularly capture our attention in television and radio advertisements. An energetic sporting atmosphere is evoked by enthusiastic spectators in an athletics stadium or by choirs composed of football supporters. In this manner, the perceptual alertness of the sports consumer is stimulated.

In practice, a sports advertising message usually arises as a mixture of these advertising formats. For example, the baseline of the campaign of VISA-Belgium in 2002 was: 'VISA, for all sorts of things.' In one of the advertisements, the emphasis lay on the role of VISA as sponsor of the Belgian mountain-bike team. This advertisement showed a bewildered Filip Meirhaeghe. The mountain bike of the silver-medal Olympic champion in Sydney had apparently just been stolen, the lock having been cut through. The advertisement stated: 'A new bicycle and next time a better lock.' This advertisement is a mix of three formats: celebrity endorsement, humour and fear.

4.5 Media selection for advertising in sport

The most important part of the advertising investment concerns the purchase of space in the media. When commissioned by companies, advertising agencies buy broadcasting time or pages from the media groups. Via TV stations, radio stations, magazines, newspapers and cinemas, they come into contact with the general public. The task of an advertising agency also consists of filling the garnered media space with content, which is developed creatively. Synonyms for all promotional instruments in the mass media are 'above-the-line communication' and 'theme communication'. Outline 4.10 lists the most important instruments of theme advertising in sport: the audiovisual media, the print media and the outside media.

Outline 4.10 Instruments of theme advertising in sport

- TV advertising
  - spot advertising
  - non-spot advertising
- Radio advertising
- Cinema advertising
- Advertising in printed media
- Advertising in outside media

Above-the-line promotional instruments usually generate an agency commission for an advertising agency. This media commission used to amount to 15% of all media space purchased,[21] but currently it is generally less than 10%. For below-the-line communication instruments (any marketing activity except mass media advertising), in contrast, the commission guideline is not applied. Despite the fact that this terminology has lost its significance – because advertising agencies increasingly often charge on the basis of hours worked – this distinction in the practice of marketing communication is used frequently.

The great advantage of communication via the mass media is that, because of its huge reach, the cost per contact is relatively low. On the other hand, in contrast to instruments of personal communication, such as personal sales in direct marketing, there may be a lot of waste in the communication message.

The main aspects involved in media selection are 'Where?' and 'When?'. In which mass media should the advertising be communicated? What is the anticipated frequency for insertions? Typical of advertisements referring to a current sporting event is the concentration of advertising efforts during peak periods. Also, budget restrictions force an advertiser to make choices. In addition, the creative concept determines which media to choose.

To achieve the desired effect on the knowledge, attitude and behaviour of consumers or companies, instruments are employed simultaneously or successively. In the media strategy for advertising campaigns, a distinction is usually made between main media and support media. The campaign theme is carried by the main medium, while the support media remind us of the theme or elaborate it further for subgroups.[27] Depending on the case, sport-linked outside media could be a main medium or a support medium within the marketing communication. For instance, promotional signage as the core of a sports sponsorship package is usually more a form of passive confirmation communication. Therefore, these advertising carriers in sport might be supplemented and supported by a well-thought-out campaign of theme and action communication.

There are different forms of sponsorship-related television advertising (see Outline 4.11). TV spots or commercials lasting 20–30 seconds dominate the advertising broadcast. Trailers are spots lasting five seconds that are usually shown just before and just after a programme and that act as an attraction for a sports event.[23] Synonyms for non-spot advertising include 'broadcast sponsoring'. In the case of medium sponsorship, the advertiser can influence the editorial content of the television programme.[24]

Outline 4.11 Forms of sponsorship-related television advertising in sport

	Explanation	Example
Spot advertising		
• 10, 15, 20 and 30 seconds on a one-minute spot	Spots that are usually shown just before and just after a programme	Pepsi – David Beckham Ask for more -campaign
• Trailer, five seconds		Tennis federation sponsor announces a tennis event
Non-spot advertising		
• Product placement	Brand is displayed during the sports programme	Provisioning of cyclists in the Tour de France with cans of Coca-Cola
• In-script sponsorship	Brand or product name is incorporated into the script	Awarding of a sporting honour by a sponsor's representative
• Bill boarding or broadcast sponsorship	Advertiser is mentioned before and/or after TV programme	'... this game is made possible by the following sponsors ...'
• Price sponsorship	Winner of a sporting event receives a present from the sponsorship brand	Kim Clijsters, winner of the WTA tournament in Antwerp in 2004, was offered a new Alfa Romeo GT

Outline 4.12 Criteria for mass media selection

• Quantitative criteria:

  - range

  - frequency

  - selectivity

  - geographic flexibility

  - speed

  - quantity of editorial attention paid to sporting object

- Qualitative criteria:

  - 'clutter' in the medium

  - emotional involvement in the medium

  - impact of the medium

  - memorability of message

  - quality of reproductions

  - content of editorial attention paid to sporting object

- Technical criteria:

  - availability of medium

  - features of media purchase

  - production costs

Source: Based on De Pelsmacker, P., Geuens, M. and Van den Bergh, J. (2004), *Marketing Communications: A European Perspective*, 2nd edn. Harlow: FT- Prentice Hall.

Media planning is receiving more and more attention, since the cost of buying advertising time and space amounts to 80–90% of the advertising budget.[25] The selection of mass media as part of an advertising campaign in sport depends on the quantitative, qualitative and technical criteria (Outline 4.12). The reach reveals how many consumers are contacted by the form of advertising. The frequency, or the number of desirable contacts per medium, depends on the medium. Thus, the number of desirable contacts in the context of an average advertising campaign differs for television (three to six), radio (five to 14) and printed media (four to nine).[26] The selectivity of a mass medium indicates the effectiveness with which the target group is being reached. Other quantifiable criteria include the geographic flexibility and speed of a mass medium. It is strategically efficient to base an advertising campaign on the publicity generated. This makes the editorial attention paid by a mass medium to a sporting project an important starting point.

Qualitative criteria determine the selection of a mass medium. The question arises as to which medium has a great or little concentration of advertising messages ('clutter'). The impact of the medium, emotional involvement of the reader or viewer, level of memorability and quality of broadcasts or reproductions are other qualitative criteria.

Technical criteria are also involved in the selection of mass media. The production costs of, for example, a printed advertisement and a radio or television commercial are not equivalent. Other technical criteria for mass-media selection are the availability of the medium and the features of the media message. For example, what are the reservation costs for the advertisement? What is the deadline for the final text of a tie-in advertisement? Outline 4.13 lists the strengths and weaknesses of the most important mass media.

Outline 4.13 Strengths and weaknesses of the most important mass media

Medium	Strengths	Weaknesses
Television	Wide market reach	High absolute costs
	Low costs per reach	Lots of noise
	Combines visual, sound and emotion	Fleeting impact
	Attention-getting	Limited selectivity of public
Newspapers	Flexible	Short-lived
	Good coverage of local market	Low reproduction quality
	Accepted widely	
	High credibility	
Magazines	High geographic and demographic selectivity	Long advertising purchase in relation to time
	Prestigious	High costs
	High reproduction quality	No positioning guarantee
	Long-lived	
Radio	Good local acceptability	Sound only
	High geographic and demographic selectivity	Poor attention
	Low costs	
Outside media	Flexible	Limited selectivity of public
	High repetition rate	Limited creativity
	Low costs	
	Low message competition	
	Good position selection	
Cinema	Selective	Low frequency
	Geographically flexible	Short existence of message
	Rapid reach	Lots of noise
	Emotional and informative impact	
	Intense attention	

Outline 4.13 continued

Medium	Strengths	Weaknesses
	Active medium	
	High reproduction quality	
	Flexible purchasing arrangements	

Source: Based on Shank, M.D. (2002), *Sports Marketing: A Strategic Perspective.* Upper Saddle River, NJ: Prentice Hall; and De Pelsmacker, P., Geuens, M. and Van den Bergh, J. (2001), *Marketing Communications.* Harlow: Pearson Education.

4.6 Summary

Advertising, presently the core of marketing communication, plays a crucial role in the establishment and maintenance of strong brands. The creation of an advertising campaign in sport involves outlining an advertising, creative and media strategy. The starting point in a brand's creative strategy is the formulation of the brand promise, because an important challenge for a brand consists of summarizing its main message in a key sentence or concept. Since both classical and modern idols personify key values, celebrity endorsement is the most significant advertising format in sport. Working with sporting heroes is, however, not without risk. Sports advertising can also associate with sporting atmosphere and experiences instead of celebrities. Finally, sports advertising utilizes everyday life, humour, eroticism, fear and music as part of its format.

The largest part of a brand's advertising investment is devoted to the purchase of space in the mass media. Television remains the dominant medium of theme advertising in sport, with spot advertising being the most significant form of television advertising. The final selection of mass media depends on quantitative, qualitative and technical criteria. In the next two chapters, the interaction between sports sponsorshop and action communication will be elaborated.

Key terms

Above-the-line campaigns
Advertising campaign
Advertising expenditure
Below-the-line campaigns
Brand value

Celebrity endorsement
City dressing
Communication cues
Effect aims
ESP
Image rights
Inflatable
Mass media
Media selection
Non-spot advertising
Outside media
Print advertising
Process goals
Signage
Speciality media
Sport advertising formats
Sports brands
Sport-linked outside media
Spot advertising
Television advertising
USP
Virtual promotional signage

Questions

1. How do the following non-sports brands communicate their key benefits by means of sports sponsorship-driven advertising: Vodafone, Gillette and Siemens Mobile?

2. How do the following sports brands communicate their key benefits by means of sports sponsorship-driven advertising: Adidas, Red Bull and The North Face?

3. Describe different categories of promotional signage of the following Formula 1 sponsors: Marlboro, Tag Heuer and NiQuitin.

4. Illustrate the potential risks of celebrity endorsement with authentic examples. Which top athletes would you select for endorsing new sports sponsorship-related advertising campaigns for the following fast-moving consumer goods: McDonald's, Snickers and Pringles?

Endnotes

1 Sponsorship Research International (2001), *Worldwide Sponsorship Market Values Report*. London: Sponsorship Research International, SportBusiness Information Resources.

2 De Pelsmacker, P., Geuens, M. and Van den Bergh, J. (2001), *Marketing Communications*. Harlow: Pearson Education.

3 De Pelsmacker *et al*. (2001), op cit.

4 Amis, J. (2004), Beyond sport: imaging and re-imaging a transnational brand. In: Silk, M., Andrews, D. and Cole, C. (eds), *Corporate Nationalism: Sport, Cultural Identity and Transnational Marketing*. Oxford: Berg, in press.

5 Shank, M.D. (2002), *Sports Marketing: A Strategic Perspective*. Upper Saddle River, NJ: Prentice Hall.

6 Van Staveren, H. (1998), Het recht op broek en trui, *Communicatie*, 5, 24–5.

7 Bilsen, R. and Van Waterschoot, W. (1983), *Marketingbeleid: theorie en praktijk*. Deurne: MIM.

8 De Pelsmacker *et al*. (2001), op cit.

9 Floor, J. M. and van Radij, W.F. (1998), Marketing-communicatiestrategie, Groningen: Stanfert, Kroese.

10 Adfo Specialists Group (2000), Nationale-Nederlanden en de KNVB. In: *Adfo Sponsorship Cases*, no. 7. Alphen aan den Rijn: Samsom.

11 Floor *et al*. (1998), op cit.

12 Mullin, B., Hardy, S. and Sutton, A. (2000), *Sports Marketing*. Champaign: Human Kinetics; Irwin, R., Sutton, W.A. and McCarthy, L. (2002), *Sport Promotion and Sales Management*. Champaign: Human Kinetics.

13 Van Spauwen, B. (2001), *Waarom reclame niet werkt*. Tielt: Lannoo.

14 Van Spauwen (2001), op cit.

15 De Pelsmacker *et al*. (2001), op cit.

16 Brooks, C. (1998), Celebrity athlete endorsement: an overview of the key theoretical issues, *Sport Marketing Quarterly*, 7(2), 34–44; Thwaites, D. and Chadwick, S. (2004), Sponsorship and endorsement. In: Beech, J. and Chadwick, S. (eds). *The Business of Sport Management*. Harlow: Pearson Education, pp. 350–67.

17 Scott, L. (2003), Impact of advertising on sports. Impact of sports on advertising, presented at the World Federation of Advertisers' Congress, Brussels, 28 October 2003.

18 De Pelsmacker *et al*. (2001), op cit.

19 Raphael, L. (2003), 'Stickman', roi du freesyle. Campagne de la semaine, *La libre Belgique; La Libre Entreprise*, 1/3/2003; www.nikefreestyle.com

20 Van Spauwen (2001), op cit.

21 Van Spauwen (2001), op cit.

22 Floor *et al*. (1998), op cit.

23 Floor *et al*. (1998), op cit.

24 Adformatie Groep (2002), Compaq en BMW Williams F1. In *Adfo Sponsorship Cases*, no.10. Alphen aan den Rijn: Kluwer, pp. 29–48.

25 De Pelsmacker *et al*. (2004), op.cit.

26 De Pelsmacker *et al*. (2004), op.cit.

Case 4 Virtual advertising: real winners

Key learning points

After studying this case, you will be able to:

- interpret new applications of virtual imaging and virtual advertising;

- analyse sports sponsorship leverage through virtual advertising;

- compare the (dis)advantages of virtual advertising vis-à-vis real advertising.

Situation of virtual imaging in Europe

Virtual imaging has two important applications in sport. One is the virtual additions to the game, and the other is virtual advertising. The first category involves images and statistics that are added to provide extra information about the game. Classic examples for a football game shown on television are images added to the screen for virtual offside lines, estimated distance to the goal, virtual penalty-kick circles, virtual video walls, digital club logos and virtual scoreboards. In other sports, the possibilities offered by virtual game additions also have been introduced: in rugby, in the form of the angle along which the rugby player kicks towards the goal, in swimming, by projecting the world-record line in the 100-m crawl on the water, in ice-hockey, where the viewer is informed of the speed of the puck, and in horse-racing, where a virtual finish line can be added and information supplied about the acceleration of the winning horse in the last 100 m.

Virtual advertising is a new advertising carrier in sport. Virtual advertising is the digital addition of 'attention-getters' for brand names or products during the television reporting of sports events. These attention-getters can be placed on electronic message boards or next to the field, scoreboards or posters. Examples include incorporating brand names on the road surface of the Champs Elysées during the final section of the Tour de France, on the background to a baseball game, and on the tarmac of a Formula 1 race. In the UK, the BBC has incorporated such advertising in the Six Nations Rugby tournament, the boat race between Oxford and Cambridge, and in the reporting of rugby games, cricket and horse races, including Ascot. In Belgium, virtual imaging was utilized by Canal+ Belgium for reporting the Belgian football first division: logos and scores were shown in the middle circle, along with offside lines, the penalty-kick circle and distances from the goal. Similarly, virtual advertising can be linked to the virtual game additions. For example, statistics can be associated with a brand name, or a brand name can appear at the same time as the offside line.

Explanations for the rise of virtual imaging

The rise of virtual imaging can be explained by four factors. First, virtual imaging is an answer to the inherent disadvantages of traditional TV advertising, which does not allow selectivity of the viewing public (one message for one target group in one region) and is characterized by a rapid and fleeting exposure to the advertising message. In addition, TV advertising often is associated with high absolute costs and competition from other TV advertisements in the same advertising block ('clutter'), which can limit the visibility. Virtual advertising is the solution. Images can be adjusted to suit the region where the sporting event is being transmitted. With digital television, even a sociodemographic segmentation by target group is possible. Also, recall of the brand names by sports consumers is higher with virtual imaging than with traditional TV advertising. A study involving 406 interviews conducted in 1999 on the impact of virtual advertising on the recall of brand names revealed that 84% of the respondents recalled commercials in virtual advertising. The same study also concluded that the level of importance of a brand name was higher when it was advertised through virtual advertising.

Second, the rise of virtual advertising is due to the technological developments in the medium. The driving forces were the advances in the field of information and communication technology in both hardware and software in the 1990s and the improved capacity of memory chips.

The growing advertising market is a third factor explaining the rise of virtual advertising. Virtual advertising was developed to use the resources invested annually more efficiently; thanks to virtual advertising, it became possible to get the message across faster to different target groups.

Finally, applications in the field of virtual advertising were stimulated by the high cost prices of broadcasting rights for national and international sports events. The holders of these rights sell virtual advertising space to recoup part of the cost price of, for example, the football broadcasts for the various European footballing competitions. A similar approach was taken by TWI for its three-yearly international broadcast rights of the English Premier League football competition. To recover some of the £180 million fee, TWI allowed Scidel Technologies to integrate the logos of the Premier League sponsors Barclaycard and British Tourist Authority in the international reporting of the English football competition.

Advantages and disadvantages of virtual advertising versus classic advertising

Advantages and disadvantages for the advertiser

For an advertiser, the medium of virtual advertising possesses interesting features that are not found in the 'real' mass media. First, virtual imaging has a greater effectiveness compared with TV commercials. The channel-hopping behaviour of viewers lowers the effectiveness of classic advertisements before, during and after a broadcast. With virtual advertising, in contrast, the brand names are displayed live during the game, which means that the sports consumer is exposed to them directly. This makes virtual advertising channel-hopping-proof. In addition, the brand stimulus is introduced into the consumer's world in a less aggressive manner by linking it to the provision of information. The statistics concerning the speed of the tennis ball may interest the viewer, even if the information is placed on a Coca-Cola crown cap, and a brand name can be added to the virtual scoreboard of the tournament.

Virtual advertising also generates improved logo visibility. Because the logo is added digitally, the visibility remains at an optimal level and is independent of changing weather conditions. In addition, logos can be superimposed on places that are not normally suited for logo placement, such as grass, snow, water and tarmac, e.g. German television station ADR added its Sportschau logo to the ski-jump during the Lathi Ski Jump World Cup.

Another advantage of virtual advertising is its flexibility and application. On the one hand, the brand name is displayed live, which permits a greater identification with the emotion of the moment. On the other hand, it can allow segmentation by country, target group or even culture. For example, during the broadcast of the football game between Glasgow Rangers (Scotland) and Parma (Italy) in the UEFA Cup in 1998, Scottish and Italian viewers saw different advertising.

Finally, virtual advertising permits greater buyer flexibility as it can be sold up to several minutes before the start of the game and can even be changed between the start and the finish of the game. With classic advertisement via the mass media, these options are not as readily available and the time elapsing between the decision to buy and transmission is longer.

For the advertiser, there are also disadvantages linked to this medium. First, there is a lack of harmonization between the different national regulations in Europe, which is a significant disadvantage. In mid-2003, virtual advertising was banned in France, Portugal, Italy and Norway, but it was permitted in Germany and the UK under certain conditions, and it was allowed without restriction in Greece and Spain. Austria and Belgium have, as yet, established no legal foundation for controlling virtual advertising. Second, a sufficiently large critical mass for digital television has not yet been achieved. The number of viewers of digital television is still limited, and so the strong point of virtual advertising, namely one-to-one communication, cannot be realized optimally. For advertisers, this can be sufficient reason not to choose virtual imaging at the moment. Also, not every television station can offer virtual advertising. Many television stations still consider virtual imaging to be an uncertain investment project with set costs but unknown returns. Another disadvantage of virtual advertising is the linking of a brand stimulus to sports information, which can be considered unnecessary or useless. Finally, the risk exists that traditional advertisers in sports stadiums will pull out because their advertising can be digitally overwritten.

Advantages and disadvantages for the viewer

For the viewer, virtual imaging can result in better viewer experiences and a greater appreciation. This can be realized through graphic game analyses and lists of team members, real-time two- or three-dimensional statistics and topographic data. Examples include three-dimensional team arrangements, estimates of the distance from the goal in football games, tables showing speeds, inclinations and G-forces in ski-jumping, and graphic representations of the perfect putt in golf. In turn, increased viewer satisfaction can be translated into more subscribers to pay-television and a higher sponsorship income.

Disadvantages for the viewer include overkill of brand information (before, during and after the game), which displaces the sports information. In addition, this form of intrusion marketing can be perceived as disturbing, particularly when the brand names are linked to outdated or irrelevant sports information.

Advantages and disadvantages for the rights holder

The owner of the television rights also can generate extra income with virtual imaging. An important extra source of income is the sale of better and more expensive advertising spaces. Virtual imaging by its very nature can increase the volume of marketable advertising space. The space can be sold several times – in fact, as many times as there are different countries, cultures, regions and target groups. One possibility is to overwrite the physical boards with virtual advertising and, thus, obtain income several times from one board. Another example is the cam carpets in football games. These are advertising boards placed just next to the goal, at the height of the lines of the football field. FIFA regulations do not permit advertising boards here, but with virtual advertising these places can be used after all. This is very effective and, in consequence, virtual imaging can demand higher advertising prices. The prices of virtual cam carpets in Spain, Italy and Germany are, on average, 25–35% higher than the prices of the physical boards just behind the goal. For some top games, the prices can be 50% higher. Other sources of income are linked to the fact that via virtual imaging, new viewers can be attracted or referred more efficiently to the advertiser's website. This is achieved by adding hyperlinks, which produces extra income for the advertiser every time the viewer clicks on the advertiser's website. This concept has been implemented on several television station websites. For example, the website of TF1 in France offered a reconstruction of the most important moments in a France–Germany football game. The visitor could see Zinedine Zidane shoot at the goal or watch the goalkeeper try to stop the shot. On the website, other websites were located just a hyperlink away from the viewer. Because many of the high-tech Internet applications are still in an experimental phase, the potential use is still unclear. A last possible source of income involves percentages of the sales that could take place due to the hyperlinks. This is still very speculative. There are also no figures about the potential income that could be generated in this way.

The most important disadvantage for the owner of the television rights involves the legal restrictions placed on the medium in Europe. European regulations do not permit advertising at all possible locations and times. For example, virtual advertising during a football broadcast is permitted only in the middle circle and the penalty zones when there are no players on the field. Another disadvantage is the immaturity of the market. This means that the range of virtual imaging packages on offer is not yet matched to the television stations' and viewers' demands. Television producers are collaborating to correct this problem. One example is the 'missed shot distance', which was developed by Symah Vision and TF1. This virtual game application measures the distance between the goalpost and the shot that just missed in football games. This advance was first used by TF1 in the France–Slovenia football game on 12 October 2002.

Conclusion

Virtual imaging has two important applications in sport: virtual additions to the game – the so-called game enhancements – and virtual advertising. The former adds images and statistics to the game, while the latter covers the digital addition of attention-getters for brand names. The rise of virtual

imaging in sports can be explained by the inherent disadvantages of traditional TV advertising, the technological developments that made virtual
imaging possible, the high cost prices of broadcasting rights for sports
events and the growing advertising market. Virtual advertising has some
advantages compared with classical advertising for the advertiser, the
viewer and the rights holder. These groups are, however, also confronted
with some disadvantages of the new medium.

Questions for discussion

1. Under what conditions would you develop a sponsor investment via virtual advertising instead of classic sports advertising?

2. Give a number of virtual advertising carriers for:

   (a) an indoor sport;

   (b) a sport played in a stadium in the open air;

   (c) a sport played on a race track;

   (d) a sport played on public roads.

3. Visit www.virtualimaging.org, the website of the Virtual Imaging
   Alliance (VIA). What are this organization's objectives?

References and further reading

Irwin, R.L., Sutton, A. and McCarthy, L. (2002), *Sport Promotion and Sales
   Management*. Champaign: Human Kinetics.
Mendez, H.Y. (1999) Virtual signage: the pitfall of 'now you see it, now you
   don't', *Sport Marketing Quarterly*, 8 (4), 15-21.
Mullin, B., Hardy, S. and Sutton, W. (2000), *Sport Marketing*. Champaign:
   Human Kinetics.
Pinon, B. (2001), Virtual advertising and its legal environment, *Sportel*,
   October, 40.
Rines, S. (2001), A change of image, *Sportel*, October, 41-2.
Scholl, J. (2001), Klementine nimmt effenberg in die Mangel, *Sport Business*,
   July, 74-5.
Schultz, A. (2000), Is it live, or is it Princeton Video?, *FSB*, July-August,
   67-74.
Shank, M. (2002), *Sports Marketing: A Strategic Perspective*, Upper Saddle
   River, NJ: Prentice Hall.
Technology Underground (2001), Use the superbowl to quickly double your
   money, www.cuttingedgeonline.com, accessed 3 June 2001.

Interesting websites

www.symahvision.com: the website of Symah Vision, European market leader in the field of virtual advertising applications in sport. An interesting related website is www.epsis.com, concerning the EPSIS hardware from Symah Vision.

www.virtualimaging.org: the Virtual Imaging Alliance (VIA) is a forum that assembles and defends the interests of the most important players in the sector with regard to the EBU, the EU, national governments, press and opinion leaders.

www.akisport.cz, www.aki.cz: Aki Sport is a small local Czech player in the field of virtual advertising applications in sport.

www.virtualvas.com: Finnish producer of virtual sport applications.

www.vizrt.com: Viz-RT is a software producer for television and sport broadcasts.

5

SPORTS SPONSORSHIP AND DIRECT MARKETING

Sport at the top is now a career, but a special career, because sport is a special business. *(Sebastian Coe)*

Overview

Direct marketing and customer relationship management

Direct mailing

Other forms of direct marketing

Internet communications

Aims

After studying this chapter, you will be able to:

- gain insight into the different forms of sponsorship-related direct marketing communication;

- compare classical and new media in direct marketing communication;

- gain insight into the various phases of an Internet marketing strategy in sport;

- state the marketing functions that can be best served via a sports-related website.

5.0 Introduction

Happy customers are usually loyal customers. Having close and personal contact with customers is the marketing philosophy behind the success of direct marketing (DM). In comparison to traditional mass marketing, the importance of one-to-one communication has grown, based on lifetime bonding with customers. Also, surrounding sports sponsorship with direct marketing communications techniques might result in more creative and effective marketing communication than with mass media advertising. However, instruments of action communication are rarely employed alone, more usually being used in combination with thematic communication instruments. Achieving a synergy between the action- and theme-oriented instruments of marketing communication is, therefore, a main aim. By combining the cumulative effects of theme and action elements, they can strengthen each other in the marketing communication mix, which makes the whole stronger than the sum of the separate instruments.

In this chapter, DM in sponsorship communication is elaborated upon. We also introduce sales promotion in the sponsorship process. The DM approach will first be considered in terms of the philosophy of customer relationship management (CRM) and the technique of database marketing (Section 5.1). Then we examine the activation of sports sponsorship with direct mailing (Section 5.2). Third, there are various other forms of DM in which sports sponsorship can be used, such as television, radio, newspapers, magazines and telephone (Section 5.3). Fourth, we discuss the use of Internet communication, a relatively new and interactive medium in sport (Section 5.4). The importance of websites as an instrument of sports marketing will be elaborated upon in Case 5, analysing the websites of European football clubs from a marketing perspective.

5.1 Direct marketing and customer relationship management

Direct marketing

DM is a form of marketing targeted at creating and maintaining a structural, direct relationship between the supplier and the customer. In order to achieve such a direct relationship it is essential that the supplier obtains relevant information about customers and prospects. Along with direct communication, DM is characterized by direct delivery. In the case of DM communication, the message is adjusted to suit the individual consumer (see Outline 5.1), in contrast to what happens in the one-to-many communications in the mass media. Also, the production, distribution and commercial stimuli are matched to the individual customer profile. Typical of one-to-one (1-to-1) marketing is the two-way traffic that develops between the sender and the receiver of the commercial message. The central aim is to increase the returns per customer. In a 1-to-1 approach, the focus is on keeping profitable customers.

Outline 5.1 Points of interest in one-to-one (1-to-1) marketing versus mass marketing

1-to-1-marketing	Mass marketing
Individual consumer	Groups of consumers
Customer profile	Customer anonymity
Tailored production and supply	Standard production and supply
Individualized distribution	Mass distribution
Individualized commercial stimuli	Mass promotion
Two-way traffic	One-way traffic
Profitable customers	All customers
Retention of profitable customers	Attract prospects

To apply DM communication successfully, a number of steps must be followed (see Outline 5.2). It is evident that the size of the budget available to a company determines the scope of the campaign.

Outline 5.2 The direct marketing (DM) communication plan

1. Set budget limits.
2. Define DM communication target group.

3. Set DM communication aims.

4. Determine DM communication strategy

   – develop campaign

   – select media.

5. Pre-test DM campaign.

6. Execute DM campaign.

7. Study effectiveness of DM campaign.

A step-by-step plan in integrated DM communication can start with a teaser (Outline 5.3).[1] For example, through a telephone call or direct mailing, attention is stimulated in the prospective consumer in a sympathetic manner. One such example is a fitness chain trying to recruit customers. Following the phone call or direct mailing, the company waits for a response from the consumer to the offer of a free trial session at the fitness centre. The follow-up concentrates on the addressees who did not react to the teaser. For example, any addressees who do not become members of the fitness club within a week receive an extra reduction on the subscription fee. Good after-sales service or retention marketing then ensures that the once-only transaction grows into a relationship with the customer. Also, the managers of the fitness centre must pay extra attention to customers who are thinking of leaving. In a further stage, cross-selling is likely to act in more depth on the relationship that has developed after the transaction and might stimulate the customer to make use of complementary services or products on offer. For instance, members of the fitness centre might be stimulated to buy sports equipment or drinks.

Outline 5.3 Steps in an integrated direct marketing (DM) communication trajectory

1. Teaser

2. Response

3. Follow-up to non-response

4. After-sales

5. Cross-selling

6. Relationship management

7. Member-gets-member

Customer relationship management

The main goal of a direct marketer is to increase the quantity and frequency of purchases of each individual customer (customer share) rather than market share. However, before the returns per customer increase, the customer has to become loyal. Marketing aimed at retaining customers falls under the term 'relationship marketing' or 'loyalty marketing'. According to De Pelsmacker and colleagues, when customer retention rises by 5%, profit might increase by 25–30%.[2] Nevertheless, the marketing budgets allocated to promotional actions to attract new customers often are five times higher than those allocated to keeping existing customers. It is thus essential to nurture carefully the relationship with the existing customers.

Within the philosophy of the retention of customers and increasing the returns associated with them, CRM is catching on. CRM originally involved a collection of databank software in which vast quantities of customer data were held. However, it has broken out of its IT straitjacket and grown into a new customer-oriented philosophy, based on the thought that it is cheaper to keep existing customers, and to realize improved returns from them, than to attract new customers. Typical CRM instruments are customer-retention programmes such as company magazines and customer cards. A company magazine offers the space to tell the brand's story. In this way, a link is built to the customer, who trusts the organization, which leads to a sort of club feeling.[3] Likewise, a customer card might bind the consumer strongly to the brand. Such a card may give a member of a fitness centre the opportunity to visit other centres of the chain locally and abroad for free. Moreover, for loyal customers a club could be established. When a customer pays for a year's subscription, he or she becomes a member of the club. Club members then receive free admission to events or a catalogue of special offers. For members of the fitness club, there could be free sauna, solarium and crèche facilities.

Finally, member-gets-member means that existing customers act as ambassadors and are rewarded if they recruit new members or customers. For example, members of a fitness centre are rewarded if they motivate friends or colleagues to come for a free trial session in the fitness centre. In this way, the fitness chain maintains the relationship with its existing customers and expands its pool of prospects.

Database marketing

The success of CRM, and of any DM campaign, depends heavily on the quality and structure of the database used. A database is a collection of market information data, relationship data and company data that can be used for different applications such as analysis, individual selection, segmentation and customer retention, loyalty and services support.[4] Evolutions in technology and automation have encouraged marketers to conduct their marketing with database-supported marketing activities. In the realm of sport, there are several databases, e.g. of participants at grass-roots sports events, that can be rented or bought from list brokers or specialized sports marketing agencies.

A good database should be updated regularly. The database could be incomplete if data fields are missing or incorrect data have been entered, or the user of the file could incur extra expenses because of the presence of so-called 'duplicates'. Equally important is the extent to which the database can be segmented. This is done according to the customers or prospects who are interesting, i.e. profitable, without wasting resources on unrewarding customers or prospects, as is the case with mass communication.

An example involves the manufacturer of sanitary napkins and tampons, which wanted to promote its products as very comfortable while practising sports. To accomplish this, a direct mailing was planned to sporting women, using a database created by merging the participants' lists of different sports competitions. However, no segmentation was done on the basis of gender, which meant that all men in the original file received a brochure about sanitary napkins! Aside from the 50% pure waste, this was also embarrassing for the manufacturer's image.

Outline 5.4 lists the various media that can be called on in DM communication. These media will be discussed further, starting with direct mailing. Sponsored magazines are another important instrument employed in the sports sponsorship context. Action communication in the mass media, telemarketing and personal selling (see Chapter 6) are other forms of DM. Finally, the Internet is well suited to providing an individualized, tailored value approach.

Outline 5.4 Direct marketing (DM) communication media in sport

- Direct mailing (Section 5.2)

- Sponsored magazines (Section 5.2)

- Action communication in the mass media (Section 5.3)

- Telemarketing (Section 5.3)

- Internet communications (Section 5.4)

5.2 Direct mailing

Direct mailing is a target-oriented and personal instrument of DM communication. It is a commercial message addressed to a person or a location and sent by mail. An example is a company catalogue, describing the range of products offered by the company and detailing how the customer can order these products.[5] In addition, a number of other communication and promotion actions reach addressees through the letterbox.

In a sporting context, very flexible use can be made of achievements in a particular sponsored sport form (see Outline 5.5). Usually, special reference is made to the sports sponsorship object in already running direct-mailing campaigns. For example, Belgian bank BACOB, sponsor in the 1990s of the national judo team, included congratulations cards along with the customers' bank statements. These

cards could be posted at the bank, where they were forwarded to the European medal winners. The congratulations cards were an expression of the customers' involvement with judo.

Outline 5.5 Distinctive features of direct mailing

- Target-oriented
- Personal
- Flexible
- Measurable
- Testable

Sponsored magazines

One of the instruments used by CRM and direct mailing in a sports sponsorship context is the sponsored magazine.[6] These magazines are commissioned by third parties; the choice of target group and the editorial content serve the marketing and/or communication aims of the client.

Sponsored magazines, also known as loyalty magazines, consumer magazines and customized media, are a relatively new medium that has definitely found a place in the marketing communication mix. With the growth of this medium, there has been a shift from internal production, or production by an established mass-media communications agency that took on the production of the company magazine as a sideline, to a professionally structured editorial team of dedicated magazine designers and publishers. These specialists consider custom publishing to be their core business. In the past few years, some of the large international advertising multinationals have created their own specialized business units for custom publishing, which has further stimulated the explosive growth in this area.

Sponsored magazines are (usually) free publications that are edited, produced and distributed by an organization for a clearly defined target group. An essential ingredient is that the client pays for the costs (production or otherwise).[7] A good sponsored magazine lies on the interface between marketing and journalism.[8] It meets the standards of a normal popular magazine in terms of concept, form and content (journalism). In addition, it must be geared towards the objectives of the sponsoring organization (marketing). This makes the identity of a sponsored magazine a hybrid: on the one hand, it wants to be a trustworthy and attractive magazine for its readers; on the other, it wants to present its message with the signature of the company or brand. Therefore, the message cannot be transmitted in a tough 'advertising' manner but rather in an indirect manner in the journalistic context.

The first aim of a sponsored magazine is to catch and hold the reader's attention. This is achieved by presenting contents that the reader considers neutral, interesting and worth reading. Only once the reader's attention is ensured can the sponsor's message be presented in a relaxed, subtle and almost subliminal manner, and then the magazine becomes an effective marketing instrument for the client. In brief, it has some advertising, but the customer barely notices this. And by including external advertisers in this almost journalistic whole, the magazine's concept resembles a normal popular magazine even more, and it will often be considered more neutral, however contradictory this is.

Outline 5.6 lists the strong points of sponsored magazines as a marketing instrument. Sponsored magazines are an excellent multifunctional tool that the sponsor can use for various purposes. It is an image instrument, as most advertising expressions are, or it can aim at familiarity with the sponsor or its products. Sponsored magazines also can be employed as a loyalty instrument in all sorts of CRM/customer-bonding programmes and can inform customers about new or existing products. Sometimes they provide space for background information. Sales promotions can be incorporated, such as competitions, savings coupons, joint promotions and savings campaigns. Also, two-way communication can be initiated, for instance through reply coupons.

Outline 5.6 Sponsored magazines: a multifunctional marketing instrument

Multifunctional instrument	Example
Providing information	Daikin cycling newsletter (as subsponsor of the Lampre-Daikin cycling team)
Image instrument (corporate image)	Citroën explains its sponsorship of Justine Henin in the newsletter
Entertainment	Helly Hansen magazine
Customer bonding programmes (CRM)	Rabobank magazine
Interactive communication	Dialogue with target group, e.g. readers' letters
Competitions	The OPEL (sponsor of Kim Clijsters) newsletter presents a competition in which participants can win VIP tickets for Roland Garros
Savings programmes	Collect points in several editions of a newsletter and win a DVD of Euro 2004
Traffic building	Exchange this coupon at your nearest point of sale

In Outline 5.7, the possibilities of sponsored magazines are compared with the limitations of classical media advertising. Through this classical print advertising, a brand could hardly start a dialogue and present the customer with a subtle and trustworthy message. Sponsored magazines, in contrast, provide more detailed information in a journalistic context.

Outline 5.7 Sponsored magazines versus classical print advertising

Sponsored magazines	Classical print advertising
Journalistic	Copywriting
Complex and detailed information	Slogan-like and single-minded
Periodical	Ad hoc
High trustworthiness	'It is just advertising'
Typical magazine layout	Advertising 'look'
Direct	Indirect
Multifunctional (everything in one tool)	Make choices
Interactive	Limited possibilities for dialogue
Exclusiveness	Affected by competition

Mini-case study – You feel … alive!

Captain Helly Juell Hansen began producing and selling waterproof outdoor clothing in 1877. Over 125 years later, the brand Helly Hansen takes pride in its rich tradition. It claims that its products and their owners have been tested to the limits, from the North Pole, over Mount Everest, to the South Pole. Currently, the company produces over 500 different products for outdoor sports.

In 2001, this sports clothing brand launched the sponsored magazine *Alive*, which was devoted completely to outdoor sports. This free magazine is published twice a year in six languages and is distributed through sports shops, sporting locations and the company website. *Alive* targets both professional athletes and recreational sports people. The brand wants to inform, entertain and inspire. In both text and images, considerable attention is devoted to athletes sponsored by Helly Hansen, who participate mostly in mountaineering, skiing, snowboarding, sailing, mountain-biking and trail running. What is the message this company wants to present to its readers between the lines of this attractive magazine? With Helly Hansen sports clothing, you can enjoy outdoor sport without restrictions, you feel free and appropriately dressed, you feel … alive!

5.3   **Other forms of direct marketing**

Action communication in the mass media

In the mass media (primarily television and printed media), DM communication is utilized to introduce products and services, make contact, generate addresses and request catalogues. In direct response advertising in the printed media, a coupon is included that the customer can send in. To inspire the consumer to act, a telephone number, email address or Internet site may be given. On television, DM communication utilizes direct response commercials. Commercials can aim to stimulate the use of catalogues or to increase the interest in a direct mailing action. The 'infomercial' is information packaged in a commercial. For instance, during a television programme, some fitness clothing is presented. The viewer might be stimulated during the programme to order this clothing by telephone or via the Internet. Infomercials are more behaviour-oriented than 'advertorials' (advertisement + editorial).

In an advertorial, editorial information in the form of an advertisement is communicated to the consumers. An example of an advertorial involves laminate flooring brand Quick.Step explaining the advantages of the product. In order to stimulate the consumer to read this commercial information, testimonials of sponsored cyclists are employed, who demonstrate the user-friendliness of the product. In an editorial, a journalist of a lifestyle magazine may examine, in a neutral way, the (dis)advantages of different types of laminate flooring.

Telemarketing

When the telephone is used in DM communication, it is called telemarketing. There is both outgoing and incoming telemarketing. Sporting organizations are making more and more use of call centres to handle the demand for tickets optimally. Outgoing telemarketing is employed to sell a product or service, to establish or maintain a relationship, or to prepare a personal sales talk. Outline 5.8 presents the sales process involving telemarketing. For example, temp agency Adecco is an example of outgoing telemarketing. Adecco sponsored the football championship Euro 2000 to boost its international brand familiarity. As part of the sponsoring, Adecco committed itself to recruiting 2600 volunteers to work in and around the stadiums. To accomplish this, Adecco employed an external call centre. In addition, potential temporary employees were tempted to buy game tickets via direct mailing actions.

Outline 5.8 The sales process via outgoing telemarketing

Process	Example
Planning before the telephone call	Fitness club responsible collects data regarding prospects
Determining approach/position	Selects the sales promotions offer for the prospect
Proposing solutions	Proposes a guest card to the prospect
Concluding call	Summarizes the offer the fitness club makes
Confirming agreements	Prospect agrees to visit the fitness club next week

5.4 Internet communications

The next stage in access to each member of the target group on an individual basis is the trend towards real interactivity. The increasing penetration of the Internet is bound to change the nature of marketing communications interactivity. As the fastest growing communication medium and marketing tool,[9] the Internet is concurrently a vector of external and internal communication and a support for promotion and advertisement. Internet marketing is the application of the Internet and related digital technologies to achieve marketing objectives.[10] Table 5.1 classifies websites offering sport-related information into five major categories.[11]

Table 5.1 Categories of sport-related websites

Category	Examples
Sports media sites	www.eurosport.com www.espn.com
Sports business goods sites	www.footlocker.com www.nike.com
Sports betting sites	www.eurobet.com www.mrbookmaker.com
Club, competition and sport federation sites	www.acmilan.com www.uefa.com www.uci.ch
Sports sponsorship-related sites	www.guinness.com (non-sport brand) www.adidas.com

Various reasons seem to ensure that sport is a focus of attention on the Internet (see Table 5.2).[12] In addition, these factors are considered by the sports marketer as stimuli to consumers to go online and to use the website as a marketing tool.

Table 5.2 Stimuli to use a website as a marketing tool

Advantage of websites	Explanation
Unlimited capacity	Sponsor can provide faster and more detailed information and entertainment compared with newsletters or brochures
High speed and flexibility	Fans obtain faster competition information than via newspapers or magazines
Interactive medium	Fans can click through from the club's site to the site of the main sponsor
Worldwide access	A fan of football club Inter Milan who lives in Japan can receive news about his or her favourite club via the official club website of Inter Milan
Improved availability	The website of a favourite football club can be visited 24 hours a day, seven days a week, at home, at work and elsewhere
High customer service	Through interaction and improved availability, customers' expectations can be met more easily, which might improve the fans' loyalty

Source: Chaffey, D., Mayer M., Johnston K and Ellis-Chadwick, F. (2000). *Internet Marketing: Strategy, Implementation and Practice*. New York: Financial Times Prentice Hall.

Although there are clearly many advantages of putting your sports club online, disadvantages must also be mentioned.[13] There is quite a lot of junk on the Internet in addition to the high-quality sites. Then there is no guarantee of safety regarding the distribution and receipt of information on the Internet. As a consequence, many Internet users are suspicious or hesitant to buy tickets and merchandising online.

Mini-case study - Sign your contract in Sydney

Against the background of the 2000 Olympic Summer Games in Sydney, the Dutch section of the international consultancy office Ernst & Young started a recruitment action called 'Sign your contract in Sydney'.[14] Through radio spots, final-year-student tax specialists, accountants and actuaries were invited to take part in a competition with questions about the Olympic Games. Some 394 students responded to the invitation. The winners of the competition were rewarded with an employment contract, which they signed in the office of Ernst & Young in Sydney. At the same time, they had a unique sporting experience by attending a number of competition days of the Olympic Games. The eight students chosen had six fantastic days in Sydney.

Another example is the Internet exploitation by Compaq Nederland of the international sponsorship rights of the BMW Williams Formula 1 team.[15] The Formula Compaq was an Internet game aimed at business target groups and employees of Compaq. The original target was to have 1500 participants. Ultimately, 3000 people became interested, of whom 2000 actively played the game from beginning to end. The game showed strong similarities to the classic Formula 1 competition. In the two weeks before each Formula 1 race, participants were requested to carry out an assignment three times on Compaq's website. The assignments consisted of expert questions and games. The players were divided into leagues of 22 players each, and the quickest six earned points per Grand Prix. At the end of the season, it was possible to use the collected points to obtain Formula-1-related prizes, such as caps and jackets. The final winner of the game was taken on a VIP trip to the Monaco Grand Prix in 2002.

Internet marketing strategy

Integrated marketing communication implies that the Internet marketing strategy can link up with the existing offline marketing concept.[16] An important factor of success for a sports-related site is setting up an Internet marketing strategy. Outline 5.9 lists the five phases involved in establishing such a strategy.

Outline 5.9 Phases involved in an Internet marketing strategy

1. Analysis

2. Planning

3. Implementation

4. Communication

5. Follow-up

Analysis

In the analysis phase, a sports sponsor considers whether and when it would be attractive to go online. There appears to be an interesting correspondence between sport and the Internet.[17] The average Internet user seems to visit sport and football sites regularly (see Table 5.3).[18] The sports profile of an Internet user is interesting information for a sports sponsor. If the sponsor wants to exploit sports sponsorship via marketing communication, then he must be able to trace the target group well.

Table 5.3 Demographic data of Internet users (general), sports fans, visitors to sports websites and visitors to football websites

	Internet users	Sports fans	Sport website visitors	Football website visitors
Male	70%	64%	75%	75%
Female	30%	36%	25%	25%
Mean age (years)	32.7	34	34	26
Average annual income	€62 500–€75 000	€62 500 +	€50 000–€75 000	€56 250

Source: Delpy, L. and Bosetti, H. A. (1998), Sport management and marketing via the world wide web, *Sport Marketing Quarterly*, 7 (1), 21-7; Church, R. (2000), Massive revenue growth forecasted for internet sports sites, www.screendigest.com/press_sportonthei.htm, accessed 25 April 2002.

Planning

In the planning phase, the goals of the website of the brand are formulated. A primary aim is usually establishing an interactive, educative, long-term relationship with the consumer. Table 5.4 illustrates the steps by which such a relationship can be established.

Table 5.4 Steps in establishing an interactive, educative, long-term relationship

	What?	How?	Example
1	The existing or potential supporters are lured to the website	Website promotion	Real Madrid puts its website URL on its football shirts.
2	An 'interactive relationship' is built up	By offering information and services that have an added value for the visitor[19]	Leeds United fans are given the opportunity to help create the club site by providing their own photographs and personal reports
3	An 'educative relationship' must be built up[20]	Using the club site to collect information about supporters (email address, place of residence, demographic data, interests)	This can be done by offering, for example, a free club screensaver in exchange for some information
4	A 'long-term relationship' is established with the supporter who becomes a loyal customer	Maintaining a dialogue with the individual supporter[21]	The fan receives birthday congratulations from his favourite player because he or she has already downloaded several photographs of the player in exchange for information

Other aims of such websites include geographic expansion, providing content (detailed information about the club), supporting public relations, improving the club's fame, improving supporter services, and making transactions easier (online sales). Further possibilities include improving internal communications via a newsletter, transferring data rapidly and cheaply (e.g. a financial report), and distributing human resources information.[22]

Implementation

These postulated aims must lead to the creation of a website. This can be done by converting the marketing functions (information, communication, promotion, interaction, transaction and user-friendly function) into real-life Web applications (see Section 5.5). This is the starting point of Case 5, in which the marketing of the official websites of European football clubs is analysed.

Communications

Once the club website has been created, this must be communicated properly. The potential visitor must know about the existence of the site before he or she can decide to visit it, so a suitable communication plan will be needed.[23] With a cunning combination of offline and online media, it is possible to attract visitors and get them to return. Possible online communication channels include registration of the website address on search engines, exchange advertising, links and creating other websites. Possible offline communication channels include printing the website address on name cards, letter heads and advertisements. An example could be a sports club printing the URL of the official club website on the players' shirts or on other signage, which again increases the exposure of the website.

Follow-up

The follow-up phase evaluates the success of the site. Measurement instruments might include feedback from website visitors, log-file analysis (when do visitors log on, how many are there, which pages are viewed) and offline or online market research. Furthermore, the site must be checked regularly to make sure that it has the latest information (i.e. updating the site) and has been modified to suit the visitors' wishes.

5.5　Summary

DM actions are important elements of action communication in the extension of sports sponsorship. DM communication focuses on creating and maintaining a structural, direct relationship between a sales person and a buyer. The commercial message is adjusted to suit the individual consumer, and increasing the returns per customer is the main goal. DM communication utilizes various media to make products and services known, establish contacts, generate addresses or request catalogues. Examples of classical media of DM communication are telemarketing and direct mailing.

The Internet is a rapidly growing communication instrument. The communication style, the social impact and the checking of content and contact seem to differ fundamentally from those of the more traditional media. The Internet offers a brand the possibility to communicate with, and to distinguish between, customers, to create a personal relationship with them, and to reward them. Finally, the quality of websites as an instrument of sports marketing is determined by the quality of the information, communication, promotion, interaction, transaction and user-friendliness.

Key terms

Action communication
Advertorial
Communication function of website
Cross-selling
Customer relationship management
Database marketing
Direct mailing
Direct marketing communication
Infomercial
Information function of website
Interaction function of website
Internet communication
Internet marketing strategy
One-to-one marketing
Promotional function of website
Response
Sponsored magazines
Sports website
Teaser
Telemarketing
Transaction function of website
User-friendliness of website

Questions

1. Explain how sponsorship-related direct marketing communications can contribute to relationship marketing.

2. Discuss the similarities and differences between classical and new instruments of direct marketing communications in the setting of sports sponsorship.

3. Analyse how and illustrate why sponsored magazines are a multifunctional marketing communications tool.

4. Visit the website www.fitnessfirst.com. Analyse the various techniques of direct marketing communications that are employed on the site.

Endnotes

1 Floor, J.M. and van Raaij, W.F. (1998), *Marketing-communicatiestrategie*. Groningen: Stenfert Kroese.

2 De Pelsmacker, P., Geuens, M. and Van den Bergh, J. (2001), *Marketing Communications*. Harlow: Pearson Education.

3 Luijk, A. (2000) Sponsored media. Trends, ontwikkelingen en strategie, thesis. Amsterdam: University of Amsterdam.

4 De Pelsmacker *et al.* (2001), op cit.

5 Floor and van Raaij (1998), op cit.

6 Verdonck, E. (2001), Marketing met koppen, *Pub Magazine*, 2, 24–5.

7 Sterkendries, H. (2001–02), Sponsored maar vrijgevochten, *Media Marketing*, 64, 54–7.

8 Verdonck (2001), op cit.

9 Internet World Stats (2003), Internet world usage statistics, www.internetworldstats.com/stats.htm, accessed 10 September 2003.

10 Nielsen/NetRatings (2003), Voetbalclubs Scoren op het Internet, www.nielsen-netratings.com/pr/pr_030826_nl.pdf, accessed 12 September 2003; Chaffey, D., Mayer, M., Johnston, K. and Ellis-Chadwick, F. (2000), *Internet Marketing: Strategy, Implementation and Practice*. New York: FT Prentice Hall.

11 Caskey, R. and Delpy, L. (1999), An examination of sport web sites and the opinion of web employees toward the use and viability of the world wide web as a profitable sports marketing tool, *Sport Marketing Quarterly*, 8(2), 13–24.

12 Brown, M.T. (1998), An examination of the content of official major league baseball team sites on the world wide web, *Cyber-Journal of Sport Marketing*, 2(1), www.cjsm.com/Vol2/brown.htm, accessed 5 December 2001; Janal, D.S. (1995), *Online Marketing Handbook: How to Sell, Advertise, Publicize, and Promote Your Products and Services on the Internet and Commercial Online Systems*. New York: Van Nostrand Reinhold; Johns, R. (1997), Sports promotion and the internet, *Cyber-Journal of Sport Marketing*, 1(4), www.cjsm.com/Vol1/johns.htm, accessed 5 December 2001; Kahle, L.R. and Meeske, C. (1999), Sports marketing and the internet: it's a whole new ball game, *Sport Marketing Quarterly*, 8(2), 9–12.

13 Duncan, M. and Campbell, R.M. (1999), Internet users: how to reach them and how to integrate the internet into the marketing strategy of sport businesses, *Sport Marketing Quarterly*, 8(2), 35–41; Johns (1997), op cit.

14 Adfo Specialists Group (2001), Ernst&Young, partner in sport van NOC*NSF. Van Sydney naar Salt Lake City en verder naar Athene – een route richting rendement. In: *Adfo Sponsoring Cases*, no. 8. Alphen aan den Rijn: Samsom, pp. 7–40.

15 Adformatie Groep (2002), Compaq en BMW.Williams.F1. In: *Adfo Sponsoring Cases*, no. 10. Alphen aan den Rijn: Kluwer, pp. 29–48.

16 Chaffey *et al.* (2000), op cit.; Janal (1995), op cit.; Pope, N.K.L. and Forrest, E.J. (1997), A proposed format for the management of sport marketing web sites, *Cyber-Journal of Sport Marketing*, 1(2), www.cjsm.com/Vol1/Pope&Forrest.htm, accessed 5 December 2001; Sterne, J. (1995), *World Wide Web Marketing: Integrating the Internet into your Marketing Strategy*. New York: John Wiley & Sons.

17 Brown (1998), op cit.; Caskey and Delpy (1999), op cit.; Johns (1997), op cit.; Duncan and Campbell (2000), op cit.

18 Church, R. (2000), Massive revenue growth forecasted for internet sports sites, www.screendigest.com/press_sportonthei.htm, accessed 25 April 2002; Johns, R. (1997), Sports promotion and the internet, *Cyber-Journal of Sport Marketing*, 1(4), www.cjsm.com/Vol1/johns.htm, accessed 5 December.

19 Chaffey *et al.* (2000), op cit.; Duhamel and Edlund (1999), op cit.

20 Chaffey *et al.* (2000), op cit.

21 Janal (1995), op cit.

22 Pope and Forrest (1997), op cit.

23 Chaffey *et al.* (2000), op cit.

Case 5 Football websites: you'll never surf alone

Key learning points

After studying this case, you will be able to:

- illustrate the marketing functions that can best be served via a sports-related website;

- gain insight into the success factors of the website of a professional football club.

Introduction

Communication is one of the most important success factors for a professional football club. An interesting means of communication is the website of a club. Table 5.5 presents the amount of time that football fans in mid-2003 spent on the websites of their favourite clubs.

Table 5.5 Top ten football club websites

Club	Country	Visitors per month	Visits per person per month	Time per person per month
Bayern Munich	Germany	342 000	4.38	0:14:28
Inter Milan	Italy	326 000	6.65	0:38:33
Manchester United	UK	273 000	3.11	0:15:02
AC Milan	Italy	218 000	6.28	0:11:16
Borussia Dortmund	Germany	194 000	8.18	0:16:58
Liverpool	UK	184 000	4.23	0:15:54
Ajax	Netherlands	160 000	3.48	0:14:33
Real Madrid	Spain	147 000	2.34	0:09:36
Juventus	Italy	141 000	2.11	0:08:20
Olympique Marseille	France	124 000	9.42	0:30:28

Source: Nielsen/NetRatings, 2003.

The most popular football club on the Internet in 2003 was Bayern Munich, followed by Inter Milan and Manchester United. However, the fans of Inter Milan and Olympique Marseille apparently visited the websites of their clubs the longest.

Selection of official websites of clubs

To what extent do official websites of clubs fulfil the marketing functions introduced in Section 5.5? For the analysis, the official websites of 21 top clubs from European football competitions were selected. For each country, three clubs were chosen that participated in the Champions League or the UEFA Cup in the 2000-01 or 2001-02 seasons or were ranked among the best clubs in April 2002 (Naessens 2002). The most important competitions include the Premier League (the UK), the Bundesliga (Germany), the Primera Division (Spain), the Serie A (Italy) and Le Championnat (France). Also, three clubs from the Jupiler Liga (Belgium) and from the Holland Casino Eredivisie (the Netherlands) were included in the analysis. Table 5.6 lists the 21 official websites that were analysed.

Table 5.6 Overview of the selected and analysed websites

No.	Country	Football club	Website address (URL)
1	Belgium	RSC Anderlecht	www.rsca.be
2	Belgium	Club Brugge KV	www.clubbrugge.be
3	Belgium	KRC Genk	www.krcgenk.be
4	France	FC Girondins de Bordeaux	www.girondins.com
5	France	Olympique Lyonnais	www.olympiquelyonnais.com
6	France	RC Lens	www.rclens.fr
7	Germany	FC Bayern München	www.fcbayern.de
8	Germany	FC Schalke 04	www.schalke04.de
9	Germany	Hertha Berlin SC	www.herthabsc.de
10	Italy	Internazionale FC	www.inter.it
11	Italy	Juventus FC	www.juventus.com
12	Italy	Milan AC	www.acmilan.com
13	Netherlands	PSV Eindhoven	www.psv.nl
14	Netherlands	Feyenoord	www.feyenoord.nl
15	Netherlands	AFC Ajax	www.ajax.nl
16	Spain	FC Barcelona	www.fcbarcelona.com
17	Spain	Real Madrid CF	www.realmadrid.com
18	Spain	Valencia CF	www.valenciacf.es
19	UK	Manchester United FC	www.manutd.com
20	UK	Liverpool FC	www.liverpoolfc.tv
21	UK	Leeds United AFC	www.leedsunited.com

   In the analysis of the websites, the focus lay on the extent to which they were used as a marketing tool. Thus, the football websites were investigated for their information function, promotion and communication function, interaction, transaction function and user-friendliness. The analysis of the sites was carried out in April 2002 as part of a study by Naessens (2002).

Information function

As evident from Figure 5.1, the findings revealed that the marketing function 'information' was present in most of the sampled club websites. In particular, around 90% of the websites provided information about the particular club's organization, the club's record of achievements, the team, the competition (results, ranking, games still to be played, other competitions), the stadium and links to websites of other teams. However, some club sites gave a written report of the last game played, with highlights and photos, whereas other websites presented a high-quality interactive report with extensive series of photos and video images, associated game statistics, interviews after the match, etc.

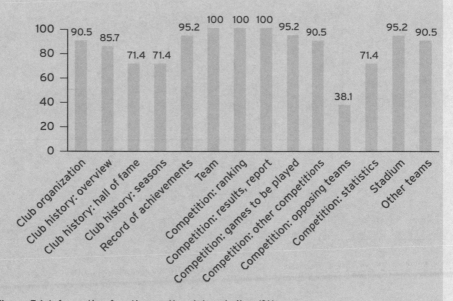

Figure 5.1 Information function on the club websites (%).

Communication function

All clubs offered news about their sport and organizational activities, ranging from the most recent news about the players, transfers, injuries, commentary on the last game, associated details and new equipment, through to weather forecasts. Daily news is an important factor to attract visitors, and get them to return, to the website. The news archive stores these reports. Another news item is the sports calendar. Here, fans can follow their favourite team hour by hour throughout each day. Figure 5.2 illustrates that almost 50% of all clubs provided press releases referring to the club. It was remarkable that all three Italian club sites offered this item, while none of the French club sites did. Via e-marketing, information is sent to other mail addresses. For instance, Juventus FC and Real Madrid each had a separate section, 'Press Room', with password-protected news information for journalists. Also, multimedia items were found on many club sites, including audio fragments (e.g. interviews, press conferences), video fragments (goals, interviews, photo galleries, images from the last game). And 61.9% of the clubs providing live reporting via the Internet produced another great variation between the different clubs.

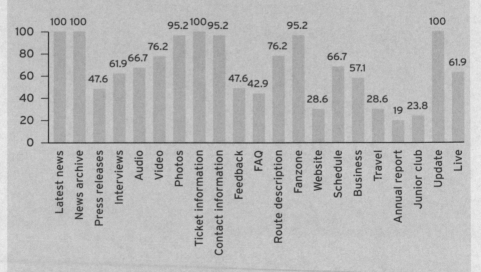

Figure 5.2 Communication function on the club websites (%).

Promotion function

The club website can also be employed as a communication channel for the promotion of the club's own products and activities. Almost all clubs provided online information about how and where to obtain merchandising products and a presentation of all the merchandising products (description, price, photo) (see Figure 5.3). The club magazine was also promoted on the club site. The profile of visitors to the club site is known, and the club can offer this information to its business partners. A website permits a more user-oriented communication than other media, as the profile of the user is better defined. Many sport sponsors (90.5%) make use of the club site to promote themselves or to make direct contact with a clearly defined target group. There are links on the club site to the official sponsors of the club. Some 71.4% of the clubs also utilized their website as an extra source of income by placing banners on their website. Commercial organizations pay the club to place their banners on the club site. Banner advertising improves brand familiarity, communicates added value and offers the possibility of a link to the brand's website.

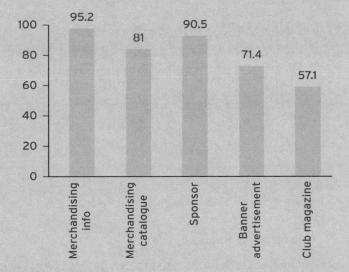

Figure 5.3 Promotion function on the club websites.

Interaction function

Football club websites appeared to be very interactive. At least 95% of the club sites investigated used the forum (chatbox, suggestion page, message board, discussion room) to enable interaction between supporters and between the club and supporters, as shown in Figure 5.4. Online newsletters, questionnaires and contests are ideal means to establish an interactive relationship with the website visitor. These were present on the vast majority of the club sites. E-zines and email allow the club to communicate at little expense with the fans. Webmail is a creative Internet application. The granting of a personalized email address linked to the club (e.g. stevenadams@manutd.com) is an excellent instrument for the club and its commercial partners to improve the loyalty of fans and expand the database at the same time. To obtain a club mail address, the fan has to provide his or her name, address, date of birth, income, job, gender, hobbies, interests, etc.

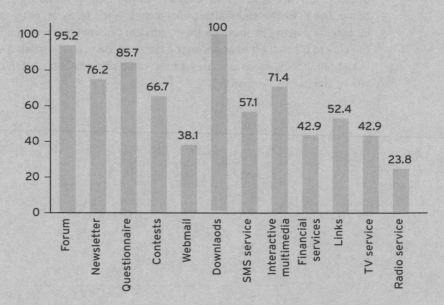

Figure 5.4 Interaction function on the club websites (%).

Transaction function

Online transactions are used to generate income. Figure 5.5 shows that most of the clubs were making use of online sales of merchandising articles by mid-2002. For example, on the websites of the three Dutch clubs, the club magazine was sold online, while via the club website of Leeds AFC, online travel arrangements were sold. In contrast to online merchandising, only a few of the websites of UK, German, French and Italian clubs sold tickets online. These differences can probably be explained by the great administrative complexity associated with ticket sales. For instance, the Belgian government restricted ticket sales through required fan cards. Strict regulations concerning ticket sales make online ticket purchasing difficult. Online betting on the results of the upcoming game was offered by only 23.8% of the club sites (primarily UK clubs).

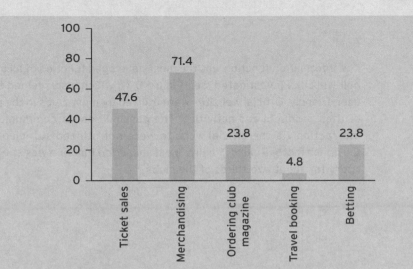

Figure 5.5 Transaction function on the club websites (%).

User-friendliness

A simple and recognizable URL, a well-maintained layout, colours and navigation contribute to the user-friendliness of the club site. As illustrated in Figure 5.6, all club sites had a consistent and user-friendly interface. By limiting the number of menu options and levels, navigation through the sites is kept simple. All club sites utilized signposts to show where the website visitor was on the site. Site maps and search tools were present on only half the club sites. All club sites had a simple and recognizable URL.

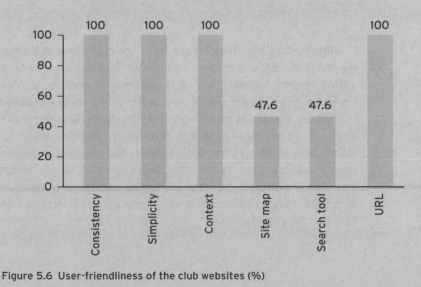

Figure 5.6 User-friendliness of the club websites (%)

Summary

The information function was the most developed function of all of the football websites investigated (see Figure 5.7), which also seemed to be very user-friendly. Official websites were utilized by most clubs in the promotion of their products and activities. The possibilities for communication and interaction via the official website were not utilized sufficiently by the European football clubs. Finally, the transaction function was still virgin territory for about two-thirds of the clubs.

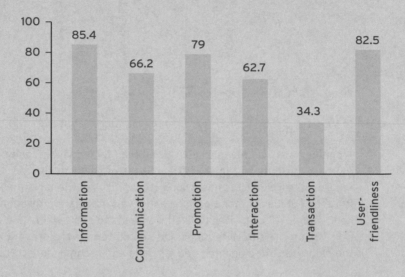

Figure 5.7 Marketing functions of the club websites (%).

Classified by club (see Figure 5.8), the club sites of Liverpool FC and Hertha Berlin SC scored best in terms of information provision, communication, promotion, interaction, e-commerce and user-friendliness. FC Bordeaux and Club Brugge had the worst-performing websites in terms of marketing. Classified by country, the UK (80%) and German (75%) club sites scored the highest for the marketing functions present. Mid-2002, Manchester United, Leeds and Liverpool had the best-developed websites from a marketing standpoint. Also, these websites were strongly business-oriented (hospitality package, financial service and e-commerce), had strong promotion channels, were interactive and attached great importance to live reporting.

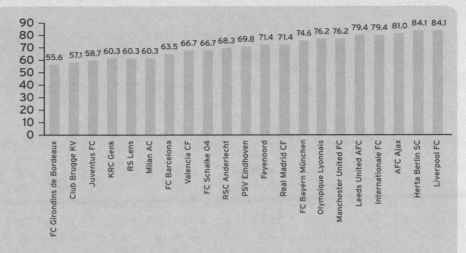
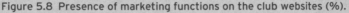

Figure 5.8 Presence of marketing functions on the club websites (%).

Questions for discussion

1. Visit the websites www.manutd.com and www.inter.it. In how many languages do these football websites provide their content? Compare how the main sponsors of the clubs develop their sponsorship.

2. Compare the marketing functions of the official website of a football club (www.liverpool.com) with the website of a cycling team (www.uci.ch) and with the website of an American team from another sport (www.nba.com/spurs).

References and further reading

Beech, J., Chadwick, S. and Tapp, A. (2000), Towards a scheme for football clubs seeking an effective presence on the internet, *European Journal for Sport Management: Special Issue Managing Professional Football in a Changing Environment*, July, 30–50.

Brown, M.T. (1998), An examination of the content of official major league baseball team sites on the world wide web, *Cyber-Journal of Sport Marketing*, 2(1), www.cjsm.com/Vol2/brown.htm, accessed 5 December 2001.

Brunelli, M. and Semprini, M. (2000), The Internet and professional football: a European perspective, *European Journal for Sport Management: Special Issue Managing Professional Football in a Changing Environment*, July, 120–48.

Chaffey, D., Mayer M., Johnston K. and Ellis-Chadwick, F. (2000). *Internet Marketing: Strategy, Implementation and Practice*. New York: FT Prentice Hall.

Church, D. (2000), Massive revenue growth forecasted for internet sports sites, www.screendigest.com/press_sportonthei.htm, accessed 25 April 2002.

Delpy, L. and Bosetti, H.A. (1998), Sport management and marketing via the world wide web, *Sport Marketing Quarterly*, 7(1), 2–7.

Duncan, M. and Campbell, R.M. (1999), Internet users: how to reach them and how to integrate the internet into the marketing strategy of sport businesses, *Sport Marketing Quarterly*, 8(2), 35–41.

Ellsworth, J.H. and Ellsworth, M.V. (1995), *Marketing on the Internet: Multimedia Strategies for the World Wide Web*. New York: John Wiley & Sons.

Mullin, B.J., Hardy, S. and Sutton W.A. (2000), *Sport Marketing*. Champaign, IL: Human Kinetics.

Naessens, D. (2002), De officiële websites van professionele footballclubs als een marketingtool, thesis, European Master in Sport Management. KU Leuven: Faculteit Lichamelijke Opvoeding en Kinesitherapie.

Smith, R.L., Pent, A.K., Pitts, B.G. (1999), The world wide web as an advertising medium for sports facilities: an analysis of the current use, *Sport Marketing Quarterly*, 8(1), 31–4.

Sterne, J. (1995), *World Wide Web Marketing: Integrating the Internet into your Marketing Strategy*. New York: John Wiley & Sons.

6

SPORTS SPONSORSHIP AND SALES PROMOTIONS

> Twenty days after his signing, Real Madrid sold 70 000 Ronaldo shirts. This is 3500 per day, 146 per hour, 2.5 per minute. A shirt costs 72 euros ...
> (*Het Nieuwsblad*, 24 September 2002)

Overview

Importance of sales promotions

Consumer promotion tools

Point-of-purchase communications

Personal selling and trade promotion tools

Sampling

Merchandising and licences

Aims

After studying this chapter, you will be able to:

- recognize the range of available methods of sales promotion developing sports sponsorship in consumer markets;

- explain the various tools of sponsorship-driven sales promotions;

- grasp the opportunity presented by sampling as an instrument of sports sponsorship development;

- provide an overview of different aspects of merchandising and licences.

6.0 Introduction

In contrast to thematic communication instruments, action communication aims to increase sales in the short term. These promotional activities are characterized by their temporary nature and the immediate behavioural response that they want to elicit. Along with the generation of direct sales, action communication can also be employed to support sales and improve brand loyalty. Despite these clear objectives, promotions must be used sparingly, since they might give a brand a 'cheap' image because promotions could undermine the effect of strategic marketing communications instruments such as advertising, which try to build long-term brand image effects.[1] Promotions might also result in negative effects in the long run because of neutralizing competitive campaigns, resulting in an increase in promotion costs for the same amount of sales.

In this chapter, the following facets of sports sponsorship and sales promotion will be discussed. After a consideration of the importance of sales promotion actions linked to sports sponsorship (Section 6.1), we consider the variety of consumer promotion tools (Section 6.2). Since many consumers seem to make choices at the point of purchase and do not know in advance what product they are going to buy, the integration of sports sponsorship at the point of sales might be very useful (Section 6.3). However, sports sponsorship can also be developed in trade promotions in a business-to-business context (Section 6.4). Receiving more and more attention as a specific sponsorship-driven example of sales promotion is sampling (Section 6.5). This chapter concludes by looking at merchandising and licensing in sport (Section 6.6). As has been discussed elsewhere in this book, a sporting environment is likely to lend itself to distinctive communications. This is illustrated in Case 6, explaining the sampling strategy used to introduce the sports drink Aquarius into the Belgian market.

6.1 Importance of sales promotions

Sales promotions are the set of activities conducted by marketers to stimulate sales in the short run. These promotions could offer an extra value to the sales force, distributors or the consumer, aimed at increasing sales in the short run.[2] Through this channel, loyal customers can be rewarded for their loyalty, and existing customers can be made loyal. Because it might be less expensive to retain a loyal customer than to convince a competitor's client to switch brands, promotions frequently reward loyal customers.

These promotions might also serve as reinforcers of other communication tools. For instance, a sponsorship campaign could have a greater impact if a promotion is included. This synergy can be explained by the fact that sponsorship works more indirectly on brand awareness and image in the long run, while most promotion campaigns might be effective in the short run, leading to a substantial increase in sales. A study of the impact of the sponsorship of Euro '96 showed that through the leverage of sports sponsorship, behavioural aims might be achieved (see Table 6.1).[3] After the European football championship, an extra 10% of the people interviewed were prepared to buy more products from the sponsors. Football sponsorship proved to be equally effective in attracting new customers, as demonstrated by an extra 14% of the people interviewed being prepared to try the products of sponsorship brands for the first time.

Table 6.1 Impact of the sponsorship of Euro '96 on consumer behaviour

	Intention to buy more products (%)	Intention to buy products for the first time (%)
All countries	+10	+14
UK	+10	+13
France	+6	+9
Germany	+9	+15
Russian Federation	+16	+18

Source: Easton, S. and Mackie, P. (1998), When football came home: a case history of the sponsorship activity at Euro '96, *International Journal of Advertising*, 17(1), 99–114.

6.2 Consumer promotion tools

In order to increase sales in the short run, a number of specific tools of sales promotion can be used. Outline 6.1 lists the most important techniques of sales promotion that are employed regularly in the activation of sports sponsorship. These promotion instruments typically work via discounts, product promotions or competitions, or a combination thereof.

Outline 6.1 Techniques and examples of sponsorship-driven consumer promotions

Technique	Example
Monetary incentives	Discounts on market prices of specific products as part of Olympic conditions
Cash refund	Refunds in cash when buying products during soccer championships
Contest	Meeting sponsored athletes as the award in a context (e.g create a baseline for a sponsorship activation campaign)
Lottery	Football ticket as a competition prize
Premium	Free T-shirts and caps when buying products
Self-liquidating premium	Sports videos/DVDs offered at or below cost prices
Savings card	Merchandising items as a result of sponsorship-related savings formulas
Sampling	Sports nutrition bars offered free of charge

Sponsorship-related monetary incentives include coupons, cash refunds and savings cards. Coupons are vouchers representing a monetary value with which the consumer can get a discount on a specific product.[4] For example, a sponsored top athlete states in an advertisement that the product he or she is recommending is currently on sale. The company can name a discount action after the sponsored event, e.g. a car manufacturer offers 'Olympic Conditions' in the run-up to and during the Olympic Games. Cash refunds are discounts offered to the customer that involve refunding part of the purchase price or transferring the money to the customer's bank account after sending a proof of purchase.[5] In the case of cash-refund coupons, an individual contact is made between a company and a customer. Sometimes the exchange of a cash-refund coupon is associated with receiving free tickets to a sports match, e.g. the one-hundredth or one-thousandth customer to send in a coupon receives tickets as well as the cash refund, perhaps after formulating a slogan to encourage the national team.

Contests and lotteries also can be linked to sponsorship projects. In the case of contests, some intellectual or other effort of the consumer is needed, e.g. consumers may be asked to propose a new baseline for a sponsorship project of a brand. Lotteries, in contrast, are based purely on chance. The prizes offered as part of competition formulas might in many cases be unique sport experiences that money cannot buy, e.g. a meeting with an athlete or a range of sports clothes.

In sales promotions, there also are a lot of different savings systems, of which savings cards are one example. To stimulate store loyalty, savings cards are promotion techniques on the basis of which customers receive a discount provided they have bought a certain number of units of the product during a specified period of time. For example, as soon as your savings card is full, you receive a ticket to a game of the sponsored football team or a poster of a sponsored athlete. Savings actions are also employed to stimulate consumers to buy and increase brand loyalty. The attractiveness of a savings programme depends not only on the amount of the reward but also on the time at which the reward is made available. Obviously, the effectiveness of a promotions campaign can be increased by integrating it in a marketing communications campaign, and thus supporting it by advertising campaigns, personal selling efforts or sponsorship campaigns. This is why brands are eager to take advantage of the hype surrounding sponsored top sporting events by awarding extra savings points. During Euro 2000, for example, Shell and the Postbank organized a joint savings action to obtain gadgets.

Premiums – items given away with the sponsor's product as part of the sales promotion – are a highly attractive tool of sales promotions. There are promotions in which the consumer receives a premium when buying a particular brand, e.g. football-player stickers enclosed in chewing-gum packs. Self-liquidating premiums are gifts that can be obtained in exchange for an extra amount of money.[6] The trick is to choose a premium that matches the advertising theme. During Euro 2000, for example, buyers of a JVC television set in the Netherlands received a ball from Adidas.

Sometimes, two brands combine different promotional actions. An example of this is the joint promotion between Coca-Cola and the Dutch distributor Albert Heijn during Euro 2000. After buying three 1.5-litre bottles of Coca-Cola, children could register for a Euro 2000 ball boy/girl selection day.[7]

Lotteries also offer a wide range of options of making links to sports sponsorship. Examples of prizes are free travel or tickets for the sporting event or merchandising.

Promotional actions are also important in the marketing communication of sports clubs. The organization of ticket sales for large sporting events, for example, is not always without problems and demands a well-planned action communication. The image of professional football clubs is associated closely with the number of subscriptions and tickets sold. To raise the ticket income, club managers employ sales promotion actions. Fans are given a commercial stimulus via a temporary savings action to arrange a subscription during the summer months. Another possibility is to give fans a free gift from the merchandising shop when they purchase a season ticket. To organize such promotional actions and reach the target group efficiently, a good database of club visitors is essential.

6.3 Point-of-purchase communications

Announcing and supporting classic sales promotions is accomplished through the combined input of retail communication and/or direct marketing communication (see Chapter 5). Retail communication, point-of-purchase (POP) communications or point-of-sales (POS) communications can be defined as any promotional material placed at the point of purchase, such as interior and window displays or printed material available at shop counters. For example, fashion retailer Hugo Boss installed a 106-inch screen in its Regent Street store in the UK to show its latest collections as well as fragments of the sporting events it sponsored.[8] The attractive exterior of this store was designed to distinguish it from its competitors and to attract customers' attention. Inside the store, eye-catching displays drew consumers' attention to specific products and induced them to buy the product.

There are many examples of integrated public relations (PR) and action communication at the point of sales; the presence of a sponsored top athlete at the opening of a refurbished or new retail outlet is one example. In this way, members of staff can show off 'their' star players and transmit this proud ambassador feeling to other people present. For example, displays of David Beckham lure the consumer to Adidas products.

However, increasing the traffic to the stores is not enough to be successful, as illustrated by the sponsorship campaign of Hyundai Belgium as the official partner of Euro 2000. Hyundai had already started advertising campaigns in April 2000, which were linked to the European football championship.[9] Consumers could obtain tickets for Euro 2000 via the Internet. Additionally, in the Hyundai customer magazine, a competition was proposed, with the main prize being tickets for Euro 2000 games. During the most important car trade fair in Belgium, Hyundai sent out a classic mailing that linked the brand to the Euro 2000 events. In the mailing, 80 000 copies were sent out, of which 26 000 were directed at existing customers and 54 000 at prospects. The purpose of the mailing involved the recipients visiting a local dealer and participating in a competition in the showroom, with the chance of winning a car. In addition, the interested customer could pick up a gadget at the dealer's point of purchase. Hyundai managed a response of 25% among existing customers and 7% among customers from competitive brands. However, the concession holders were not happy, because the consumers came in only to pick up the free gadget. This example illustrates that sales actions must do more than just make links to sports sponsorship: they must also be sales-oriented.

Sponsorship-related POS communications can be supported by a wide range of POS materials. Important tools are displays, mobiles, posters, shelf liners and inflatables. Nike displays in outlets featuring Nike-sponsored Manchester United goal keeper Fabien Bartez are examples in the fast-moving consumer-goods sphere. An illustration in the durable goods sector is the sale of BMW Williams merchandising material in showrooms of BMW dealers.

Mini-case study - Sponsorship-driven sales promotions during Euro 2000

The sales promotions used in national football championships come in all shapes and sizes. For example, during Euro 2000, Sony launched a competition on the Internet. The prizes included dozens of tickets for the Euro 2000 games. In this way, Sony promoted its home entertainment range along with its virtual shop Sony Style.

Another example from Euro 2000 is Philips and its shaving appliance, the Philishave Cool Skin, developed from a cobranding with Nivea. A large-scale promotion was started several months before the football tournament, combining a free gift with a purchase, a tombola and a competition formula. With the purchase of a Philishave Cool Skin, the customer could win a prize package by filling in a coupon at the point of sale, attaching the sales slip and barcode proof of purchase, and putting everything in the post. The prize package consisted of a mini radio and a football rattle, in the form of the shaving appliance, that made the appropriate supporter sounds. After scratching a few lottery tickets, participants knew immediately whether they had won one of 300 tickets for the Euro 2000 games, a coupon for a McDonald's Euro 2000 hamburger, a calendar with all of the games noted, or an invitation to a game projected on a giant screen. The more dedicated football fans could become members of the Fanclub Cool Skin Euro 2000. This promotion was announced at the end of every TV commercial involving the shaver and was supported by POS material and advertisements.

Credit cards are another important player on the sponsorship market. For instance, in its mass sponsorship programme, Europay International - official sponsor of Euro 2000 - gave its customers the opportunity to use the official logo and emblem of the tournament on their EuroCard/MasterCard credit cards. Citibank introduced a Euro 2000 MasterCard, which carried a permanent credit of €1875; the card cost €20 per year. When registering, the customer received an official Euro 2000 football signed by Pélé, who had been the ambassador for Europay International for all football events for some time. After the launch of the card, a lottery was organized every month in which cardholders could win tickets for Euro 2000 games. In the sponsor communication of Euro 2004, this theme was expanded further: Eusebio (Portugal), Klinsmann (Germany) and Pfaff (Belgium) were selected for Portugal 2004 along with Pélé as MasterCard ambassadors.

① 6.4 **Personal selling and trade promotion tools**

Sports sponsorship can be developed via sales promotions not only in consumer markets but also in business circles. The most important business-to-business instruments are trade fairs and personal selling. Trade fairs are considered to be a more personal and thus a below-the-line communications tool. In this medium, one-to-one contacts with customers and prospects, PR and personal selling are combined.[10] Trade fairs frequently offer the opportunity of building relationships with stakeholders, who feel important if they are treated as VIPs at fairs and exhibitions; for example, novelties or meet-and-greet activities as part of a sports sponsorship project might offer powerful experiences to VIPs.

The aim of sports sponsorship development at trade fairs is to generate extra traffic to the stand. For example, on the Belgian construction trade fair Batibouw in 2002, construction materials manufacturer Mapei and laminate flooring brand Quick.Step asked sponsored cyclists to come to their stand. This PR activity gave extra attractiveness to the stand, which was decorated with displays of cyclists from the Mapei Quick.Step team. A quiz formula was developed to stimulate trade fair visitors to stop for a moment at their stand.

Personal selling also involves direct contact between the seller and the customer, which allows for personalized and often rapid contact. Most personal selling occurs in the arena of business-to-business activities.[11] One example of this involved the negotiations conducted by the sponsor committee of Tennis Club Baseline (TCB) with prospective sponsors (see Case 2). The mini-case below describes the personal selling tactics employed by TCB to win over the prospect.

Mini-case study – The personal selling tactics of Tennis Club Baseline

'You never get a second chance to make a good first impression.' This slogan applies well to the sponsorship recruiters in TCB, who have invested considerable time in the preparatory phase. Naturally, it is very important to know who the sponsorship recruiters will be meeting and to what extent they are involved in the club. Because everything depends on the presentation, the TCB sponsor committee makes sure that its approach is professional, using a laptop and projector, and that the presentation is clear.

From attending courses on presentation techniques, TCB chair, Ms Volley, has learned to explain what you are going to say, say it, and summarize what you have just said. Clarify the purpose of the discussion (e.g. another appointment or sending of a concept contract). The TCB presentation is structured as follows: introduction of club history, structure and future plans, role of sponsorship, starting points of the sponsor policy, the concrete offer, and a proposal for further dealings. One strong point of TCB is that it devotes attention to specific returns that are important to the sponsor, e.g. the organization of a tennis clinic for their personnel, a special event for friends and family or a sales drive among the members.

TCB wants to show what the options and opportunities of a partnership are and to demonstrate that sponsoring of the club goes much further than just including a logo on a sponsor board or shirt. Such an approach demonstrates respect and interest in the company and might often generate considerable respect and continuing interest by the potential sponsor. The directors of TCB make sure that they have several copies of the presentation that they can leave behind. Generally, the company will conduct an internal discussion, in which the decision will be made as to whether to sponsor TCB. Sometimes, more information will come up in the first discussion that leads to new ideas and initiatives and can provide the stimulus for a second discussion. Therefore, the TCB sponsor committee agrees in advance on the follow-up procedure. In order not to depend on the other party contacting them, the TCB sponsor committee always tries to keep the initiative, e.g. by sending out follow-up sponsorship letters.

Ms Volley has also learned that when a sports club and a potential sponsor sit down together to negotiate and possibly conclude an agreement, the club must consider in advance their tactics for winning over the company. Possible difficulties that the company might anticipate must be listed, and the club must think of a way to deal with each one of these. If the potential sponsor brings up one or more difficulties during the negotiations, then the club has a ready-prepared answer, thus removing the sponsor's arguments against entering into the sponsorship contract. In addition, the company will be pleasantly surprised at the club's thorough and professional preparation of the negotiations. TCB considers the personal selling tactics listed in Table 6.2 for winning over the prospect sponsor in advance.

Table 6.2 Personal selling tactics of Tennis Club Baseline

Tactic	Example
Differentiate the sponsor contribution	Distinguish between 'match', 'set' and 'game' sponsors
Propose an active media policy	'Match' and 'set' sponsors receive a newsletter four times a year
Be flexible in setting sponsor duration	'Match' = three years; 'set' = two years; 'game' = one year

Offer sector exclusivity	Sector exclusivity offered for 'match' sponsors
Set evaluation deadlines	Twice a year: sponsorship contract evaluation
Be flexible in payment arrangement	Payments for 'match' (or 'set') sponsors may be split over three (or two) years
Stimulate the employees' involvement	Offer tennis clinics for employees of 'match' and 'set' sponsors

6.5 Sampling

Retail communication can also find an application on the sports terrain through sampling. This sales promotion technique, which is very popular in sporting environments, consists of distributing a free or low-priced sample of the product.[12] Sampling is the ideal promotion instrument to allow the consumer to try a product. Sampling is certainly recommended for products with benefits that become evident after tasting just small quantities, such as chocolate bars and soft drinks. Sampling might also be of interest in circumstances when purely thematic communication instruments would find it difficult to convince the consumer of the product's unique features.

Because they are characterized by an exciting and relaxing environment, where many powerful experiences can be had, sporting environments are eminently suitable for sampling activities. There is also a concentration of a target group in a sporting environment, which allows for targeted distribution of the free samples. Interestingly, in sport, there is a wide range of possibilities for sampling. Experiential sampling in sport means that the samples are distributed on the spot, at that moment, for that target group, with the timing that the consumption of the sample becomes a unique experience. For example, recreational joggers or mountain-bikers enjoy 'provisioning' even more when they are feeling hungry, so the chocolate bar or sports drink consumed provides greater satisfaction. In this way, athletes become ambassadors for a brand, and positive word-of-mouth publicity is generated. Outline 6.2 lists the product features of a brand that can make sampling an effective technique of action communication. For example, sports drinks and chocolate bars benefit greatly from sampling actions. Sponsorship-related sampling is not limited to fast-moving consumer goods or food products; it can also be used in consumer durable products, e.g. a prospective new car buyer can be offered a test drive.

Outline 6.2 Product features that favour effective sampling

- Low price

- Large potential turnover

- High turnover rate

- Packaging, transport and distribution in large volumes

- Unique properties (e.g. taste)

- Brand advantage evident after consumption of just a small quantity

- Readily available in stores

- Better quality than competing products

Source: Based on Floor, J. and van Raaij, F. (2002), *Marketing-communicatiestrategie*, Groningen: Wolters-Noordhoff.

Because the personal brand experience has a stronger effect than a commercial message, sampling is an excellent means to allow the consumer to try a brand. The story of the launching of the sports drink Aquarius in Belgium tellingly illustrates the power of experiential sampling in sport (see Case 6). The breakthrough of Aquarius in Belgium was due primarily to successful action communication. Through free trials – the free provision of cans of Aquarius to young and active athletes in a sports setting – the brand successfully entered the market. Through powerful experience communication, athletes received the right stimulus of the sports brand, at the right time and in the right place. By combining this sampling with effective communication on site, the qualitative and direct contacts with the target group were strengthened.

6.6 Merchandising and licences

Alongside sampling, merchandising is a special form of action communication in sport. In the sporting world, merchandising is described as the sale of a variety of products or services displaying the official logo and the brand name of a sports brand. Merchandising has taken off in sport because it is linked to sometimes worldwide sports brands such as the Olympic Games, the NBA or Manchester United. Originally, merchandising focused primarily on the local market. Quite rapidly, however, it became evident that the real commercial opportunities lay beyond national borders. The language, country and cultural independence of the sports brand allowed the marketing area to be sensitively expanded. European examples include football club FC Barcelona and Zinedine Zidane or the Formula 1 Ferrari racing team with Michael Schumacher. The success of merchandising is a logical consequence of the strong involvement and identification of the fan with the sports brand. Merchandising articles act in this case as souvenirs, reminders or symbols of the emotions and tension felt during the unique sporting experience.[13] Consequently, merchandising articles become a brand for which the fan is prepared to pay.

Brand equity

Merchandising is primarily important for strong brands where the added value of a product is due to its brand name. The concept of brand value includes both financial and consumer brand value.[14] Financial brand value refers to the financial value of a brand to a company, estimated for organizations listed on the stock exchange by stock market capitalization (value per share multiplied by the number of shares).[15] In contrast to financial brand equity, it is much more difficult to measure consumer brand equity. The concept of consumer equity reflects the extent to which a brand gives a product extra marketing power. First, the strength of a brand is determined by the consumer's familiarity with the brand (see Outline 6.3). The brand familiarity of strong brands extends much further than a familiar name and passive brand knowledge and stands for active brand knowledge. Second, there is the quality perception of a brand, i.e. the consumer's opinion of the features of the product or service compared with competing brands. Third, there are the strengths and the unique character of the brand associations that are aroused. Brand loyalty is by far the most important component of a strong brand, as evidenced by season-ticket holders of football clubs who apply for a repeat purchase. In addition, research has revealed that the costs of convincing prospects are more than six-fold those of keeping existing consumers.[16] A fifth component of brand strength is the quality of the remaining marketing factors, such as the distribution policy, the protection afforded by patents, quality labels, or the quality of the staff behind the brand.

Outline 6.3 Components of strong brands

Component	Example
Brand familiarity	Adidas
Quality evaluation of brand	Rolex
Brand associations	Rebel image of Nike
Brand loyalty	Manchester United season-ticket holders
Legal protection of brand	Adidas Roteiro
Other strengths (quality of personnel, quality labels, etc.)	A.S. Adventure distribution channel

Mini-case study – Building the 'Chelski' brand

Aside from the transfer of top players such as David Beckham, football fans tend not to notice much about what takes place away from the pitch of their favourite club. But fans and investors alike were left stunned when Peter Kenyon resigned from Manchester United to take a position at Chelsea, the club's west London rival recently acquired by Roman Abramovich, the Russian billionaire.

The departure of one of the sport's most highly regarded administrators and brand-builders from Manchester United to Chelsea – which is seeking to claim United's crown as English champions – could have ominous repercussions for the north-west club. During his three years as chief executive of Manchester United, Mr Kenyon has overseen unprecedented expansion at the club. He was the architect of United's record-breaking 430 million euro marketing deal with Nike – which adds, on a yearly basis, a minimum of 28 million euros a year to profits.

His success at turning Manchester United into a heavyweight global brand should not be understated. The club has spent the past few summers touring new markets in an attempt to turn some of its estimated 50 million fans into customers, culminating recently in a coast-to-coast tour of the USA. Under Mr Kenyon, Manchester United also agreed to a unique marketing tie-up with the New York Yankees.

Source: Garrocham, M. and Harris, C. (2003), Man U man joins 'Chelski' brand-wagon, *FT.com*, 8 September 2003.

The perception of brand strength is a subjective element. *Sport Business International* polled the perception of a number of opinion leaders about sports management for strong sports brands.[17] The brand specialists interviewed cited Nike and Adidas as strong sports brands. The modern, dynamic, clean, simple and 'cool' brand image of Nike, the strong logo, and the successful brand diversification into other sports are always supplied as explanations. Also, the brand Adidas, with its strong three-stripes logo, has also successfully undergone brand-stretching. Adidas eyewear, watches, deodorant and perfume are some examples. The Olympic rings and the Champions League, symbolized by its logo of the star ball, were cited as strong brands. Other strong brands include the Ferrari Formula 1 team, the NBA competition, basketball legend Michael Jordan and the Wimbledon tennis tournament.

Licensing

Merchandising products are usually the result of a licensing process.[18] Licensing can be defined as the act of granting a second party, the licensee, the right to produce merchandise bearing an associated mark, symbol, logo or likeness.[19] The benefits of licensing, enjoyed by the licensor as well as the licensee, are two-fold. First, licensing should include protection against unauthorized, counterfeit or improper logo usage. Second, licensing provides promotion through the increase in popularity of both the sports property and the manufacturer and, ultimately, the ability to profit from merchandise sales.

Protection and control of logo usage have been identified as the fundamental benefits of establishing a licensing programme. Therefore, the logos used by sporting organizations are recognized as trademarks, permitting sporting organizations to capitalize on trademark law intended to restrain the unauthorized production and distribution of merchandise bearing these trademarks. Handtags affixed to all licensable property help the consumer identify authentically licensed merchandise. For the ice hockey world cup, held in the spring of 2003 in Finland, nine licence holders bought the rights to the official logo and the mascot of the Finnish organization (see Table 6.3) in order to use them for merchandising purposes.

Table 6.3 Official licence holders for the 2003 ice hockey world championships

Company	Products
Fanituote TJP	Carnival products
Goodgame	Textiles, mascots, toys, souvenirs
Jettaset	Flags, caps
Marja Kurki	Ties, shawls, umbrellas
Maurix	Leather articles, bottle-openers
Rahapaja	Medallions, jewellery, watches, money
Sidoste	Socks
Suomen Kuvataide	Maps
TMF-trade	Pins, keychains, magnets

Source: Based on European Association of Sport Management, Finland (2002), World championship ice hockey Finland 2003, European student management seminar, September 2002, Kannononski, Finland.

Promotion of the sports merchandise and the manufacturer through licensing is generated by the exposure of the available licensed products in the marketplace. It is plain that both Real Madrid, as licensor, and shirt sponsor Adidas, as licensee, will profit from an increased exposure of merchandise. Furthermore, licensing products can serve as a means of accessing a new market through the availability of branded products. For instance, by providing merchandise for children, a sporting organization targets the potentially (future) important 6- to 12-year-old children's market.[20] Ultimately, licensing provides an alternative stream of revenue. The sports merchandise, or licensor, derives its earnings in the form of a royalty fee – generally 6–10% of the product's wholesale price – which is charged to the licensed manufacturer.

Several types of licensing agreements between the licensor and the licensee can be distinguished. An exclusive licensing agreement enables the licensor to restrict the number of licensees producing in a particular product category or geographical region. Advantages of licensee exclusivity are a strong partnership with the licensor, easier detection of unauthorized, counterfeit merchandise, and good communication between the licensor and the licensee. Moreover, the licensee benefits from the exclusive classification as well as the limited competition. The licensor, however, runs the risk of limiting the product availability, service and creativity that often result from competitive business. On the other hand, a non-exclusive agreement entails competition among licensees within the same product category. The other side of the picture can be an oversaturation of the licensed product marketplace and an inferior quality of goods. A third type of agreement, the joint-use licensing agreement, arises when two (or more) licensors allow their logos to appear together on merchandise. Finally, promotional licensing agreements permit a licensee to use the sports property's symbols or logos in a short-term promotional campaign, for instance a premium product give-away by a fast-food restaurant. In such an agreement, the licensee is interested in making capital out of the licensor's goodwill, while both parties profit by the awareness generated.

Mini-case study – European football clubs and merchandising: the Manchester United case

Merchandising has many applications for the large football clubs in the UK, Germany, Spain and Italy. Football clubs generate income in four different ways. One important source of income comes from the media and television, including television rights and payment for the broadcasting of football games on public or pay-television stations. A second source arises from tickets sold on the day of the game and subscriptions for season tickets. A third source is the income from sponsorship, e.g. shirt sponsorship or venue branding. Finally, football clubs might also derive income from the rental of the facility (e.g. for pop concerts) and the income from catering (before, during and after football games). Income from merchandising is also included in this category. Table 6.4 presents the relative proportions of the four sources of income in the total annual income of football clubs.

Table 6.4 Proportion of sources of income for first-class football clubs in Europe, 2000-01 and 2001-02*

Country	TV rights		Tickets		Sponsorship		Merchandising, catering and stadium rental	
	2000-01	2001-02	2000-01	2001-02	2000-01	2001-02	2000-01	2001-02
England	39%	42%	31%	28%	30%	30%	-	-
Italy	54%	53%	16%	16%	13%	14%	17%	17%
Spain	51%	51%	25%	25%	9%	9%	15%	15%
Germany	45%	40%	18%	17%	22%	26%	14%	17%
France	51%	52%	16%	15%	18%	20%	15%	13%
Average	**48%**	**47%**	**21%**	**20%**	**18%**	**20%**	**12%**	**16%**
Portugal	20%		42%		18%		20%	
Netherlands	12%		34%		41%		12%	
Scotland	23%		42%		35%		-	
Denmark	4%		17%		43%		36%	
Norway	4%		40%		43%		13%	
Sweden	14%		33%		28%		25%	
Average	**13%**		**35%**		**35%**		**18%**	

*Data refer to the 2000-01 and 2001-02 seasons. Exceptions to this are Portugal and Scotland (1999-2000) and Spain (1997-1998). In England, the income from merchandising, catering and stadium rental together with sponsorship are considered as commercial income.

Source: Deloitte & Touche (2002), *Annual Review of Football Finance*. London: Deloitte & Touche; and Vandeweghe (2003), Football: grote vijf worden groter, *Sport International*, November 2003.

Nevertheless, the merchandising income, in terms of the overall club turnover, is still relatively limited. For German club Bayern Munich, for example, the merchandising income in the 1999-2000 season amounted to €11.1 million. This corresponds to 7.6% of the annual turnover. AC Milan realized €4.5 million turnover in that segment (3.1% of turnover), Juventus Turin €7.9 million (3.6% of turnover) and Borussia Dortmund €10.2 million (10.8% of turnover). Figure 6.1 shows the sources of income for England's Manchester United for the 2002-03 football season.

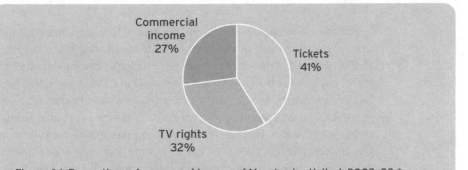

Figure 6.1 Proportions of sources of income of Manchester United, 2002–03.*
*In England, income from merchandising, catering and stadium rental together with sponsorship are considered commercial income.
Source: www.manutd.com

In the 2002–03 football season, Manchester United received 100 million euros from ticketing (41%) and 80 million euros from media (32%); 27% of the total income, or 65 million euros, can be considered as commercial income. In comparison with Italy, media do not represent a principal income source for Manchester United. Figure 6.2 illustrates the distribution of commercial income.

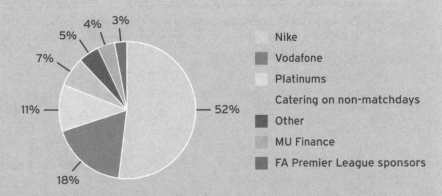

Figure 6.2 Distribution of commercial income of Manchester United, 2002–03.
Source: http://ir.manutd.com/manutd/findata/reports/.

As one of the world's football merchandising pioneers, Manchester United is connected with sports brand Nike in a 13-year multimillion-pound contract. Since August 2002, Nike holds the sponsorship, licensing and merchandising rights. Manchester United's merchandising team, Manchester United Merchandising Limited, even has its seat as a sister company in the new office blocks of Nike on Sir Matt Busby Way. During the first financial year, 3.9 million items of Nike-branded merchandise, including 2.5 million replica shirts, were sold.

Among the available merchandise, a distinction is made between the official sports equipment of the football club and products and services linked to the football brand. The first category includes the sale of specific equipment, such as football shirts and competition balls. This represents a very lucrative segment that is controlled by large sports brands such as Adidas and Nike. The second category contains all other football attributes, such as the sale of badges, rucksacks, scarves and ties marked with the club logo. The brand-stretching of large sports brands also falls under this category, i.e. the extension of the football brand to commercial activities independent of the football industry. For example, PSV Eindhoven offers group insurance, in the form of supplementary pension arrangements, and industrial accident insurance under the umbrella of its sports brand.

Even the largest European football club, Manchester United, extends its brand to financial services. Supporters can obtain a credit card of the club or open a savings account in the name of Manchester United. The club offers insurance (in collaboration with Zürich Financial Services), and a loan from the Bank of Scotland can be arranged. A significant unique selling point for merchandising is that it is not limited by national borders or language barriers. This makes the potential market much larger than that for ticket sales, which is usually limited to the club's own country. The large European clubs are angling for new growth markets, such as the Far East. In Figure 6.3, the geographical spread of merchandise sales for Manchester United in 2002–03 is shown.

Figure 6.3 Geographical spread of merchandise sales of Manchester United, 2002–03.
Source: Based on http://ir.manutd.com/manutd/findata/reports/2004.

The 2002 football World Cup tournament in Japan and South Korea provided an ideal catalyst for football brands to enter the Southeast Asian market. For example, Juventus Turin is very interested in the market potential of the Far East. Juventus planned the opening of a Juventus store in Tokyo after discovering that 20% of the visitors to the Juventus website came from

Asia. Manchester United is also exploring this growth market to the full and signed a new merchandising and licensing agreement with Japanese Sports Vision (JSV) in January 2002. JSV is the official distributor for Japan and is an important customer of Nike, the merchandising partner of Manchester United. Finally, Real Madrid developed a Japanese version of its website and toured Asia for two weeks in the summer of 2003, where the team played various demonstration games. The attraction of Asian top football players fits into this international marketing strategy for football clubs from the large football markets as well as the small football markets.

Organization of merchandising

The next question is how do sports clubs get their merchandising to the customer? The merchandising shop can be located in or outside the stadium. For example, there is a Barça-shop in Barcelona airport. Another possibility consists of channelling products through general retailers. However, the problems for clubs that secure shelf space in general retailers are that they have to split the revenue with the retailer and that they cannot control the in-store exposure that their brand gets. Also, targeting the general retail sector is time-consuming, expensive and unlikely to generate big returns. Establishing a presence in local independent sports shops is not too difficult for medium to large soccer clubs, but there are very few clubs that can secure nationwide distribution with retail multiples.

The Internet has developed into an important distribution channel. Clubs can offer replica kits, club-branded clothing, videos and DVDs and souvenirs to the whole world via their websites. The increasing importance of online stores can be illustrated by the following incident surrounding the transfer of David Beckham to Real Madrid. Within minutes of Real Madrid confirming that Beckham would play in the number 23 shirt, the domain names Beckham23.com, Becks23.com and Becks23.co.uk were all registered by an individual in the UK. Rumours of Beckham's departure from Manchester United had seen more than 75 Beckham-related domains being registered, ranging from Becksinspain.com to speculations over his shirt number, such as Beckham11.com, Beckham17.com and Beckham77.com. It was, thus, surprising that neither Beckham's agents nor Real Madrid had done anything to secure these memorable Web addresses and protect his brand in the online world. Losing these or similar Web addresses could prove to be damaging both commercially and in terms of managing Beckham's reputation online in the future.[21]

The second problem that arises is how far can a sports brand stretch? For example, Dutch club Ajax Amsterdam offers traditional merchandising articles such as replica shirts, training wear and footballs as well as new merchandising such as financial services. Less obvious products such as Ajax lunchboxes, bathing suits, rings and sunshades are also considered for merchandising.

It is clear that a sports organization can do a lot in this area. The associated danger is that clubs will 'over-merchandise' the brand, attracted by the lucrative profit margins. Over-merchandising means expanding the product range too quickly, too far and too deeply, such that the supporter becomes swamped with products. For example, Manchester United introduced six different club outfits over a period of three seasons at the end of the 1990s. It is clear that over-merchandising might upset the relationship between the sports consumer and the brand. It makes little sense to produce 15 different types of ballpen displaying the sports club logo when there is a demand for only three types. Over-merchandising is also involved when the prices of products are raised to unreasonable levels. For instance, to regulate price-fixing among competitive sports brands, the Office of Fair Trading in the UK was called in during the second half of the 1990s. This illustrates that the profiling of a sports brand as a passion brand does not mean that supporters will be prepared to pay any price. Involving fans in the development of a product line is therefore a success factor in merchandising. This increases the supporters' feeling of involvement in the club and reveals a lot about market demand. One example comes from the English Premier League football club Leicester City, which developed a customer-based product line in consultation with its supporters.[22] Consequently, the merchandising income rose from about €407000 in 1991 to €3.91 million in 2000.

6.7 Summary

Usually, sports sponsorship works indirectly and in the long term. However, supplementing sports sponsorship with sales promotional campaigns might result in short-run effects. Promotional activities are characterized by their temporary nature and the immediate behavioural response that they elicit. Along with the generation of direct sales, sponsorship-driven sales promotion might also be employed to support sales and improve brand loyalty. Despite these clear objectives, promotions should be used sparingly because they might not only elicit competitive campaigns but also give a brand a 'cheap' image, making the brand appear to be of a lower quality. Additionally, promotions could also undermine the effect of a strategic sponsorship that tries to build long-term brand-image effects.

In order to increase sales in the short term, a number of specific tools of sponsorship-related sales promotions can be used. Employed regularly in the leverage of sports sponsorship are (a combination of) discounts, product promotions and competitions. There are also many examples of integrated PR and action communication at the point of sales, e.g. the presence of a sponsored top athlete at the opening of a new retail outlet. Sports sponsorship can be developed via sales promotions not only in consumer markets but also in business-to-business circles through trade fairs and personal selling.

Sampling, or handing out samples, is a very popular technique of sales promotion in a sporting environment. Sampling consists of distributing a free or very-low-priced product, which is usually specially packaged. In a sporting environment, sampling is interesting because the consumer is stimulated to consume the product at the right moment in an environment filled with strong emotions. Merchandising is also a popular technique of action communication in sport. In the sport and media worlds, merchandising is described as the sale of a wide range of products or services carrying the logo and the name of a sports brand. For European football clubs, merchandising already has important applications.

Key terms

Action communications
Brand equity
Cash refund
Consumer brand equity
Contest
Discount
Financial brand equity
Licence
Licensee
Licensor
Lottery
Merchandising
Monetary incentives
One-to-one-marketing
Over-merchandising
Personal selling
Point-of-purchase communications
Point-of-sales communications
Premium
Royalty
Sales promotions
Sampling
Savings card
Self-liquidating premium
Trade promotions

Questions

1. Visit the official website of Manchester United (www.manutd.com). How is the merchandising range presented? Describe how e-commerce is encouraged.

2. Locate some sales promotion tools employed in the leverage of a sports sponsorship programme. Discuss the relative importance of product promotions, discounts and competitions.

3. Give additional examples of sponsorship-related point-of-sales and trade-fair communications.

4. Describe your experiences as a consumer with sampling in both a sporting and a non-sporting context.

Endnotes

1 De Pelsmacker, P., Geuens, M. and Van den Bergh, J. (2002), *Marketing Communications*. Harlow: Pearson Education.
2 Pope, N. and Turco, D. (2001), *Sport and Event Management*. Roseville, NSW: McGraw-Hill.
3 Easton, S. and Mackie, P. (1998), When football came home: a case history of the sponsorship activity at Euro '96, *International Journal of Advertising*, 17(1), 99–114.
4 De Pelsmacker, P., Geuens, M. and van den Bergh, J. (2004), *Marketing Communications. A European Perspective*. Harlow: FT Prentice Hall.
5 De Pelsmacker *et al.* (2004), op cit.
6 De Pelsmacker *et al.* (2004), op cit.
7 Adfo Specialists Group (2000), Euro 2000: het geld, de koorts en het rendement. In: *Adfo Sponsorship Cases*, no. 7. Alpen aan den Rijn: Samsom, pp. 7–34.
8 De Pelsmacker *et al.* (2004), op cit.
9 Lagae, W. and Baccarne, J. (2002), De inzet van sportsponsorship in de marketingcommunicatie van Daewoo en Hyundai. In: Van Tilborgh, C. and Duyck, R. (eds), *Marketingjaarboek* 2002. Zellik: Kluwer.
10 De Pelsmacker *et al.* (2004), op cit.
11 Pope and Turco (2001), op cit.
12 Floor, J. and van Raaij, F. (2002), *Marketing-communicatiestrategie*. Groningen: Wolters-Noordhoff.
13 Irwin, L., Sutton, W. and McCarthy, L. (2002), *Sport Promotion and Sales Management*. Champaign, IL: Human Kinetics.
14 De Pelsmacker *et al.* (2004), op cit.
15 Miyazaki, A. (2001), Assessing market value of event sponsorship: corporate Olympic sponsorships, *Journal of Advertising Research*, 41(1).
   Miyazaki discovered a significant increase in the market value of an organization after the announcement of an Olympic sponsorship agreement.

16 De Pelsmacker *et al.* (2004), op cit.
17 Gillis, R. (2002), Branded good, *Sport Business International*, 70, 32–4.
18 Pope and Turco (2001), op cit.
19 Irwin *et al.* (2002), op cit.
20 *Football Business International* (2003), Beyond the megastore, *Football Business International*, August 2003.
21 *Sportbusiness International* (2003), Real domain for Becks, *Sportbusiness International*, August 2003.
22 Pierpoint, B. (2002), Clubs bank on retail therapy, *Football Business International*, March 2002.

Case 6 The sampling strategy of the sports drink Aquarius

Key learning points

After studying this case, you will be able to:

- illustrate the importance of marketing communications of sport;
- discuss sports sponsorship leverage through sampling;
- elaborate a sampling strategy for a fast-moving consumer good.

Introduction

In the 1980s, a century after The Coca-Cola Company was created, a new phenomenon appeared in the strongly dominated soft-drinks market: the sports drink. In the USA, Powerade was Coca-Cola's answer to the already successful Gatorade, a drink created in Florida and named after an American football team. In the first half of the 1990s, Gatorade came to Europe and The Coca-Cola Company quickly had to find another sports drink to construct a dam against its threat. This sports drink was Aquarius, a drink that The Coca-Cola Company had already introduced to the Japanese market. In Japan, Aquarius was not specifically advertised as a sports drink, but rather as a type of leisure drink, e.g. to be consumed after bathing, a very popular activity in the Japanese culture. During the 1992 Olympic Games in Barcelona, Aquarius was launched in Europe. Two years later, the sports drink was introduced into the Belgian market.

The sports drinks market

A sports drink is described as 'a healthy or stimulating drink, often enjoyed after sports activities in sports schools'. Market research has revealed, however, that only 13% of sports drinks are drunk during and immediately after sporting activities (see Table 6.5). This implies that the greatest competition to Aquarius comes from outside the market segment of sports drinks.

However, the boundary between what is and what is not a sports drink is rather vague. An energy drink provides extra energy, a sports drink compensates faster for what is lost during sporting activities, and a soft drink is a refreshing, non-alcoholic drink. In certain statistical analyses, high-caffeine 'energy drinks' are included with the sports drinks, which may produce a distorted image.

Table 6.5 Consumption of drinks during and immediately after sporting activities

Drink	%
Sports drinks	13
Water	33
Iced tea	20
Other drinks	34

Source: Heijl, M. (2000), *De marketingcommunicatiemix van het 'sportmerk' Aquarius in België*, final thesis, Master of Sports Management. Brussels: Vlekho Business School.

It is evident from Figure 6.4 that the market for sports drinks is growing. Sports drinks have three unique advantages. First, they contain a small amount of salt and an adjusted amount of carbohydrates, which allows them to pass through the intestinal wall and be taken up into the blood more rapidly. Second, a sports drink provides energy. During sporting activity, the body creates power by burning fats and carbohydrates. There are usually sufficient fat reserves in the human body, but it is possible to run out of carbohydrates. Aquarius contains between 6 and 8% carbohydrates, sufficient to replenish the energy reserves; a higher percentage is not advisable because it would inhibit gastric transit and the drink would not be taken up as rapidly by the blood. Third, sports drinks are not fizzy and, thus, are easy to digest; therefore, they do not produce intestinal or gastric symptoms if drunk during sporting activities.

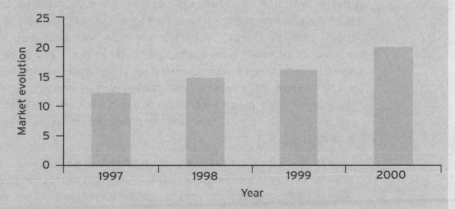

Figure 6.4 Growth of the market for sports drinks in Belgium (millions of litres).
Source: Heijl, M. (2000), *De marketingcommunicatiemix van het 'sportmerk' Aquarius in België*, final thesis, Master of Sports Management. Brussels: Vlekho Business School.

Other statistics indicate that the sports drink category grew 13-fold between 1991 and 2002. Aquarius has a growing share of the expanding market of sports drinks. In 1994, that market share was 40%; in 2000, the market share of Aquarius in Belgium was 58% (see Figure 6.5).

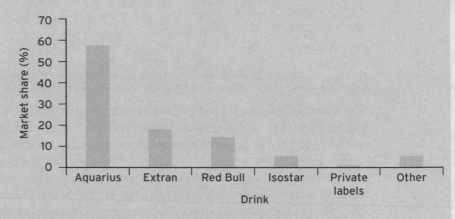

Figure 6.5 Market share of Aquarius and other drnks in 2000
Source: Heijl, M. (2000), *De marketingcommunicatiemix van het 'sportmerk' Aquarius in België*, final thesis, Master of Sports Management. Brussels: Vlekho Business School.

Despite the lack of clearly defined data about the market for sports drinks, we can conclude that Aquarius is unmistakably a successful product with a growing market share in an expanding market segment. Six per cent of the population aged between 12 and 49 years drink Aquarius daily, while 11% of the population drink it weekly. These numbers are very low in comparison with the market leaders in the USA and Australia, where the consumption of sports drinks per capita is three times and twice as much, respectively. In Anglo Saxon countries, sport has a more prominent place in society, and hence the sports drinks market is in a more advanced phase of development than in continental European countries. Aquarius wants to position itself in this market environment. The mission statement of Aquarius claims:

Aquarius is a drink for recreational athletes, when practising sports, who want to bring fun and pleasure to their lives. Aquarius is the beverage for sports thirst, that brings them physically and mentally back in balance, allowing them to have fun, feel alive and relieve tension through sports. Because only Aquarius provides:

1 rapid thirst quenching and body replenishment, sustaining effort and aiding recovery
2 with a unique and great taste.

Aquarius is distributed through traditional food channels (60%). Sports centres (30%) are the central distribution channel. This is where the authority of the product is fostered among opinion leaders and the target group. In this way, the consumer becomes acquainted with the fun, pleasant taste and healthy aspect of Aquarius. This is essential for the brand and is one of the most important underlying reasons for the 'Aquarius Challenge', the cornerstone of the success of Aquarius, which was based on sampling the product.

Strategy and practical elaboration of the sampling

Sampling intends to achieve two effects. First, Aquarius wanted to acquaint the target group with the benefits of consuming the sports drink (good taste, thirst-quenching and refreshing) at the right moment. One unique advantage of the drink lies in its consumption during or after intensive 'hot and sweaty' sports. Second, the Coca-Cola group wanted to establish Aquarius as a strong brand in the sports drinks segment.

To support the brand's authority, a strong and active presence was required at sporting events, which had to meet three criteria:

- an intensive, 'hot and sweaty' nature;

- no high sensation, risk or adventure content;

- corresponds with the target group of the sports brand (young and dynamic men and women).

In 1999 and 2000, some 390 and 480 sporting events, respectively, met the Aquarius criteria. This led to 500 000 contact moments between athletes and Aquarius in 1999 via sampling. Each sampling activity of Aquarius usually consists of three parts. First, the sports drink is given away free, which is ultimately the essence of sampling. Then the communication carriers of the brand are specifically positioned at the sports event. For example, every sampling opportunity was announced by a poster placed 100 metres before an Aquarius stand, announcing: 'Don't give up! Only 100 metres more to earn a free Aquarius drink!' Other communication carriers mentioning the brand name and the logo of Aquarius included banners, coolers, flags, posters and inflatables. Finally, an Aquarius event was created inside the sporting event. By organizing the Aquarius Challenge, an extra competition inside the sporting event, the sports drink became distinctive. Because several sponsors are active at sporting events, Aquarius intended to use this to reduce the risk of displacement in the multisponsor environment.

Integration of sampling in the strategy of sports sponsorship communication

The Aquarius Challenge was the key element in the sports sponsorship programme of the sports drink. The Aquarius Challenge consisted of an integrated sports programme that was intended to ensure the presence of the drink at every sporting level in the Belgian sporting world. Aquarius was put in the spotlight at various sporting moments, ultimately to increase the sales of the sports drink. Table 6.6 lists the five phases of the sampling process.

Table 6.6 Phases in the sampling process

Phase	Aim
I see	To improve familiarity with the brand by being actively and repetitively present at sports events
I feel	To acquaint the athlete with the brand; the emphasis lies primarily on the drink's taste and benefits
I like	To achieve a positive attitude in the athlete with regard to the sports drink
I switch	Attention is transferred from the sporting event to the shop by means of sales material linked to the sport at the point of sale
I buy	To sell the sports drink

In the Aquarius Challenge, five different sponsorship programmes are distinguished: sports federations, professional sporting events, top athletes, recreational sports people, and young people. Each level has its own function and interpretation. Joint projects are set up with the sports federations, which enables both sampling and the use of visible communication carriers of Aquarius. At professional sporting events, the aim is to achieve a prominent presence for Aquarius on the sports terrain. The use of the sports drink by top athletes is essential in connection with their role as brand ambassadors. On the one hand, the top athletes consume Aquarius as celebrity endorsers. On the other, they are employed as speakers or special guests at sporting events. For Belgium, Aquarius selected Frederik Deburghgraeve (swimming, Olympic Gold Medal winner 1996), Luc Van Lierde (triathlon, twice Iron Man winner), Ulla Werbrouck (judo, Olympic Gold Medal winner 1996), Jonathan Nsenga (athletics), Kim Clijsters (tennis, number one in women's tennis 2003) and Yseult Gervy (swimming). Finally, recreational sports people and youths are approached through sampling and communication carriers at events.

The programme does not target all sports. The Aquarius Challenge concentrates on 'pillar sports', along with a number of important recreational events. A pillar sport is one:

- in which athletes want to excel;

- in which top athletes excel;

- that receives extensive media attention;

- in which many athletes participate.

Based on these criteria, cycling, hiking, swimming, fitness, jogging, mountain-biking, triathlon, judo and athletics were selected.

Effectiveness of the sampling action

The sampling strategy of Aquarius appears to have worked very well. Research, the most important results of which are given in Table 6.7, has revealed a statistically significant difference between groups that participated and those that did not participate in the Aquarius Challenge. In particular, a positive link can be demonstrated between participation in Aquarius events and brand familiarity, brand preference, purchasing frequency and brand image. After the sampling action, the purchasing intention of participants in the Aquarius Challenge amounted to 52%, an increase of 13% over the level before the action.

Table 6.7 Link between Aquarius events and key indicators

	Participated in Aquarius event (%)	Did not participate in Aquarius event (%)
Aided brand familiarity (Aquarius)	94	87
Assisted brand familiarity (Orange, assisted)	83*	66
Preference	40	32
Several times per week	38*	11
Never	42*	68
Purchasing intention	52*	22
For active people	48	42
For people like me	51	43
For sociable and extrovert people	35*	19

*Statistically significant difference between the two groups.
Source: Heijl, M. (2000), *De marketingcommunicatiemix van het 'sportmerk' Aquarius in België*, final thesis, Master of Sports Management. Brussels: Vlekho Business School.

The Aquarius Challenge sampling programme has achieved more than just introducing Aquarius into the market; it has also created a very successful product. In a period of five years, sales volume tripled, the Aquarius range took over 64% of the sports drinks market, and Aquarius realized a brand familiarity of 97% among athletes (figures from 2002). After the successful launch, the brand continuously renewed itself. In the midst of a developing market, this primarily meant product innovation for Aquarius.

In 1997, Aquarius introduced a second flavour on to the market, Orange. Orange grew immediately to become the most popular flavour and is a favourite primarily with the younger market. In 1999, the grapefruit flavour was introduced, which appealed more to women. Later, kiwi-watermelon–galangal and orange–carrot were added, which aimed to capitalize on the health and wellness trend. The five different flavours of the Aquarius range motivate the athlete to drink sufficient fluids thanks to the generous variety and choice. In addition, The Coca-Cola Company introduced Aquana Sportwater to the market along with the five flavours of Aquarius. Aquana is a specially prepared water for athletes, with zero calories, five vitamins, minerals and a light refreshing taste.

As well as the new flavours, there were other innovations, such as packaging in a squeezable sports bottle with a sports top. Also, the look of the Aquarius range was restyled. The Olympic rings remained the central focus, as in the original Aquarius packaging. This logo is accompanied by the message that Aquarius is the 'Official Sports Drink of the Olympic Games'. This association with one of the world's strongest logos and with the world's greatest sporting event is an extra trump card for Aquarius, which is not only made clear on the packaging but also is utilized in a number of other forms of communication around the brand. It helps the sports drink to identify with top sport and quality, and it helps to create a clean image around the brand.

Gradually, the marketing approach is being modified further. Along with sampling, which made the brand great, an extensive marketing communication through television spots was established. This gradual transition to above-the-line communication, however, does not disguise the fact that the success of Aquarius had little to do with theme advertisement and far more to do with action advertisement in the form of sampling or experiential marketing. Ironically, all this concerns a subsidiary brand of Coca-Cola, the world's strongest marketing brand, which owes its greatness to classical above-the-line communication.

Questions for discussion

1. Discuss an alternative sponsorship development strategy for Aquarius, with theme communications instruments such as advertising and PR being central channels.

2. What bottlenecks could arise in the execution of the sampling strategy of Aquarius? How far should one go to account for this kind of unforeseen circumstance in a sponsorship communications plan?

3. Imagine you are responsible for the sponsorship of Red Bull. What sports sponsorship form would you select? How would you develop this sports sponsorship from a communicative point of view?

References and further reading

De Pelsmacker, P., Geuens, M. and van den Bergh, J. (2004), *Marketing Communications*, 2nd edn. Harlow: Pearson Education.

Frank, J. (1995), Hot spots, *Beverage Industry*, 86 (4), 58–9.

Gardner, R. (2003), Strategy of the week: Liptonicetea, *Campaign*, 24.

Hargrave-Silk, A. (2003), Nestea lines up for $1.3m for ice Rush's HK entry, *Media Asia*.

Heijl, M. (2000), *De marketingcommunicatiemix van het 'sportmerk' Aquarius in België*, final thesis, Master of Sports Management. Brussels: Vlekho Business School.

Lefton, T. (1998), Pepsi steps up to the plate with youth sampling tied to MLB deal, *Brandweek*, 39 (8).

Thompson, S. (2000), Pepsi favors sampling over ads for fruit drink, *Advertising Age*, 71 (4).

7

THE EFFECTIVENESS OF SPORTS SPONSORSHIP COMMUNICATIONS

You miss 100% of the shots you never take *(Johan Cruyff)*

Overview

Ambush marketing in the sponsorship clutter

Exposure

Communication results

Commercial results

Aims

After studying this chapter, you will be able to:

● detect and block ambush marketing;

● evaluate the media value of sports sponsorship;

● measure the communication results of sports sponsorship;

● evaluate when it makes sense and how to measure the commercial results of sports sponsorship.

7.0 Introduction

Communication managers are measured against the returns from all instruments employed in the communication mix. Even sponsorship does not escape this estimate of their effectiveness. Too often, sponsorship is still being evaluated through the sports sponsorship manager's intuition or personal interpretation. Ideally, clear objectives must first be formulated, and time and budget for the evaluation phase reserved, before the start of the sponsorship project. In practice, this rarely happens. Research conducted by the European Sponsorship Consulting Agency discovered that at least 32% of sponsorship decision-makers do not allocate money to research, while 48% spend less than 1% of the rights fee on research.[1]

In this final chapter, the effect of sports sponsorship communication will be evaluated from the sponsor's viewpoint. Ambush marketing represents a nasty threat to official sponsors because their exclusivity, and thus their effectiveness, is undermined (Section 7.1). Three types of sponsorship effectiveness can be measured: exposure, communication and commercial results. A crude evaluation tool for the effectiveness of sponsorship awareness is media exposure measurement (Section 7.2). A stronger test for sponsorship accountability is the measurement of the communication results (Section 7.3). Moreover, in selected cases and under very strict conditions, the effectiveness of sponsorship can be assessed by estimating the commercial results (Section 7.4). However, usually, sponsorship measurement seems to cope with serious limitations.

7.1 Ambush marketing in the sponsorship clutter

Ambush marketing concerns tactics used by brand competitors to spoil official sports sponsorship activation campaigns. An example of ambush marketing is the conflict between private bank and insurance company Delta Lloyd Belgium and Kim Clijsters. Delta Lloyd Belgium, main sponsor of the Flemish Tennis

Federation (VTV), designed an advertisement around Kim Clijsters's first Grand Slam final at Roland Garros in 2001. Delta Lloyd neglected, however, to negotiate the portrait rights of Clijsters with the International Management Group (IMG), Clijsters's sports-management agency at that time. Despite the fact that this advertisement, which was printed in the weekend editions of the Flemish newspapers, won public awards, IMG threatened to take Delta Lloyd to court. After mediation by the VTV, the case was settled out of court.

Sandler and Shani describe ambush marketing as '... a planned effort by an organisation to associate themselves indirectly with an event in order to gain at least some of the recognition and benefits that are associated with being an official sponsor ...'[2] In ambush marketing, a brand profits from the image of the sport without paying the appropriate sponsorship costs. The ambusher wants to deceive the public into thinking that it paid for the sponsorship rights linked to the association possibilities. Synonyms for ambush marketing are guerilla, parasite[3] and vigilante marketing.[4]

Outline 7.1 Types of ambush marketing

- Advertising ambush
- Sales promotion ambush
- Spectator ambush
- Event-competitor ambush
- PR ambush

An ambushing organization employs several promotional tactics in order to confuse the consumer regarding its application status.[5] The ambush can take many forms: advertising, sales promotion, public relations (PR), spectator and event-competitor[6] ambushing (see Outline 7.1). Advertising ambush is probably the most calculated form of all and aptly illustrates the shady aspect of ambush marketing. It is not forbidden to take advantage of strongly mediatized or unique events, such as a royal wedding or the triumphs of a national football team. For example, American Express's campaign in the 1994 Winter Olympics (sponsored by VISA) featured the slogan 'If you are travelling to Lillehammer, you will need a passport but you don't need a Visa!'[7] Examples of sales promotional ambush tactics include sampling actions at or around an event for which no rights have been bought and distributing flyers along the course (see Table 7.1).

Table 7.1 Techniques of advertising and sales promotion ambush

Technique	Example
Coordinating advertisement campaigns to the duration of the sport project	Euro 2000: Daewoo (ambusher) (official sponsor Hyundai) - advertising ambush
Collaborating with the media sponsors	Belgian soccer prizes 2004: Nivea (ambusher) (official sponsor Rexona) - advertising ambush
Creating advertising campaigns	Delta Lloyd Belgium (federation sponsor; ambush brand) versus Kim Clijsters - advertising ambush
Owning former sports personalities in advertising campaigns	Nike (ambusher) and Michael Johnson - advertising ambush
Distributing flags, baseball caps or flyers along the course or in the stadium	Nike (ambusher) - around events officially sponsored by Adidas - PR ambush
Carrying out sampling actions without permission	Red Bull Belgium (ambusher) - sales promotional ambush

Spectator ambush marketing tactics of non-official sponsors include having displays outside the venue or along the track or giving away merchandise. For example, Belgian supporters were not admitted to the stadium during a World Cup football game in the Japanese city of Saitama because they were wearing caps emblazoned with the Belgian beer brand Jupiler (a brand of the American brewer Anheuser-Busch).[8] Because care was taken to ensure that no brand other than official World Cup 2002 sponsor Budweiser was present in or around the stadiums, the Jupiler logo of the Belgian supporters had to be covered. The story of a group of Chinese supporters all wearing Samsung caps is similar: Samsung is a competitor of the official World Cup sponsor Philips.

Event competitor ambush marketing consists of an ambusher who is connected only indirectly with the event taking over the communication options of a more highly placed sponsor. For instance, the team sponsor of the Spanish cyclist Miguel Indurain, who won the Tour de France five times, was Banesto. However, this team sponsor crowded out the main official event sponsor, Crédit Lyonnais.

Finally, PR ambush tactics consist of the improper exploitation of hospitality possibilities. At the FIFA World Cup in France 1998, Nike set up its alternative Nike Village in Paris near to the official sponsor's village. An example of this is the guerilla or ambush marketing between Nike, apparel sponsor of national football teams and individual athletes, and Adidas, the official sponsor of international football tournaments. During Euro 2000, the organizers attempted to safeguard the rights of the official sponsors by refusing ambushers the right to conduct promotional actions within a radius of three kilometres around the stadium.

Ambush marketing prospers even more if there are many sponsor categories or if there is a large group of sponsors per category (Outline 7.2). Ambush marketing also arises if the sponsorship is not distinctive enough. Additionally, excessively strict exclusivity rules could limit the number of official sponsors and motivate ambushers to grab something from the sporting event. Ingenious ambush concepts include indirect references to the event in advertising.

Outline 7.2 When does ambush marketing appear?

- Wide variety of categories of sponsors
- Many sponsors per category
- High official sponsorship rights
- Inadequate exploitation by official sponsors
- Limited number of sponsors admitted to a sporting project
- Pooling of different categories of sponsors
- Peripheral events outside the central event

Ambush marketing makes it difficult for the official sponsor to develop its sponsor investment maximally, because ambushers match the duration of their communication campaign to the duration of the sporting event. The problem with this is that the medal rights belong not to the personal sponsors of the win-ning athlete but to the organization and the official event sponsors. This is why official sport sponsors should be wary of any dilution of their efforts as a result of the aggressive behaviour of ambushers.

However, the legal battle against ambushers is not straightforward. Since ambush brands operate in a grey zone, clever ambushers can and will avoid using the official symbols and brands in their campaigns. In addition, an ambush cam-paign is usually short and unique. However, the complaint and the subsequent legal procedure could take a long time, which tends to discourage the victim from pressing charges in court, especially if the incident was small. Nevertheless, several legal cases have been fought. Ansett, official airline sponsor of the Olympic Games 2000, issued a summons against its competitor Qantas. Ansett had paid up to 30 million euros to be the official airline for the Sydney 2000 Olympic Games. However, Qantas ran an advertising campaign that featured close-ups of various athletes accompanied by the words 'Spirit of Australia'. This won Qantas about 44% consumer recognition, compared with 27% consumer recognition for competitor Ansett.[9] The courts declared Qantas to be in the wrong and forced the company to report in a disclaimer that it was not an Olympic sponsor.

Certainly in Europe, the legal aspects have to be developed further because there are few legal precedents. In the Netherlands, for example, a judge decided in summary proceedings that Daewoo's ambush campaign did not have to be stopped. To take advantage of the football fever in the Netherlands, and not to lose ground to Hyundai, the official Euro 2000 sponsor, Daewoo created an ambush campaign during Euro 2000. Against a background of ecstatic football players, Daewoo communicated that a customer would receive a discount of 2000 euros when buying a new car. Nevertheless, the judge pronounced that this advertisement was not a transgression on the registered brand Euro 2000.

Blocking ambushers is therefore a more efficient strategy than taking legal action (Outline 7.3). Protecting sports sponsorship investments can take different forms. Ambush could be countered by making use of unique and clear brand symbols and logos of the official sponsors. A clear exclusivity plan for official partners will make it very difficult for ambushers to break the association between sponsor and sport. An exclusivity action plan could imply, among other things, a ranking of exclusivity rights and assignment of a negotiating range to sponsorship items that require exclusivity.[10] A sponsor protection committee, directed by competent sports lawyers, is another tool for blocking ambushers. Finally, professional leverage of sponsorship rights might discourage ambush brands from their spoiling activities.

Outline 7.3 How to block ambushers

- Use unique logos and brand names for official sponsors

- Make clear exclusivity agreements

- Form a sponsor protection committee

- Official sponsors elaborate integrated sponsorship communication:

    - (exchange) media campaign for official sponsors

    - organize associated events for official sponsors

    - encourage pooling between official sponsors

Ambush shows how complex the sports environment can be in which the sponsors have to operate. Ambush adds clutter to the situation, weakening the branding opportunities and benefits for the sponsor. Ideally, event organizers must ambush the ambush marketers by taking away the main incentive: a confused consumer (see Outline 7.4).[11] Successful ambush strategies feed on ill-conceived sponsorships (complex multisponsor environments) and inept sponsors (inadequate communication in sports sponsorship, inadequate fit between the sport and the brand). Sports sponsorship confusion is due mainly to the complexity of the multisponsor environment.

Outline 7.4 Reasons for low effectiveness of sports sponsorship

- Inadequate communication in sports sponsorship

- Complex multisponsor environment

- Inadequate fit between sport and brand

- Ambush marketing

7.2 Exposure

As mentioned previously, ambush marketing tactics could hinder the effectiveness of official sports sponsorship, because ambush marketing campaigns are likely to add clutter to the situation, which may weaken the exposure and leverage possibilities for official sponsors. The existence of ambush marketers seems to be an extra argument for official sponsors to analyse the effectiveness of their campaigns. Three types of sponsorship effectiveness measurement can be distinguished (see Outline 7.5): measurement of exposure, communication results and commercial results.

Outline 7.5 Types of sports sponsorship effectiveness evaluation

- Media exposure measures (see Section 7.2)

- Monitor changes in communications indicators (see Section 7.3)

- Monitor changes in commercial indicators (see Section 7.4)

The most controversial method is exposure measurement. Two main techniques are included in the group of exposure-based measurement methods of sponsorship effects (see Outline 7.6): estimating direct and indirect audiences, and monitoring the quantity and nature of the media exposure obtained for the sponsorship property.[12] Sponsorship is largely a mute medium.[13] Given the fact that signage is often limited to a brand logo and name (non-verbal), one could argue that the effectiveness of sports sponsorship is based on the mere exposure effect.[14] This means that increased familiarity with the brand as a result of exposure to a sponsor's name generates a preference for the brand.[15] In addition, the sponsorship stimulus jogs the consumer's brand memory or can cause the consumer to remember the brand when shopping.

Outline 7.6 Exposure-based methods of sponsorship evaluation

- Estimating brand exposure to direct and indirect attendances

- Measuring brand exposure in the media

Media evaluation is the measurement of television, radio, press and Internet exposure resulting from sports sponsorship.[16] There are specialized sponsorship agencies that will conduct media evaluation, such as International Events Group, Sponsorship Consulting (SLC),[17] IFM[18] and Sports Marketing Surveys.[19] These sponsorship agencies have developed independently a model in order to arrive at a value for the advertising equivalent of publicity (AEP), based on the media rate card.

Evaluation of TV coverage is usually done by noting the exact duration of time that the sponsor's brand name is seen on the screen.[20] Some agencies assume that the sponsor's brand name or logo needs to be 75% visible for at least one second.[21] AEPs evaluate the seconds of exposure on the basis of relevant TV audience data (audience levels, profiles and ratings). Next, seconds of exposure are weighted according to figures relating to cost per thousand per 30 seconds on each channel on which the sponsorship appears.[22] The relevant impact of the screen sponsorship images is also taken into account. For example, a brand name on perimeter boards could be weighted 0.1, logos on clothing 0.2 and text on screen 0.4.[23]

An interesting case study of sponsor communication involves the Korean car brand Hyundai, which has been establishing and expanding strong relations with sport. By linking itself to Euro 2000, Hyundai wanted to:

- build strong brand identity associated with world-class football;

- increase and optimize sales;

- strengthen the morale and pride of the Hyundai Motor Company family;

- kick off its FIFA World Cup Japan–South Korea sponsorship 2002 programme in Europe successfully.

Through the communications from Euro 2000, the brand name and the logo of Hyundai were associated continuously with the logos of world brands such as Coca-Cola, McDonald's and PlayStation. During Euro 2000, Hyundai kept the brand permanently in the spotlight and conducted a strong promotion campaign. For example, an international football-oriented television and billboard campaign for the Hyundai models Athos, Coupé and Accent was conducted between May and June 2000.

In all venues, the Hyundai brand was exposed to 1 202 250 spectators through four perimeter boards installed at each side of the pitch. Through TV broadcasting, the Hyundai brand was exposed for six hours, 18 minutes and one second across 31 matches, or an average of 12 minutes and 12 seconds per match. The brand exposure of the Hyundai brand name amounted to 153 hours, six minutes and 23 seconds for the coverage in only 26 European countries. This figure could be interpreted to have $240 million visualized media value in Europe, based on one-seventh of the advertising value of media buys during Euro 2000.

The presence of a sponsorship object in the printed media is another important component of visibility. This includes the visibility of the sponsorship brand name in general daily newspapers, weekly periodicals and the specialized press. Reporting of the sponsor's name in an editorial context (text and title mentioned) and its presence on photos and captions are recorded. Just like the auditory reinforcement of a brand name in the audiovisual media, a printed recording of the sponsor's name is positive for a sponsor.

AEPs can provide useful information on year-on-year comparisons, on comparisons with competing sponsors or properties, and on maximizing future exposure. However, media exposure evaluation is the subject of considerable debate within the sports sponsorship industry. Although often used by business, exposure-based methods have been heavily criticized.[24] There are substantial limitations to measures of exposure, since these frequently inflate the real value of AEP. Typically, article length is equated with advertising space, even though the sponsor's name may be mentioned occasionally in the article.[25] Another source of inflation is that when quantifying the AEP the maximum rate card value is assumed, while few organizations have to pay these full rates. Furthermore, the question also arises as to how verbal mentions of brand names, the tone of the broadcast, and specific positive or negative references to the sponsorship or property should be weighted. Also, the frequency and reach of exposure may give an indication only of the probability of having contacted the target group and nothing about the quality or impact of the contact.[26]

7.3 Communication results

In the case of brand tracking, the brand itself is the subject whose effect is being measured.[27] This provides information with which to measure the effect of the integrated sports sponsorship communication. Brand tracking is difficult, however, since the main problem with the evaluation of sports sponsorship is differentiation of its effect from the impact of advertising and other promotional techniques.[28] Isolating sports sponsorship and its communication forms is made difficult by:[29, 30]

- simultaneous use of other marketing and communications mix variables;
- carry-over effects of earlier marketing (communications) activities;
- the pursuit of multiple objectives;
- the complex relation between sponsorship rights and communication;
- the indirect and implicit nature of sports sponsorship;
- uncontrollable environmental factors.

Setting measurable objectives

Sponsorship testing, if used effectively, starts with measurable objectives at the outset of the sponsorship decision. According to Stotlar, sponsorship should begin answering the crucial question, 'Did the sponsorship accomplish our objectives?' and has to stop asking the question, 'What did the sponsorship do?'[31] Indeed, it is a challenge to convert non-quantifiable objectives into quantifiable objectives (see Table 7.2 for an example). However, setting sponsorship objectives is not enough. Some objectives may be much harder to quantify empirically, which does not imply that they are any less valid. Examples of difficult-to-quantify sponsorship objectives include improvements in employee relationships and in the relationships with the neighbourhood of the organization.

Table 7.2 Replacing non-quantifiable objectives with quantifiable sponsorship objectives

Non-quantifiable sponsorship objective	Quantifiable sponsorship objective
Increase brand awareness	Increase aided brand awareness from 27% to 45% by the end of the rugby season
Change brand image	Increase the values of winning, team spirit and flexibility
Increase employee motivation	Reduce job-changing by employees by 20% on a year-by-year basis
Increase sales	Create incremental sales of 20% during the four-week sponsorship-related sales promotional action

Sponsorship awareness

An extension of exposure measurement is measurement of sponsorship aware-ness. In this type of test, a list of sponsored properties is presented to a sample of the target group, who are asked to name (aided or unaided) the sponsors of the property. A good example is Flora and the London Marathon. Flora is a popular low-fat spread in the UK. It is positioned as being a healthy alternative to butter. Apart from achieving opportunities for visibility and saliency, one of the key objectives of the sponsorship of the London Marathon is, for those aware of the sponsorship, to link Flora to the general message of 'healthy' (see Kolah (2003)).

Sponsorship-related ad awareness

Developing upon previous work, the Hyundai Motor Company (HMC) also evaluated the communications effects of their sponsorship activities during Euro 2000 by comparing their advertisements with those of other sponsors. The ad-tracking study had a coverage of six countries, including Belgium, the Netherlands, Germany, the UK, Spain and Italy. The target group comprised males and females aged 20–59 years, with a quota by gender set on a nation-wide sample of 70% male and 30% female, expected in accordance with the population of the target group. The study consisted of two waves of telephone interviewing for quota by gender. The first wave was organized before the start of Euro 2000 (end of April) and the second wave took place right after the final match (early July). A total of 3000 interviews were executed, 500 for each country.

The advertisement recall rate in the second wave of advertisement tracking appeared to be much higher than that in the first wave. The unaided recall rate increased to 6% from 1%, and the aided recall rate increased to 69% from 59%. In

Belgium and Holland, these changes appeared to be much higher than in other countries: unaided recall in the Netherlands increased to 13% from 6%, while aided recall in Belgium increased to 46% from 36%. In the evaluation of the advertisements, a change of the Hyundai image could be noticed with respect to the values 'advanced technology', 'durable', 'innovative' and 'familiar'.

Brand awareness

While sponsorship awareness measures do not answer the crucial question of whether organizations succeeded in accomplishing their communications objectives, a more reliable test is being provided by brand awareness testing. The official sponsors of the European football championships in 1996 were Carlsberg, Canon, Coca-Cola, Fujifilm, General Motors, JVC, McDonald's, MasterCard, Philips, Snickers and Umbro. Table 7.3 lists the changes in aided brand awareness or brand recognition of the sponsoring brands in July 1996 compared with the benchmark in November 1995. Euro '96 increased the brand awareness of the official sponsors by 12% on average. Primarily in the Russian Federation and in Germany, there was a strong increase in perceived awareness of the brands; in France, the increase in brand perception was limited to 4%.[32]

Table 7.3 Impact of sponsorship (development) of Euro '96 sponsors on brand awareness

	Change in aided brand awareness (%)
All countries	+ 12
UK	+ 13
France	+ 4
Germany	+ 15
Russian Federation	+ 16

Source: Easton, S. and Mackie, P. (1998), When football came home: a case history of the sponsorship activity at Euro '96, *International Journal of Advertising*, 17(1), 99-114.

Measuring hospitality feedback

Influencing stakeholders is likely to be an important communication objective of sponsorship-driven hospitality management. Feedback from stakeholders can be measured in different ways: response/reaction, thankyou letters, word of mouth, upward selling, improved relationships, etc. Techniques to measure the effect of hospitality include self-completion questionnaires, internal interviews, audits, event research, intranet, market research and diverse evaluation forms.

Persuasive impact of sports sponsorship

The effectiveness of sports sponsorship communications can be summarized by the 'persuasive impact equation' of Crimmins and Horn, which integrates a number of important sponsorship impact factors at the communications level (see Outline 7.7).[33]

Outline 7.7 Persuasive impact of sport sponsorship

$$\text{Persuasive impact} = \text{strength of the link} \times \text{duration of the link} \times (\text{gratitude felt due to the link} + \text{perceptual change due to the link})$$

Source: Crimmins, J. and Horn, M. (1996), 'Sponsorship: from management ego trip to marketing success', *Journal of Advertising Research*, (15)4, 11-21.

From this representation, it can be noted that the strength of the association is evaluated by whether the target group realizes that a competitor is not a sponsor of the sport or object. For example, the exclusive awareness reveals the percentage of members of the target group who recognize the link between the sponsoring brand and the sports object (desired link) minus the percentage of the target group who believe incorrectly that there is a link between the same sports object and a non-sponsoring competitor (ambush link). For example, 64% of Olympic sponsors who surrounded their sports sponsorship with advertising activities succeeded in creating a link in the consumer's mind between the Olympic Games and their brand. However, only 4% of the Olympic sponsors who did not run an advertising campaign succeeded in creating a link between the Olympic Games and their brand.[34]

The effectiveness of the sports sponsorship project is also determined by the duration of the link. A short-term association is evident only during the sporting event. A long-term association continues before, during and after the sporting event. The persuasive impact is influenced also by the appreciation and the change in brand perception of the target group as a result of the association. Appreciation is translated into sympathy for sponsors ('I feel I am contributing to the Olympics by buying the brands of Olympic sponsors'). If consumers ultimately revise their perception of the sponsoring brand, then the sponsorship has had a strong impact. For instance, during the Atlanta '96 Olympic Games, Olympic sponsor VISA doubled its lead over MasterCard as the leading credit card brand.[35]

7.4 Commercial results

Most evaluations do not attempt to measure the direct impact of sports sponsorship on sales. This is because the sports sponsorship objective is usually to generate awareness and change the brand image, and not to generate sales directly. Impact on sales is measurable only if localized or short-term sponsorship is used, since this makes comparison easier with control areas or periods and determination of the incremental sales volume generated by sports sponsorship. It is clear that these measurement limitations substantially complicate the analysis of sponsorship effectiveness on 'real-life' commercial data. From this, the issue of return on investment has been addressed by monitoring reaction to a sponsor's on-site and broadcast sponsorship[36] or promotional efforts[37] in an experimental setting.[38] The direct impact on sales can also be measured when there are sales promotions accompanying the event. For example, by distributing coupons along the track or at the venue, and then tracking how many were redeemed, the commercial effectiveness can be measured.[39] Scanner data or on-site sales also can provide useful data on the success of the sales promotional development of sponsorship.

However, the ultimate objective of a sponsorship communications campaign is to make consumers buy the product. In behavioural tests, the relation between sponsorship and buying behaviour is studied directly. Various behavioural measures of sponsorship effectiveness can be distinguished, such as the sales evolution, the market share evolution, the degree of loyalty to a brand, and trial purchases. Sales data could be quantified further into new customers, increased loyalty and up-selling. In addition to these classic indicators of commercial success, tracking tools for websites are becoming increasingly sophisticated and enjoy a high degree of accuracy. Websites can not only record the number of individual visitors and click-throughs but could also measure the incremental change in e-commerce. Sponsorship managers seem to attach a medium degree of importance to sales data, website visitor feedback and Internet data in the many information areas.

7.5 Summary

Successful sports sponsorship managers plan and develop sponsorship and, as clever marketers, are likely to block or counter competing ambush brands. With the huge sums paid for sports sponsorship, alertness with regard to ambush brands has intensified. Advertising ambush, spectator ambush and event ambush are the most important types of ambush marketing.

Measurement audits should answer the question, 'Where is the sponsorship organization now in relation to where it wanted to be in its objectives?' Sponsorship achievement of effectiveness, from the sponsor's viewpoint, could be measured on the basis of exposure, communication results and commercial results. The exposure measurement is only a rough test of sponsorship effectiveness. On the basis of the number of seconds that sponsorship is on air, the monetary value of the exposure could be measured. However, consultants seem to disagree on exposure measurement methods, on the correction factors for the multisponsor environment and – above all – on the correction factor to convert publicity into advertising equivalences.

Despite these substantial limitations associated with measuring media exposure, the advertising equivalent of publicity measures seems to be used widely. Correct sponsor attribution, sponsorship awareness and brand image are important indicators of the measurement of the communication results of a sponsorship campaign. Nevertheless, brand tracking is likely to be the most comprehensive effect measurement in sports sponsorship communication. From this, most audits do not attempt to measure the direct impact of sports sponsorship on sales. However, sales promotion-related sports sponsorship and the commercial effectiveness of sponsorship could be assessed by estimating the sponsorship's impact on sales or market share.

Key terms

Accountability
Advertising ambush
Advertising equivalent of publicity
Ambush brand
Ambush marketing
Audience measurement
Brand awareness
Brand image
Brand tracking
Commercial results
Communication results
Event ambush
Exposure
Feedback from stakeholders
Hospitality feedback
Media evaluation
Persuasive impact equation
Post-testing
PR ambush
Sales promotion ambush
Spectator ambush
Sponsorship attributes
Sponsorship awareness
Television coverage
Vigilante marketing

Questions

1. Provide recent examples from your sporting environment of advertising, spectator and event ambush marketing.

2. What are the communications objectives that Flora is trying to realize with its sponsorship programme?

3. The effect of sports sponsorship, and its communication, can be difficult to isolate. Illustrate this using the example of Siemens Mobile and David Beckham, shirt sponsor and star player, respectively, of Real Madrid.

4. Comment on the following statement: 'Sports marketers must be prepared to evaluate sports sponsorship in the same manner as other marketing tools.'

Endnotes

1 European Sponsorship Consulting Agency (2003), Report. In: Kolah, A. (ed.), *Maximising the Value of Sponsorship*. London: SportBusiness Group, pp. 84–8.
2 Sandler, D.M. and Shani, D. (1989), Olympic sponsorship vs 'ambush' marketing: who gets the gold?, *Journal of Advertising Research*, August/September, 9–14.
3 Mullin, B., Hardy, S. and Sutton, W. (2000), *Sport Marketing*, 2nd edn. Champaign, IL: Human Kinetics.
4 Kolah, A. (2003), *Maximising the Value of Sponsorship*. London: SportBusiness Group.
5 Irwin, R., Sutton, W. and McCarthy, L. (2002), *Sport Promotion and Sales Management*. Champaign, IL: Human Kinetics.
6 Kolah (2003), op cit.
7 Kolah (2003), op cit.
8 *De Morgen*, 2002, *Interbrew via Budweiser* aanwezig op WK, *De Morgen*, 25 June 2002.
9 Davidson, J. and McDonald, J. (2001), Avoiding surprise results at the Olympic Games, *Managing Intellectual Property*, December/January, 115.
10 Kolah (2003), op cit.
11 De Pelsmacker, P., Geuens, M. and van den Bergh, J. (2004), *Marketing Communications. A European Perspective*. Harlow: FT Prentice Hall.
12 Cornwell, T. and Maignan, I. (1998), An international review of sponsorship research, *Journal of Advertising*, 27(1), 1–21.
13 Meenaghan, T. (1991), Sponsorship – legitimising the medium, *European Journal of Marketing*, 25, 5–10.
14 Zajonck, R. (1968), Attitudinal effects of mere exposure, *Journal of Personality and Social Psychology*, 9, 1–12.
15 Hoek, J., Gendall, P., Jeffcaat, M. and Orsmar, D. (1997), Sponsorship and advertising: a comparison of their effects, *Journal of Marketing Communications*, 3, 21–32.
16 Segers, K. (1997), Sponsorvermelding in de pers: impact en effectiviteit. In: Roomer, J. and Van Tilborgh, C. (eds), *Intern/Extern. Communicatie voor Organisaties, Bedrijven en Instellingen*. Deventer: Kluwer.
17 Kolah (2003), op cit.

18 Van Drunen (1999), Meten is weten in sportsponsorship, *Sponsorship en Fondsenwerving*, 11(8), 14–16.

19 Sports Marketing Surveys (1996), *Analyse de la Couverture Télévisée et des retombées de sponsorship de Mapei-GB: saison 1995 et 1996*. Paris: UCI.

20 Busby, R. (1997), *Measuring Successful Sponsorship: Evaluation Strategies for Justifying Investment*. London: FT Pearson Professional.

21 Kolah (2003), op cit.

22 Crimmins, J. and Horn, M. (1996), Sponsorship: from management ego trip to marketing success, *Journal of Advertising Research*, 36(4), 11–21.

23 Kolah (2003), op cit.

24 Sleight, S. (1989), *Sponsorship: What It Is and How To Use It*. Maidenhead: McGraw-Hill; Crimmins, J. and Horn, M. (1996), Sponsorship: from management ego trip to marketing success, *International Journal of Advertising*, 17(1), 99–114; Cornwell, T. and Maignan, I. (1998), op cit.

25 Crompton, L. (1994), Measuring the return of sponsorship investments at major recreation events, *Journal of Park and Recreation Management*, Summer, 73–85.

26 Sponsorship Research International (1999), *How to Get Most Out of Your Sponsorship Marketing: Selecting and Measuring Effectiveness*. Limelette: Institute of International Research, Colloquium Sponsorship Marketing.

27 Erdogan, B. and Kitchen, P. (1998), Managerial mindsets and the symbiotic relationship between sponsorship and advertising, *Marketing Intelligence and Planning*, 16(6), 369–74.

28 Cornwell, T. and Maignan, I. (1998), op cit.

29 Hoek *et al*. (1997), op cit.

30 Hastings, G. (1984), Sponsorship works differently from advertising, *International Journal of Advertising*, 3, 171–6.

31 Stotlar, D. (2004), Sponsorship evaluation: moving from theory to practice, *Sport Marketing Quarterley*, 13, 61–4.

32 Easton, S. and Mackie, P. (1998), When football came home: a case history of the sponsorship activity at Euro '96, *International Journal of Advertising*, 17(1), 99–114.

33 Crimmins and Horn (1996), op cit.

34 Crimmins and Horn (1996), op cit; Erdogan and Kitchen (1998), op cit.

35 Crimmins and Horn (1996), op cit.

36 Lardinoit, T. and Derbaix, C. (2001), Sponsorship and recall of sponsors, *Psychology and Marketing*, 18(2), 167–90; Lardinoit, T. (2001), Attitudinal effects of combined sponsorship and sponsor's prominence on basketball in Europe, *Journal of Advertising Research*, 41(1), 48–59.

37 McCarville, R., Flood, C. and Froats, T. (1998), The effectiveness of selected promotions on spectators' assessments of a nonprofit sporting event sponsor, *Sport Management Review*, 12(1).

38 Hansen, F. and Scotwin, L. (1995), An experimental inquiry into sponsoring: what effects can be measured?, *Marketing and Research Today*, 23(3), 173–81.

39 Crompton (1994), op cit.

Case 7 Cofidis, giving credit to cycling sponsorship

Key learning points:

After studying this case, you will be able to:

- explain why cycling team sponsorship is a rapidly growing instrument of marketing communication;

- illustrate the tools of sports sponsorship communication;

- distinguish between the different methods of sports sponsorship effectiveness.

Introduction

Until well into the 1970s, professional cycling was limited primarily to Belgium, France, Italy, the Netherlands and Spain. Mainly Flemish, small and medium-sized businesses were the main sponsors of the most important teams. Cyclist sponsorship was characterized primarily by hobbyism until well into the 1970s. In a period of modest budgets, a number of bicycle manufacturers, including Belgian Flandria and Italian Bianchi, could remain the main sponsor of a team. Cycling team sponsors came from the sectors of drinks (Spanish soft drink Kas, Belgian beer Maes), food and dairy products, home furnishings, car manufacturing (Fiat, Renault), truck manufacturing (Daf Trucks), mail order (La Redoute) and cigarette manufacturing (Boule d'Or).

The wages of cyclists amounted to a fraction of what top cyclists make today. For example, Eddy Merckx dominated international cycling at the start of the 1970s for an annual salary of €50 000; the annual salaries of the world top ten cyclists today are at least one million euros. There were few social security allowances for cyclists, and disturbing tales of cyclists being exploited and amateurish sponsors were common. There was also no concept of a minimum salary, and until the mid-1970s many cyclists raced for the equipment and the competition winnings.

Panasonic, trendsetter for multinationals

From the start of the 1980s, cycling was enriched with sports people from non-European countries, such as the USA, Australia and Colombia. In addition, the move of cycling towards Eastern Europe had a strong influence on the international sport. The cycling calendar thus gained an international flavour. A number of multinationals zeroed in on this growth and gradually elbowed the small companies out of the way. Trendsetter and pioneer of the group of the sponsoring multinationals was Japanese electronics giant Panasonic, which sponsored the top team of the same name at the instigation of sports director Peter Post between 1984 and 1992. Hitachi and Toshiba followed Panasonic's example and became the main sponsors of cycling teams between 1985 and 1989.

The entrance of multinationals into international professional cycling led to an increasing demand for top cyclists, which in turn led to increasing pressure on the team budgets. Bicycle brands could no longer afford to be main sponsors. They were reduced to the role of providing materials or co-sponsor. In the second half of the 1980s, brand names of supermarkets, home furnishings, audio and TV equipment, electrical appliances, clothing and lotteries discovered cycling sponsorship.

The great leap forwards for international professional cycling came in the 1990s. The catalyst for continued internationalization and professionalization was the appointment of Hein Verbruggen in 1991 as chairperson of the Union Cycliste International (UCI). In this function, he implemented various reforms, inspired by tennis and Formula 1, from which the current structure and organization of modern cycle racing developed. With a better distribution of the competitions, the UCI intended to maintain the cycling enthusiast's attention all year round and attract sponsors by providing the chance of logo visibility over a longer period. Another important improvement was the introduction of a points system that determined the market value of cyclists and their teams. In this new system, the best ranked teams received officially prescribed preferential treatment.

The explosion of the team budgets in the 1990s

During the past ten years, the budgets of professional cycling teams have exploded. This can be illustrated by comparing the annual budgets of the ten highest-ranking cycling teams at the end of a selected cycling season in 1992, 1998 and 2003 (see Tables 7.6–7.8). The team budgets indicate the promotional sports rights that the sponsors paid. Operating budgets are not included in the team budgets given. The left-hand columns in Tables 7.6–7.8 give the UCI ranking of a cycling team at the end of a calendar year.*

*The interpretation of the data must be done very carefully. Depending on the primary source (for example, the Dutch monthly *Wielerrevue*, the French daily l'*Equipe* or the Flemish daily *Het Nieuwsblad*), there can be considerable variation in the reported budgets. The actual budgets are generally underestimated, since companies are not willing to disclose the sums of money that they are pumping into a professional cycling team. Another reason is that several lines of funding have to avoid fiscal exposure. Sometimes, the budget is even overestimated; this happens when the prestige and the power of a team and of the sponsoring company have to be emphasized. For the most recent figures, the official budgets were checked against the perception of well-informed sources.

Table 7.6 Ranking and budgets of top cycling teams, 1992

UCI ranking (31 December 1992)	Official UCI designation (nationality)	Budget 1992 (millions of euros)	Business of sponsor
1	Banesto (SPA)	5.3	Bank
2	Ceramiche/Ariostea (ITA)	3.8	Ceramics/tiles
3	Panasonic/Sportlife (NETH)	3.4	Electronics/ chewing gum
4	Buckler (NETH)	3.0	Non-alcoholic beer
5	Once (SPA)	5.0	Lottery
6	Gatorade/Chateaux d'Ax (ITA)	4.6	Sports drink/hotel chain
7	Carrera (ITA)	3.4	Jeans
8	GB-MG (ITA)	2.7	Distributor/ clothing
9	PDM (NETH)	3.6	Cassettes
10	Z (FRA)	4.2	Children's wear
	Average	3.9	

Source: Lagae, W. (2000), De sponsoring van professionele wielerploegen: een economische situering [the sponsoring of professional cycling teams: an economic analysis]. In: *Mediagids: Communicatie*, 4, 1.4.5, 1-24.

The average budget of a top team in 1992 was €3.9 million. Banesto was the richest team in 1992, with an annual budget of €5.3 million (see Table 7.6), followed by the Spanish lottery Once (which benefits blind and visually impaired people). Multinational Heineken used a cycling team from 1991 to familiarize the public with its non-alcoholic beer Buckler. The Buckler team budget amounted to €3 million.

Table 7.7 Ranking and budgets of top cycling teams, 1998

UCI ranking (31 December 1998)	Official UCI designation (nationality)	Budget 1998 (millions of euros)	Business of sponsor
1	Mapei/Bricobi (ITA)	5.5	Adhesives and construction materials/DIY products
2	Festina/Lotus (FRA)	4.0	Clock manufacturer
3	Team Deutsche Telekom (GER)	4.7	Telecommunications
4	Once/Deutsche Bank (SPA)	5.6	Lottery/bank
5	Rabobank (NETH)	4.3	Bank
6	Banesto (SPA)	6.5	Bank
7	Casino, c'est votre équipe (FRA)	4.2	Distributor
8	TVM/Farm Frites (NETH)	3.7	Insurance/potato processing
9	Gan/Crédit Agricole (FRA)	3.9	Insurance
10	Saeco Macchine Da Caffe/Cannondale (ITA)	4.0	Coffee machines/ bicycles
	Average	**4.6**	
14	Cofidis	4.96	Credit supply

Source: Lagae, W. (2000), De sponsoring van professionele wielerploegen: een economische situering [the sponsoring of professional cycling teams: an economic analysis]. In: Mediagids: Communicatie, 4, 1.4.5, 1–24.

The average budget of the top ten in 1998 had increased by €0.7 million to €4.6 million (see Table 7.7). The professional season in 1998 was marred by the Festina scandal, which erupted during the Tour de France, shocking the cycling world and leaving deep wounds. Drug abuse, which was until then considered to be a marginal phenomenon practised only by a few individual cyclists, was officially proven to be structurally organized by the management of the cycling team.

Although the Festina scandal sent a shockwave through professional cycling, the market value of professional cycling teams continued to rise. For instance, in 2003, the average budget had increased to €7.76 million among the ten best-performing cycling teams that published their budgets (Table 7.8).

Table 7.8 Ranking and budgets of top cycling teams, 2003

UCI ranking (2003)	Official UCI designation (nationality)	Budget 2003 (millions of euros)	Business of sponsor
1	Fassa Bortolo (ITA)	8	Construction materials
2	Saeco-Lognoni (ITA)	7	Coffee machines
3	Telekom (GER)	15	Telecommunications
4	Quick.Step-Davitamon (BEL)	7	Laminate flooring/vitamins
5	Rabobank (NETH)	9.5	Bank
6	iBanesto (SPA)	7	Bank
7	CSC-Tiscali (DKK)	6.1	Telecommunications/Internet provider
8	Alessio (ITA)	3	Car wheel rims
9	Cofidis; le crédit par téléphone (FRA)	7	Credit delivery
10	ONCE-Eroski (SPA)	8	Lottery/distributor
Average		7.76	

Source: Interview with P. Lefevre, team manager Quick.Step-Davitamon, 2 September 2003.

Typically in cycling sponsorship, the team's income relies primarily on money from sponsors. A certain proportion of the team's budget consists of entry fees and reimbursement of expenses when participating in important competitions. Main sponsors, co-sponsors and subsidiary sponsors are cash sponsors. The most important material sponsors provide money along with bicycles, cycling clothing, cycling helmets and goggles. In addition, there also are technical and logistics sponsors that supply goods and services, from leisure clothing and caravans to a company specialized in salary administration.

Cofidis, le crédit par téléphone

Sponsorship strategy

The French firm Cofidis specializes in the granting of credit. In 1982, the company was established in France by the mail order company Les 3 Suisses to offer customers the option of paying for products in instalments. This grew into the activity of providing consumers with credit by telephone, an activity that was successful because in 1986 it was extended to Belgium, followed by Spain (1990), Italy (1996), Portugal (1996) and Argentina and Greece (2002).

However, the familiarity of the name Cofidis remained low. In Belgium, the aided name awareness in 1997 ('Have you heard of the credit provider Cofidis?') was only 12.5% and the spontaneous brand awareness ('Name the credit providers you know') was just 1%. Cofidis was also struggling with an image problem – typical for the sector, as it often has to work with threatening letters and bailiffs. Because of these problems, the company's marketing communication was completely reorganized. Until that point, Cofidis had not done anything other than direct marketing and classic above-the-line advertisement. Due to the excessively low share of voice (relative proportion of advertising budget), credit provider Cofidis did not succeed in developing sufficient brand awareness, let alone becoming top of mind.

Therefore, sports sponsorship was selected to realize the company's marketing objectives in an alternative and creative manner and to compete with the large banks. After a thorough selection process, the ultimate choice fell on the main sponsoring of a professional cycling team carrying the sponsor's name. In 1997, Cofidis invested €5 million in the cycling team. With this input, 20 cyclists were recruited with enough UCI points to create a first-class team. This allowed the team to participate in all international competitions and the Tour de France. Cofidis was the sole sponsor, which meant that the official UCI team name consisted only of the brand name Cofidis. The Cofidis budget varied in the period 1997-2004 between €5 million and €7 million.

Exposure and publicity

During its first participation in the Tour de France in 1997, the name of the Cofidis team appeared on television for 3.5 hours. Only Deutsche Telekom (with the winner Jan Ullrich) and Festina (with the French darling Richard Virenque) had greater visibility. In 1997, the spontaneous brand awareness of Cofidis doubled. In the following years, there were several sporting successes, including third place by Bobby Julich in the Tour of 1998 and the supremacy of the British cyclist David Millar in time trials. The increased brand awareness and the effect on the company's positive image were exploited further in direct mailings and advertisements.

The sponsoring also had its downside. For example, two weeks after signing the contract in the winter of 1997, the still unknown American cyclist Lance Armstrong was diagnosed with cancer. This resulted not only in an investment without any exposure but also in negative press, as Cofidis was criticized for abruptly cancelling the contract. In various interviews, Armstrong stressed repeatedly that he felt abandoned by Cofidis. He also criticized Cofidis's cold attitude. In contrast to Cofidis, US Postal believed in Armstrong. US Postal contributed to the history of modern cycling by supporting Armstrong to five Tour victories. At the end of 1997, Cofidis replaced Armstrong in extremis with Tony Rominger, another top cyclist in the team, but he broke his collarbone on the fourth day of the Tour de France. Again, no sporting success and no visibility.

Cofidis also shared in the doping scandal that plagued the professional cycling world. In 1999, Cofidis wonderboy Frank Vandenbroucke was suspended for alleged drug use. What followed was a cascade of arguments, statements, threats and accusations; in other words: negative publicity. In March 2003, during the several-day cycling race Paris–Nice, Cofidis was confronted with the fatal accident of Cofidis cyclist Andreï Kivilev.

In the spring of 2004, a new doping drama struck the Cofidis cycling team. Again, the team was in the sports headlines, since it withdrew from competition for several weeks. One might ask, 'Is any publicity good publicity?' It's an old communication adage that is certainly open to discussion.

Communications of cycling sponsorship

Sponsor activation is fundamental to enhancing the value of sponsorship. For instance, the cycling sponsorship investment is shared jointly by all European branches of Cofidis. In addition to the €500 000 per year spent on the team in 2002, Cofidis Belgium also invested €400 000 in communicating the sponsoring investment. The communication actions conducted by Cofidis Belgium in 2002 varied widely:

- €280 000 for TV commercials. Cofidis prefers simple TV spots in which the sale of credit products is highlighted. The spots are always shown before and after live broadcasts, which allows the viewer to make the link between the brand and the sponsorship.

- €84 000 for advertisements in the printed media. These advertisements appeared generally during the Tour de France and emphasized the cyclists' achievements. They were printed in the sports sections of newspapers and specialist magazines to maintain the link with cycling and the sympathetic image.

- €20 000 for a presence at the cycling event Franco-Belge. Cofidis was co-sponsor of this Belgian race and followed the action in three VIP cars, which was an excellent opportunity to invite VIPs to attend.

- €16 000 for a cycling game/competition on the Cofidis website during the Tour de France.

Communication results

Linking the brand name with a cycling team resulted immediately in improved brand familiarity. However, the problem regarding brand interpretation remained. As with so many cycling teams (Mapei, Once, Kelme, TVM, Fassa Bortolo …), more people recognized the brand name but did not have a clue what it stood for. Therefore, after 1998, the second year of cycling sponsorship, the team name was changed to Cofidis, le crédit par téléphone. In addition, all communications from the cycling team included the company's 0800 number and Web address, resulting in extra traffic, i.e. inbound calls and hits on the website.

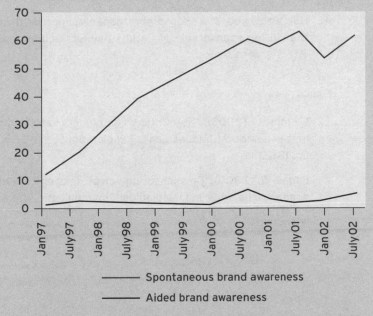

Figure 7.1 Evolution of the spontaneous and aided brand awareness of Cofidis.

Figure 7.1 portrays the communicative results of cycling sponsorship by Cofidis. At the end of 2002, after five seasons of cycling sponsorship, aided brand awareness had risen from 12.5 to 64%, and spontaneous brand awareness from 1 to 5%.

Commercial results

The commercial results from cycling sponsorship were also significant. In Belgium, for example, in five years the turnover in outstanding loans soared above the sector average by at least 111%, from €114 to €242 million. This gave Cofidis fourth place in the credit provision sector, after three large banks. Cycling sponsorship was successful for Cofidis in a commercial sense as well, since 10–15% of the telephone credit requests seemed to recognize Cofidis from the cycling sponsorship.

Questions for discussion

1. What sport- and marketing-related factors led to the professionalization and internationalization of cycling?

2. Discuss and explain the evolution in the team budgets after the eruption of the Festina drug scandal in 1998.

3. Compare the incomes of cycling teams with those of football teams. How could cycling teams reduce their dependence on sponsorship?

4. How would you, as a sponsorship manager, improve the development of the cycling sponsorship of Cofidis Belgium and increase sponsorship effectiveness?

References

Geuens, L. (2003), 'Hoe Cofidis zijn naambekendheid oppept. Scoren met een beperkt budget dankzij wielersponsoring', *Bizz*, maart 2003, pp. 18–23.

Lagae, W. (2000), 'De sponsoring van professionale wielerploegen: een economische situering; Mediagids: Communicatie, 4, 1.4.5, 1–24.

www.uaich

INDEX